COSMOPOLIS

COSMOPOLIS

Prospects for World Government

DANILO ZOLO

Translated from the Italian by David McKie

Polity Press

Copyright © Danilo Zolo 1997

The right of Danilo Zolo to be identified as author of this work has been asserted in accordance with the Copyright, Designs and Patents Act 1988.

First published in 1997 by Polity Press in association with Blackwell Publishers Ltd.

2 4 6 8 10 9 7 5 3 1

Editorial office:
Polity Press
65 Bridge Street
Cambridge CB2 1UR, UK

Marketing and production:
Blackwell Publishers Ltd
108 Cowley Road
Oxford OX4 1JF, UK

Published in the USA by
Blackwell Publishers Inc.
237 Main Street
Cambridge, MA 02142, USA

ISBN 0-7456-1300-4
ISBN 0-7456-1301-2 (pbk)

A CIP catalogue record for this book is available from the British Library and the Library of Congress.

Typeset in 10 on 12 pt Times
by CentraCet Ltd, Cambridge

This book is printed on acid-free paper.

Contents

The Newtonian image of the state as a planetary system and the power of the sovereign as a counterpart of the central force of the sun, fleshed out and added details to Hobbes' basic picture. The stability of society required not just centralized force, but also a system of fixed orbits: a modern Cosmopolis.

In both science and philosophy the intellectual agenda today obliges us to pay less attention to *stability* and *system*, more attention to *function* and *adaptability*. This shift of attention has its counterpart in the social and political realms. The task is not to build new, larger, and yet more powerful powers, let alone a 'world state' having worldwide sovereignty.

S. Toulmin, *Cosmopolis*

A forced conformity of cultures would cut back man's evolutionary prospects. Herein lies the greatest danger to any evolution planned and guided by us. As soon as we direct it to a definite goal, we run the risk of narrowing the spectrum of possibilities and thus setting in train a process of involution. Differentiation, many-sidedness, and openness to the world are human properties that must be retained.

I. Eibl-Eibesfeldt, *The Biology of Peace and War*

The opposite of war is not peace, the opposite of love is not hate, the opposite of collaboration is not harassment. Each of these dichotomous pairs is at the same end of the scale of mutual involvement and relatedness. At the opposite end of the scale lie separation, indifference, exclusion, and rejection.

H. L. Nieburg, *Political Violence*

Preface

The opinion is rapidly gaining ground among political scientists both in Europe and in the United States that conflict between the nation states of the world will only cease when the situation of international anarchy inherited from seventeenth-century Europe has been brought to an end. Many believe this step to have been made all the more pressing by the escalating globalization of the problems besetting government, economic development, the rational use of resources and control of the world's ecology. They propose the dismantling of the system of sovereign states which was established in Europe by the Peace of Westphalia and which, by the close of the nineteenth century, had become universal. It was a system which enshrined the right of the nation state to exercise exclusive power within its own boundaries and to claim absolute independence from any external authority. In place of this 'Westphalian model' it is argued that a new hierarchy of formally established and legitimated international power is necessary. In other words, a form of modern Cosmopolis is advocated, in which relations not only between one state and another but also between a state and its citizens would be subject to the control and interventive direction of a 'world government'.

According to this school of thought, political order rests on the concentration of coercive power within centralized institutions. Within each state these institutions have been used to contain centrifugal forces and to remove conflict between particular interests, through recourse, where necessary, to the use of force. Civil wars have habitually resulted in the establishment of (new) central authorities empowered to exercise this function. But institutions of this sort have never hitherto played a part in the relations between states. Here, and for many centuries, the figure at most of the mediator or arbitrator has appeared, but never that of the judge or police official. Whenever and wherever they have been able to do so, states have exercised their own form of justice by resorting to war. For this reason, while individual citizens may not normally be permitted to carry arms, there is no state in the world which has not attempted to arm itself to the maximum possible extent.

At those times when peace between nations has been guaranteed, it has been effected by means of a balance either of power or of fear. If, however, the objective is to achieve a stable and lasting peace within an international system, then some form of *pactum subjectionis*, subordinating the power of self-defence of states to the control of an appropriately armed central authority, appears to be indispensable. A reform of existing international institutions in order to increase the powers and to enlarge the functions of the United Nations follows from this as an absolute necessity.

Even without invoking so cosmopolitan a viewpoint, however, I believe it to be difficult to argue that the 'Westphalian system' has not reached a point of crisis or to claim that the structuring (and democratization) of the international community has made any great progress in its passage from Holy Alliance to League of Nations to United Nations. The last two centuries have seen no significant increase in the efficacy or authority of international institutions. Neither the peace nor the 'just' world order which these institutions were officially brought into being to promote has in fact been achieved. And in the meantime the condition of the planet has taken on alarming aspects.

Today, as Hans Küng points out in his *Project Weltethos*, each minute the nations of the world spend nearly two million dollars on armaments, each hour 1,500 children die of malnutrition, each day an animal species becomes extinct, each week more people are imprisoned, tortured, murdered or forced to migrate, each month some eight billion dollars are added to the accumulated debt – now standing at 1,500 billion dollars – of the world's poorest countries, and each year an area of tropical rainforest roughly equivalent to the total ground area of Korea is destroyed. In addition, to be added to this list, the world population is increasing at a present rate of over ninety million a year, and is likely, in the course of the next half-century alone, to double, taking its current figure of five and a half billion to eleven billion or more.

It is this context which reveals the structural unsuitability of the United Nations not simply to guarantee peace but to operate effectively in securing the international protection of human rights, the economic and social development of impoverished and backward areas of the planet and the safety of the environment. Naturally responsibility for the remedying of this situation falls most heavily on the industrialized democracies, which are the only countries with sufficient power and economic resources to bring about reform of international institutions. Even democratic countries, however, operate according to methods

which are in many respects scarcely to be distinguished from those used
by autocratic and totalitarian regimes. These methods include recourse
to war, the imposition of tariff or non-tariff strategies which result in the
marginalizing of weaker countries and restrictive or conservative immi-
gration and environmental policies. Furthermore, as a result of the
growing interdependence of political decision-making, the situation of
disorder at international level appears to be exercising an increasing
influence on the functioning of democratic institutions and the exercise
of fundamental rights within individual countries. In other words, the
conditions of 'internal democracy' are becoming more and more dependent upon the conditions of 'external democracy' and are influenced to
an ever-increasing degree by the quality of international relations.

In the face of such formidable problems it is hardly surprising that
the establishment of a 'global government' is presented by those whom
Hedley Bull terms 'Western globalists' as the sole available alternative
not simply to war and international disorder but, absolutely, to the
planet's destruction and the extinction of human beings as a species:
only in the Cosmopolis are world peace and environmental salvation to
be found. But, as I shall attempt to argue, this is a view which the
growing complexity and turbulence of international relations are rendering increasingly facile.

My own interest in this range of theoretical problems received a strong
impetus from the issues raised by the Gulf War in 1991. This is a war
which western public opinion has succeeded in allowing to fade rapidly
from its consciousness, but one which, in terms of its importance for
international organization, I personally hold to be among the most
significant events of this century. Sadly, however, this importance lies in
entirely negative directions. I remember the sharp jolt of surprise I
received when, on the morning of 17 January 1991, the Italian news-
papers announced not only that 'Operation Desert Storm' had been
unleashed during the night but that the political philosopher Norberto
Bobbio, in an interview in Milan, had declared the war to be 'just'.
Immediately I wrote an article expressing my profound disagreement
with Bobbio. Neither the theory of the 'just war', I held, nor, more
broadly, theories of ethics in international relations could provide any
justification for this war and, in particular, for the actions of the United
Nations. In modern warfare, quite apart from the now techologically
defunct distinction between conventional and nuclear attack, ethical
and legal considerations had ceased to have any commensurability.
What was needed, I concluded, was a realistic – rather than a moralistic
or legalistic – evaluation of the international political situation following
the collapse of the Soviet empire and the end of bipolarism.

Bobbio made his reply, and as a result further discussion took place between us, both in public and in an exchange of letters. In the end, the distance between our positions had appreciably narrowed, and I was left with a clear impression of the intellectual honesty and sense of public responsibility of my distinguished opponent, a man for whom my personal respect remains undiminished.

But that early shock was far from being the only disappointment I was to suffer. I was grieved by the tacit acquiescence of numerous intellectuals who for years past had argued, sometimes even against me, for the moral, even more than political, necessity of judging politics in the light of public ethics. From that point on, silence appears to have acquired something of the force of habit even across a broad spectrum of the left. There is particular cause for concern about this in that the events of the years succeeding the Gulf War have served only to lend stability and legitimacy to the political and military practices which that war established. These events may seem small in themselves but they are in my view indicative of a profound shift in international politics and balances of power. Among these I include the restrictions imposed on Iraqi territorial sovereignty by the western powers with the tacit approval of the United Nations, but quite without any formal legitimation, and the bombings of Iraq carried out on the personal orders of the United States President for reasons either of internal politics or of outright revenge. In addition there have followed the 'humanitarian' intervention of certain western powers in Somalia in 1993, the neocolonial expedition by France in Rwanda in 1994 and, in September of the same year, the invasion of Haiti by the United States, which was authorized by the entire Security Council with the sole abstention of China.

These last three instances seem to me to be typical of the institutional confusion which characterized the Gulf War and which has in succeeding years become a matter of course. This is the confusion between the powers of the formalized organs of the United Nations, the powers of national governments taking part in military intervention, and, extending over all of these, the powers of the United States. A result of this confusion has been that the 'Blue Helmets' sent into Somalia for humanitarian reasons ended by firing on defenceless crowds, while some hundreds of civilians were killed by fire from United States helicopters which had not been formally incorporated into the United Nations military force. In turn, innocent western journalists were killed at the hands of angry Somali mobs, and captured United States soldiers were subjected to torture. In Rwanda 'Operation Turquoise' repeated the model adopted by the United States in Somalia: French soldiers fought, not under the flag and military command of the United Nations, but as an autonomous force 'authorized' by the Security Council. This followed diplomatic pressure applied by France in direct opposition to the Organization for African Unity. Clearly the interests of France went beyond the simple alleviation of the sufferings of the population of Rwanda, and included promotion of its own hegemony in the region. This coincided largely with the interests of the dictatorial Hutu regime, which France had itself supported both politically and militarily.

Even more was at issue in the authorization by the Security Council of the invasion of Haiti by the United States in order to re-establish democracy (*Uphold Democracy* being the name given to the operation by the Pentagon). On a formal level this was a matter of unprecedented seriousness. For the first time the world's supreme international institution, in total disregard of the provisions of its own Charter, gave legitimation to the *Realpolitik* traditionally practised by the United States in the Caribbean and Central America and known as the 'Monroe Doctrine'. It is now easy to predict that in the near future, notwithstanding the evident mistakes and failings of this strategy for the enforcement of peace and the promotion of democracy, analogous 'humanitarian interventions' will be undertaken in the countries of Central and sub-Saharan Africa, over and beyond, naturally, further 'traditional' incursions in the Caribbean and Latin America.

Nor does the new 'global security' strategy devised by the western powers and Japan provide any less cause for concern. Following the end of the Cold War and the collapse of the Soviet empire, the security of industrialized nations, it is argued, is now threatened by the explosion of nationalism and the growing danger of anarchy. Defensive military strategies, developed in accordance with an earlier minimalist conception of collective security and international regulation, now appear inadequate. The situation of increased economic and technological interdependence requires the political stability of the planet to be guaranteed by intervention of a kind which will meet the needs of collective security both quickly and flexibly. Such intervention, greatly exceeding the traditional geographical limitation of NATO, is intended to focus above all on crisis hotspots which emerge in the non-industrialized world.

For it is from this region, it is argued, that there arises the greatest likelihood of conflict and of danger to peace as a result of the increasing economic differentials between undeveloped countries, the population explosion, climatic upheavals, ethnic warfare and terrorism. The poorest areas of the world, more than any others, are held to pose the greatest threat to the regular movement of energy resources, the security of air and sea transport, the stability of financial markets and the commitment of industrialized countries to restricting the proliferation of chemical, biological and nuclear weapons.

More questionable still, however, is the emerging cosmopolitan philosophy which, based on Kant far more than on Grotius, aims to give theoretical justification to the new strategy of the industrial powers and the role which international institutions must inevitably play in it. My fear is that 'globalistic' theoretical outlooks such as those advanced respectively by Richard Falk and David Held (or, in Italy, by Norberto Bobbio and Antonio Cassese) will be found to give unwitting support to just this type of political philosophy. They are liable, for instance, to lend justification to the theory of 'humanitarian intervention' by the great powers in the political, economic and social problems of other states, even against the wishes of their governments or of majorities or minorities within those countries. Still less confidence is inspired by ethical theories which, in the name of a moral obligation or planetary responsibility which they attribute to the United States or the West, are all too ready to produce justificatory arguments for the actions and undertakings of the 'Christian armies'.

Paradoxically, however, the concept of world government suggests itself, even to writers who have declared themselves opposed over these last years to military intervention by the great powers in countries such as Iraq, Somalia or Bosnia, as the most suitable means of engendering a more peaceful and just international order. For this reason they have declared their support for 'democratic reform' which aims to legitimize the United Nations as a provider of compulsory worldwide justice and an international police force.

The present work arises from my opposition to this view of political philosophy, an opposition which is rooted in my unwillingness to subscribe to the ethical and juridical theories on which it is based. It is intended, therefore, to be what Günther Anders would describe as a work of iconoclasm. Iconoclasm, understood as active obedience to the precept 'thou shall not make unto thee any graven image', lies for Anders at the very heart of any non-academic philosophy. In my own case it is more a matter of breaking an image – that of the moral, legal and political rationality of world government – which, despite its entirely regressive nature, or perhaps precisely because of it, has come to assume for us all the overbearing dominance of an idol. It is as if the old dream of *monarchie universelle*, criticized by Hume as well as Montesquieu, were coming to life once more after centuries of obscurity. It should cause no surprise to recall that the need for a higher political authority is a cause dear to the heart of the Catholic Church.

In contrast to this dream of old Europe, which undoubtedly underlies the organization itself of the United Nations (and accounts also for its failures), my own endeavour has been to achieve a conception of international relations which takes account of their 'complex' – that is to say, pluralistic, dynamic and conflictual – nature. I have attempted also to sketch out the elements of a theory of peacemaking which assimilates the results of recent research into human ethology and the ethology of war. It is an attempt – no more than an attempt, I fully recognize – to develop a theory which not only takes account of the growing complexity of international relations but also aims to take realistic advantage of the contributions that moral and legal philosophy have to offer.

From my own standpoint, therefore, diversity, change and differentiation should be conceived as the rule, rather than the exception, in the conduct of international relations of a kind which are capable of 'reducing fear' without attempting to remove conflict through the use of centralized and superior military force. Such relations, without claiming in the slightest to be able to eradicate war once and for all, would at least promote less destructive expressions of human aggression. The process looks, needless to say, very much towards the long term, and is subject to a multiplicity of conditions which may not be easy to realize. But its object is to take us, in Stephen Toulmin's apt phrase, away from the logic of the Leviathan to the logic of the many small chains of Lilliput. We would move, in other words, away from the logic of hierarchical centralizing which so dominates the Charter of the United Nations and towards the logic of a 'weak interventionism' – and hence of a 'weak pacifism' – which sets greater store by self-organization, co-ordination and negotiation.

The aim of this book is to present a realist approach to international politics and the problem of peace and war. The approach will, however, be found to have little in common with the classic international realism of Niebuhr, Morgenthau or Carr, but is closer, all told, to the neo-realist stance of Robert Keohane and, in some important respects, to that of a Grotian neo-realist such as Hedley Bull. If it is possible to follow Martin Wight in identifying three distinct traditions within the European philosophy of internationalism – the Hobbesian–Machiavellian, the Grotian and the Kantian – then my own position approximates most closely to the first. This will be seen in at least the sense that I find no practical value in the idea of the spiritual unity of humankind that lies at the heart of the Kantian position and exercises influence also on the Grotian. I am, moreover, little inclined to accept that Rawlsian theories of justice or Kelsenian metaphysics of law are able to offer any assistance in formulating the problems of peace and war. Nor, finally, am I able to place much confidence in the ethics of international relations.

This 'Machiavellian' realism is likely to have its roots more in my

early political experiences than in my later philosophical inquiries, and
is, at least in part, a reaction to those experiences. My interest in
international relations derives from the early 1960s and my collaboration at that time with Giorgio La Pira, Mayor of Florence, who involved
me in his mission of unofficial diplomacy in the service of world peace
which concentrated in those years on Israel, Egypt and the Arab
countries of north Africa.

My final commission for him took me to Tunis, where I was to take a
private message to the President of the Tunisian Republic, Habib
Bourguiba. The assistance of the Italian ambassador, a personal friend
of La Pira, succeeded in obtaining for me a meeting with the Secretary
General of the Ministry of Foreign Affairs.

Escorted by the ambassador, I was received in a room splendidly
decorated in Moorish style. There I spoke with passion on the opportunity to strengthen cultural links between countries lying on the shores
of the Mediterranean, on the dialogue which could be held between the
three great monotheistic religions which adjoin one another in that
region and on the need to build spiritual bases from which to resolve
the conflict between Arab and Israeli (I had been in Israel shortly
before, and my conversation on the matter with Martin Buber was fresh
in my mind). I advanced in particular the idea of an Islamic Council –
Vatican II was then coming to an end in Rome – to be held in Tunis or
the holy city of Kairouan and to be freely attended by Christian and
Jewish observers. Such an initiative, I added, would receive a warm
reception in Italian Catholic circles.

So far my Arabian host had heard me through with gracious courtesy,
but, on hearing this, he interrupted me with a tiny gesture of impatience:
'We have long', he said, 'been interested in having good relations with
the Catholic Church. That is shown by the contracts which we have
recently exchanged with the Vatican regarding substantial investment
in the housing sector here in Tunis. If you and your friend Professor La
Pira, thanks to your influence with the Vatican, could succeed in
increasing this investment for us in future years, we would be most
grateful to you and very happy to make manifest our gratitude in some
concrete way. As for the other matters, however, I will tell you frankly
that they are not ones which hold great interest for us. *Cher monsieur,
en politique nous sommes cartésiens, nous sommes réalistes . . .*'

Acknowledgements

In recognition of the many debts which I have incurred in writing this book my first thanks are due to Ezra Suleiman, Director of the Council on Regional Studies at Princeton University, for his hospitality during the period I spent in the winter and spring of 1993 as Visiting Fellow in the Department of Politics. This time at Princeton gave me, among many other advantages, the valuable opportunity to discuss the ideas of this book with Richard Falk, Director of the World Order Studies component of the University's Center of International Studies.

I was enabled to bring my work to its conclusion through the grant in 1993 of a Jemolo Fellowship at the Centre for European Studies, Nuffield College, Oxford, where I also returned for further periods of study in the autumn of 1994 and 1995. Here I was able to benefit greatly from the exceptional resources of the Bodleian and other Oxford libraries, as well as from the friendly assistance of Andrew Hurrell, David Miller and Vincent Wright, Fellows of Nuffield College.

My further thanks are due to Antonio Cassese, who has been lavish in the provision of information, advice and cautionary warnings. Without the safety net of his constant attention, this is a project I could never have dared to embark upon. This must not, however, be taken to involve him in responsibility for the theories which are here advanced and with which, I fear, he will not find himself in full agreement. Amongst others whom I wish most warmly to thank are Roberto Gilodi, who first encouraged me to write a work of political philosophy on the international questions arising from the great watershed formed by the Gulf War; Furio Cerutti, whose frequent criticisms have stimulated me to pay greater attention to the problem of relations between democracy and international issues; Patrizia Messeri, who initiated my interest in the ethology of primates and human ethology with regard to matters such as aggression, pacification rituals and war; Pietro Costa, Luigi Ferrajoli, Giorgio Gaja, Letizia Gianformaggio and Pier Paolo Portinaro, whose reading of my work in its complete but not yet final form resulted in considerable further improvement.

In addition I wish to record here the debt I owe to my friends in the Inter-university Seminar on Political Philosophy, which has met for a number of years now in Florence, and with whom I have discussed at length the arguments of this book, in particular Luca Baccelli, Franca Bonichi, Antonella Brillante, Anna Loretoni, Maria Chiara Pievatolo, Emilio Santoro, Monica Toraldo di Francia and Francesco Vertova.

My last, and crucial, debt is once again to the literary skill of David McKie, Fellow of Robinson College, Cambridge, who has, for this third time, undertaken the English translation of my work. On this occasion I am indebted in addition to Rachel Barrit for her co-operation in providing an initial English version of chapters 3, 4 and 5.

D. Z.

Oxford, September 1995

1 The Cosmopolitan Model of the Holy Alliance

> The international government of the United Nations is identical with the international government of the Security Council. The Security Council appears, as it were, as the Holy Alliance of our time. And the five permanent members of the Security Council are, as it were, a Holy Alliance within a Holy Alliance.
>
> H. Morgenthau, *Politics among Nations*

A Modern Cosmopolis

For two centuries now the winners of large-scale continental or world wars have set in motion ambitious schemes to ensure the subsequent preservation of peace. The result has not been, however, that a depletion of the military arsenals of these powers has in any way matched the growth of their schemes. On the contrary, the accumulation of weaponry has continued unimpeded and threats to use it have often been made. It would be facile, nevertheless, to conclude from this that war has all along remained the secret agenda of the great nineteenth- and twentieth-century powers. What their repeated attempts in fact amount to is pursuit of a modern Cosmopolis in which peace and stability are to be guaranteed by a legitimized power hierarchy.[1] Peace, as Bert Röling has observed, has gradually taken over from Christian and other notions of civilization in the role of a central criterion which is used to justify not only the existence of an international juridical system but also its continued expansion and the preservation of its pyramidical structure.[2]

But war has in no sense been ended by these means, nor have its intensity and violence been at all reduced. If anything, the precise opposite has been the result. Analyses of the long-term dynamics of 'global power' – such as those of Modelski, Gilpin or Wallerstein –

show that war is a process set in train by a party which believes, for the most part erroneously, that it can gain advantage from an altered situation which the use of force will bring into being.[3] Such is not the objective of a power which has already emerged victorious from a preceding 'contest for hegemony'. For, as soon as certain territorial, political or economic results have been achieved within the global political arena, preservation of a lasting and universal peace – 'hegemonic stability', in the terminology of Robert Keohane's neo-realist lexicon – becomes the prime aim of a conquering power. To this end victorious nations have on at least three occasions in modern times endeavoured to lay the basis of an international organization capable of countering the forces of anarchy and war. In constructing new forms of the concentration and legitimation of international power, they have time and again attempted to hold in check those movements which – arising principally from technological and economic developments – militate against the continuation and legitimation of their own control.[4]

The situation whereby great powers resort once more to the use of armed force – and in so doing contradict the principles and even at times violate the rules of the very international institutions which they have themselves set in place – arises from the overpowering need which they develop to counteract threats to the 'hegemonic stability' which they have so painfully built up.'[5] Action is similarly provoked if other powers disturb the world order by violently overturning legitimized hierarchies and established procedures for the allocation of international resources. On all occasions, however, the task of maintaining peace has, despite repeated historical failure, been assumed by a small nucleus of superpowers, while the great majority of other countries have acquiesced passively in the action which was taken. There has arisen, in other words, what I propose to term here 'the cosmopolitan model of the Holy Alliance': that is to say, the formation of a political entity envisaged as universal, pacific, hierarchical, monocentric and, given the natural force of circumstances, eurocentric or in any event centred on the West.

The historical events of the last two hundred years reveal, therefore, a notable recurrence to which theoreticians of international relations, with the sole exception of system analysts and a small number of the exponents of the realist school, have paid scant attention.[6] As Ian Clark has rightly pointed out, no political system over the last two hundred years has shown itself to possess greater stability than the hierarchical model adopted by the international institutions in 1815. And, paradoxically, such stability as has been achieved has received no support from any particular ability of this system to correspond to its own institutional goals.[7]

My own view is that this phenomenon, once recognized, forms a valuable starting-point for a philosophical investigation of the nature, potentiality and limitations of contemporary international organizations. A necessary first step towards this investigation will be a survey, however summary, of the historical development of international institutions over the past two centuries. The following pages of this chapter, for all their digressive and perhaps elementary appearance, will form therefore the indispensable basis of the arguments which will subsequently be developed.

The Holy Alliance

The Napoleonic Wars – truly the first cataclysmic 'world war' in the sense that, all told, the extended series of conflicts claimed the lives of some two million victims – overturned at the beginning of the nineteenth century the balanced European order of the day. This balance had grown from the accord which had developed within the 'family of nations' from the time of the Peace of Westphalia at the conclusion of the Thirty Years' War in 1648. Out of this accord arose the first recognizably 'modern' relationship between nations whereby a plurality of separately sovereign nation states did not acknowledge a higher authority of Church or Empire.[8] It was precisely this pluralism of sovereign states which Napoleon sought to replace with a personal universal empire. In addition, as his armies spread through the continent, they brought with them the nationalistic ideals of the French Revolution and the bourgeois principles which called into question the legitimation of the kings and aristocratic ruling classes of Europe. For at least these two paradoxically contradictory reasons the reaction of the absolute monarchies could not be anything other than severe.

The alliance formed by the victorious powers after the defeat of Napoleon was the first large scheme in the direction of 'international government'. It was the first attempt to find a peaceful alternative to anarchy and war which went beyond a simple return to the pre-war system of equilibrium between the European powers. In the years 1814 and 1815 Austria, Great Britain, Prussia and Russia succeeded in bringing about a genuinely 'congressional government' whose duration they envisaged as being conceivably indefinite but in any case as of no less than twenty years.

'For the benefit of the world', in the words of the protocol signed by Russia, Prussia and Austria (followed in practice by Britain also), the superpowers committed themselves to an agreed schedule of international congresses for the purpose of taking 'those measures most conducive to popular tranquillity and prosperity and to the maintenance of international peace'. The Holy Alliance was, within a short time, to embrace all other European states of whatever rank and size, with the exception of the Roman See and the Sultanate, without any of these other members making the slightest claim that they should be allowed to submit to further discussion decisions which had already been taken by the superpowers. Thus for the first time in European and in world history the principle was established of an international federation for the promotion of peace whose membership was open to all states but which was under the effective control of the major European powers. This conception, as Hegel was somewhat scornfully to remark in his *Philosophy of Right*, bore a remarkable resemblance to the idea of a federation of states acting as guarantor of lasting peace which Kant had advanced in his widely circulated work *Zum ewigen Frieden* of 1795.[9]

The Holy Alliance was, however, ripe for collapse after scarcely ten years.[10] Despite the lack of any permanent organizational structure, it had, even so, successfully created at least three specialized agencies devoted to the consideration of individual issues, one of them the abolition of the slave trade. In its congresses, furthermore, it had taken in hand the resolution of several other problems of primary importance.[11]

One major cause of the demise of the Alliance was unquestionably the conflict of interest which emerged between two of the largest powers of the time, Great Britain and Russia. These interests were to leave no doubt in the end as to whether precedence went to them or resided instead in the expressions of pious international hope and Christian rhetoric which flowed from the documents of the Alliance, filled as they were with phrases, prompted by Tsar Alexander I, such as 'reciprocal benefit', 'unalterable goodwill', 'mutual affection', 'Christian charity', 'indissoluble fraternity' and so forth.[12]

A second and deeper cause of the disintegration lay in the collision between the expectations of dynastic legitimation which formed the real basis of alliance for at least three of the four great powers – Russia, Prussia and Austria – and the growing impetus of the forces of nascent European nationalism and liberalism. Shortsightedly, but in accordance with the purposes of European restoration for which it had been called into being, the Alliance acted against these forces by giving tacit consent to recourse on the part of its members to the severest imaginable military repression, especially in Italy and Spain.

The League of Nations

The First World War mobilized some seventy million combatants and resulted in over eighteen million deaths (including those of ten million civilians) and twenty-one million casualties. Physical destruction of property was also carried out on an unprecedented scale. At the end of the war resurrection of the model of the Holy Alliance took place at the instigation of the victorious powers, Great Britain, France, Italy and Japan. Formally constituted in 1920, the League of Nations represented the second great attempt to secure for the world stable peace through the institution of a permanent organization designed to supersede the earlier principle of international equilibrium. Unlike the Holy Alliance, with which it nevertheless shared many aspects in common, the League of Nations was an international organization drawn up with specific constituent elements such as an Assembly, Council, permanent Secretariat and Court of Justice.

The Assembly was composed of representatives of the governments of all the member states. Each state was entitled to one vote, and unanimity of the members present was required to implement any decision of a political nature, including those concerned with peace-threatening international disputes. In such a case, however, the parties who were themselves involved were required to abstain from voting and could not exercise a right of veto in pursuit of their own advantage.[13]

The Council was made up of both permanent and non-permanent members, those in the latter category being nominated by the Assembly. Here too the rule of unanimity applied. All four great powers, joined later by Germany and the Soviet Union, were permanent members.[14] Clearly the influence on the League of the permanent members, and especially of France and Great Britain, was hard to resist, but this did not remove the fact that the Assembly – unlike, as will be seen, the Assembly of the United Nations – constituted an international body with the authority to take decisions on matters of vital importance, such as measures to ensure the prevention of war. It is true that the Assembly did not have the power (as neither, for its part, did the Council) to send troops against a potential aggressor, but it was able to recommend sanctionary measures, representing an effective collective response, if only on a voluntary basis.[15] In this, as in all other matters, the area of its responsibility and that of the Council's were equivalent and parallel.

The inability of the League of Nations to fulfil its potential as a source of international government is most naturally and most convincingly explained by the obsessive tendency of the great powers, France above all, to employ it as a means towards rigid preservation of the *status quo.* The League had, of course, been essentially set up with very much this end in view, given its objective of holding all states, from the most down to the least powerful, to a strict adherence to the terms of the Treaty of Versailles and the other successive treaties which had brought the war to a conclusion and had imposed conditions of peace on the defeated countries. This adherence entailed above all the permanent disarmament of Germany and its relegation to a reduced political ranking. Not only was the policy of disarmament a failure but the conservative attitude of France and Great Britain also helped to keep permanently outside the League two states which had clearly succeeded in reaching premier world status, the United States and, with the exception of a brief period of inclusion, the Soviet Union.

Second, just as had earlier been the case with the Holy Alliance, the League of Nations also was discredited and in the end paralysed by the increasing distance which developed between the interests of its two most powerful members. Although, unlike the situation which was later to obtain in the United Nations, they held no exclusive right of veto, the preponderant power which these two countries wielded prevented the League from operating, either in Assembly or in Council, as a truly collective body. A series of outright violations of international order received therefore a form of tacit legitimation. These included the Italian occupation of Corfu, the Japanese invasion of Manchuria and China and the continuous infringements by Germany of the Treaty of Versailles which culminated in the invasion of Poland in 1939. The sanctions decreed against Italy for its aggression towards Ethiopia, a fellow member of the League, remained deliberately unenforced. The expulsion, finally, of the Soviet Union in December 1939 for its attack on Finland was inevitably devoid of effect: the Second World War was already in the process of breaking out and the League was for all practical purposes defunct.[16]

The United Nations

In very many of its aspects the organization of the United Nations encapsulates the history, objectives and structure of both of its two forerunners on the international stage, the Holy Alliance and the League of Nations. As the Second World War drew to a close with its tally of tens of millions of deaths – amongst them some six million Jews exterminated in the Nazi death-camps – the representatives of the governments of the United States, Great Britain, the Soviet Union and China gathered in the summer of 1944 at Dumbarton Oaks, Washington

DC, for the purpose of laying the foundations of a new international organization.

In only one respect, the system of voting among the members of the Security Council, did the proposals put forward at Dumbarton Oaks fail essentially to match the arrangements which later materialized as the United Nations. When, on 25 April 1945, the United Nations Conference met at San Francisco to bring into being the Charter of the new organization, the fifty countries which had accepted the invitation of Roosevelt, Churchill and Stalin found themselves confronted with a clear-cut position. Although a two-thirds majority was sufficient to decide the formulation of individual articles, no overall option was open to them other than that of accepting the general lines already laid down at Dumbarton Oaks (and explicitly presented by the host governments as non-negotiable) or of bringing about the immediate collapse of the initiative.[17]

Such attempts as were made to avoid dependence of the functioning of the new organization on the will of the great powers ran into obstacles at every stage. The only exception to this of any significance was the introduction of a right of self-defence granted to states in the event of their being subjected to aggression. This effectively reduced what would otherwise have been a complete monopoly of the use of military force invested in the Security Council.[18] On the other hand the proposal to grant the International Court of Justice authoritative power of interpretation of the Charter and thus a control over the legitimacy of the acts of the organization was, along with a number of other similar proposals, withdrawn. On 26 June 1945 the constitution thus devised for the United Nations received unanimous approval and was signed by the representatives of all the countries involved.[19]

In the broad outline of its structure, i.e. General Assembly, Security Council, Secretariat and Court of Justice, the United Nations repeats the essential elements of the League of Nations. Beyond this, however, many of its points of contact are more readily shared with the Holy Alliance. Even in the grandiloquence of the preamble to its Charter – which contrasts markedly with the extreme sobriety of expression used in the League of Nations Covenant – the United Nations appears to draw on the same rhetorical tradition as that which fills the pages of the Treaty of the Holy Alliance.

More particularly, the division of functions between the United Nations General Assembly and Security Council differs radically from that which obtained between the same bodies of the League of Nations. The United Nations General Assembly possesses no power of binding decision and is limited simply to the formation of recommendations. These the Security Council is not bound to take into account. Significantly, in cases where the Council already has a dispute or situation in hand, the Assembly is not then permitted to proceed with recommendations unless requested to do so.[20]

In the United Nations the totality of powers is concentrated therefore in a Security Council which, quite unlike the Council of the League of Nations, is not a purely deliberative body. Chapter VII of the Charter is, for example, given over entirely to specification of the powers of military organization and command which belong to the Council in cases where coercive international action is under consideration.[21] In granting these most important military functions to the Council, the creators of the United Nations institutional framework at Dumbarton Oaks clearly started from the premise that the League of Nations had failed precisely because of the lack of powers given to its leading organizational body.

Decisions of the Security Council do not, as was the case with the League of Nations, require unanimity, but rely instead on the principle of a qualified majority which must include votes in favour from the permanent members, which is to say the five powers victorious in the Second World War. This formulation, which gives an effective force of veto to each of the five great powers,[22] reflects the wishes expressed by Roosevelt, Churchill and Stalin at Yalta. In effect, therefore, the Security Council members enjoy an extremely high level of discretionary power to intervene in both the political and the military spheres, and yet, as was by no means the case under the League of Nations, are not bound to abstain in instances where force is needed to resolve disputes in which they are themselves involved. The natural consequence of this is that the five permanent members of the Council have the ability to exercise the very extensive powers granted to that body without themselves, thanks to their right of veto, running the risk of being at any stage subjected to those powers.

As Hans Morgenthau has frankly and realistically observed, the Holy Alliance amounted to open and unashamed international government on the part of the great powers. The League of Nations was, on the other hand, international government by the great powers tempered by the advice and consensus of all the member countries. In principle the rule of unanimity gave them the effective ability to oppose the wishes of the great powers. The United Nations, by contrast, is international government by the great powers identical in its constitutional outline to that of the Holy Alliance. It is therefore entirely autocratic, while pretending at the same time to be open and temperate in the same way as the League of Nations was.[23] The Security Council, it may then be said, has become the Holy Alliance of the twentieth century, and its five permanent members a Holy Alliance within the Holy Alliance.[24] A similar conclusion has been reached by Ian Clark, who argues that the institutional structure of the United Nations amounts to a clear regression to the eighteenth-century position whereby the fate of all other states lay at the mercy of the changeable alliance between the great powers. The Charter of the United Nations failed even to grant the concessions in favour of the interests of weaker states which the Covenant of the League of Nations had earlier provided for.[25]

In practice, given the circumstances whereby the United States and the Soviet Union formed the only true superpowers, the Charter of the United Nations guaranteed these two countries a highly extensive coercive control over international relations without, however, providing means for the resolution of any conflict potentially arising between them. The lack of a requirement to abstain should they both be involved in a dispute which required the use of military force, and the mechanism of the veto formed two highly effective obstacles to any altercation between the countries being internationally regulated against their own volition.

The Prolonged Agony of the United Nations

In its first years the United Nations operated very much under the hegemony of the United States, one of whose actions was the decision to house the organization on its own territory and to account for at least one quarter of its expenses (a situation which continues to obtain today).[26] Evidence of this domination is to be seen in the 1947 decision to constitute the state of Israel, where it was plain not only that this decision exceeded the remit of the United Nations but that establishment of the state in Palestine ran contrary to the wishes of the great majority of the inhabitants of the territories involved. Furthermore, in 1950, the United States was able to take advantage of the temporary absence of the Soviet delegation to the Security Council and to respond to the invasion of South Korea by launching its own attack against the North under the auspices of the United Nations (whose flag remains flying to this day over the military demarcation line between the two Koreas).

From the beginning of the 1950s, however, up until the end of the 1980s the rivalry between the two superpowers (and their subsequent sharing of power along the lines of a sort of twofold 'Brezhnev doctrine') brought paralysis once again to the notion of 'international government'. The logic of equilibrium between sovereign states – this time in the form of a matched and escalating nuclear deterrent – again came to dictate the terms of war and peace between the nations of the world.

It is common knowledge that both of the superpowers repeatedly and almost as a matter of course have violated the principles set out in the preamble to the Charter of the United Nations through their attempts in the Security Council to protect their own positions, and those of their allies, by a systematic use of the right of veto.[27] Both have involved themselves in long-drawn-out armed conflicts: the United States in Vietnam, the Soviet Union in Afghanistan. And both have embarked on the pursuit of more limited military objectives such as, in the case of the United States, Guatemala (1954), Lebanon (1958), Cuba (1961), the Dominican Republic (1965), Grenada (1983), Libya (1986) and Panama (1989), and, in the case of the Soviet Union, the invasions in Eastern Europe in 1956 and 1968. In one instance only, that of the United States's support of the Contras in Nicaragua, has condemnation been forthcoming from the International Court of Justice, a result entirely ignored by virtue of its power of veto by the United States government.[28]

For over forty years now the two superpowers and their respective military alliances, NATO and the Warsaw Pact, have edged the United Nations out of the international arena and nullified the wide military and political powers formally possessed by the Security Council. Few of the Chapter VII rules, designed to bring the use of armed force under the control of the Security Council, have ever been applied. In particular article 47, which provides for the constitution of a Military Staff Committee composed of the Chiefs of Staff of the five permanent members of the Security Council, has remained entirely ineffectual. This committee was to have been responsible for the strategic direction of all armed forces put at the disposal of the Security Council. The most, however, that the Security Council has ever been authorized to do is to exercise functions of vastly inferior importance to those envisaged for it in the Charter, such as the exercise of placing invited peacekeeping forces between parties in conflict (as in the Middle East, the Congo and Cyprus).

Nor has the General Assembly achieved anything other than declarations of principle lacking legal potency such as the Universal Declaration of Human Rights of 1948 or its many long-winded and unspecific documents on such world problems as aid to underdeveloped countries, protection of the environment, development of international trade, demographic control, human rights. The vast majority of these, such as, typically, the 1974 programme for a New International Economic Order (NIEO), have never been more than dead letters. And this has been the case even in the circumstances of the 1960s when the process of widespread decolonization created favourable conditions for the entry into the United Nations of many of the Third World countries, as well as the People's Republic of China (1971). Hopes were raised by this that the General Assembly would be able to overcome its lack of power and find a way of exercising some sort of significant function. Such illusions, however, fostered as they were by the creation of a plethora of commissions on the part of the Assembly and the Economic and Social Council, were destined to wilt in the face of opposition from the United States and the western powers and indifference from the Soviet Union. The nadir of impotence, passivity and lack of status occurred – to borrow Richard Falk's observation – with the election in 1971 as Secretary General, followed by renewal in 1976, of a figure such as Kurt Waldheim.[29]

Some Political-Philosophical Questions

At this stage I propose to consider some of the political-philosophical questions which arise from the consideration of international insti-tutions as they stood at the point so far reached, the end of the 1980s. Clearly subsequent events, in the shape of the collapse of the Soviet empire and the outbreak of the Gulf War, have brought about highly significant further developments. But, before turning attention to these in the next chapter, I wish first to attempt to formulate certain questions which it will be the aim of this study to answer.

None of the three schemes for lasting and universal peace which have been brought into being over the last two centuries has, as we have seen, achieved any notable degree of success. On a strictly political level their lack of effect appears attributable to, first, the tendency of stronger states to pursue their own advantage through the practice of a power politics flagrantly contradictory to the principles to which they had previously expressed adherence; second, the lack of any provision for the peaceful resolution of quarrels which have risen between these states; third, the difficulty over the long term of reconciling, without self-contradictory recourse to the use of force, the maintenance of peace with the defence of the international *status quo* and its need for the institutional concentration and legitimation of power.

In the event, not only has peace not been maintained but the potential for world conflict has developed immensely. Worldwide military spend-ing has continued to grow unchecked, as have the global stocks both of conventional arms and of the more sophisticated weaponry and strategic nuclear arsenals held by the major powers. A recent finding of the Stockholm International Peace Research Institute is that world military spending rose from $220 billion in 1950 to $610 billion in 1970, and reached a high point of $950 billion in 1987.[30] Perhaps not unconnectedly, some 130 armed conflicts are known to have arisen in the years from 1935 to today, resulting in a total of not fewer than thirty-five million deaths.

Regardless of the military aspects, however, it is important, to my mind, to try to discover what political philosophy and what peacemaking and peacekeeping theories lay behind the failed attempts of the three schemes designed to solve the problems of international anarchy and war. One key to the problem, as I have indicated above, lies in seeing how 'the cosmopolitan model of the Holy Alliance' has been held in common by all three schemes. I define this model as comprising at least the following characteristics.

First, the task of fostering and maintaining peace is entrusted to a highly centralized locus of power, which results in the international system being conceived in terms of a very simple cosmopolitan structure. At the top stands a small group of great powers – frequently no more than two – to whom all other 'peripheral' countries are subordinate. So asymmetrical and polarized is this hierarchy that the powers which find themselves at the peak of the Cosmopolis are able to assume coercive control of the international disputes which arise between other countries, while at the same time ensuring de facto – and even, under the United Nations, de jure – that they do not themselves become subject to any form of coercive control in potential disputes concerning their own relations either with one another or with the other countries.

Second, the federative element of a cosmopolitan scheme boils down in practice to allowance for cases in which the collective use of military force will be either recommended or directly pursued. Very little importance is attached to other possible forms of cohesion or even of general international co-operation, and no consideration is taken of the part potentially available to be played by the internal political institutions of the various countries. Kant was firm in his insistence that a federation should, at minimum, be one of republican states, each one heedful of the rights to freedom of its own citizens. In the event, however, none of the three historical schemes has seen any incompatibility between the aim of peace and the despotic, totalitarian or police-state nature of certain among the regimes included in them. Article 1 of the United Nations Charter makes an idealistic reference to 'respect for fundamental freedoms and the rights of man', but, over and beyond this, the suitability of various governments to express the interests or the expectations of their respective populations has never been taken into account. Truman, Churchill and – for all his notorious hostility towards any possible interference from the West – Stalin had no difficulty in subscribing to the demands of the Charter, for the reason that these had no bearing on internal relations between governments and their citizens. In the case of the League of Nations, any reference to these relations was totally excluded, with the full agreement of the United States President, Woodrow Wilson. A Japanese proposal to include in the Covenant a clause forbidding racial discrimination within the member states was rejected.[31]

Third, for all the weakness of the federative bonds which exist within the Cosmopolis, the power of coercive intervention in peace-threatening disputes creates an outright monopoly of the international use of armed force which is granted to the institution, and so, in effect, to the superpowers. This is particularly true of the United Nations Security Council, where an extreme form of the 'domestic analogy' applies: international order is guaranteed only if the states relinquish their ability to exercise justice on their own account and agree to submit themselves in Hobbesian fashion to the absolute power of a global Leviathan.[32] What follows from this is a drastic departure both from the classic principle, dating from the Peace of Westphalia, of the sovereignty and independence of modern states and from the principle of the sovereign equality of states, vacuously and incompatibly enunciated in article 2 of the United Nations Charter.

Fourth, universal and lasting peace, seen as the greatest aim of collective endeavour, tends to go hand-in-hand with a freezing of the world's political, economic and military map as it is at the time of the constitution of the organization. Again, this involves a remarkably primitive notion of the Cosmoplis, in that the idea of peace is opposed not only to that of war but also, implicitly, to the notions of social change, development and productive rivalry.

Fifth, general references to social well-being, work security and respect for human rights forming a basis for the growth of friendly relations between the nations are to be found in the Covenant of the League of Nations as well as in the Charter of the United Nations.[33] But, apart from these, which are given no further prescriptive formulation, no general theory of peacemaking appears to have informed the minds of the statesmen who created the conceptions of the three projects for peace. It is in any case hard to envisage a coherent philosophy of peace which could, in the case of the United Nations, have been shared by such diverse figures as Stalin, Churchill and Truman. The entirely pragmatic outcome aimed for by the international organization is that diplomatic or military intervention is pursued only when a dispute emerges or armed conflict breaks out. As a result, attention is not given to any possible general strategy for the prevention of war. The Covenant of the League of Nations did at least make some reference to the problem of disarmament and the need to control arms traffic and the production of arms by private companies. None of these issues is even touched upon by the Charter of the United Nations. It is noticeable that, throughout the long Iran–Iraq War (1980–8), all five permanent members of the Security Council, and probably also Israel, derived considerable financial benefit from their sales of large quantities of arms to both sides involved in the conflict.[34]

Sixth, the cosmopolitan model of the Holy Alliance has historically been arrived at without apparent indebtedness to any particular political philosophy or social theory, or in any event indebtedness to any notion remotely comparable with the influence which philosophical theory has exercised on the growth of the modern liberal democratic state and its law-making institutions. This is surprising in view of the long European tradition of institutional pacifism and international political theory which can be traced through Erasmus, Hugo Grotius, Émeric Crucé, le duc de Sully, William Penn, l'abbé de Saint-Pierre, Rousseau, Bentham, Kant and Kelsen.[35] The question naturally arises whether this occurred as a result of a paucity of exposure to political theory on the part of the individual framers of the three political projects (including President Wilson, whose international idealism was greatly drawn upon at the formative stage of the League of Nations), or whether the mediocrity of the European philosophical tradition concerning the subject of peace and war has not instead been the principal cause. In addition, at a still deeper level, the effect should also be considered of the lack of a political theory of international relations which was identified by Martin Wight at the end of the 1960s.[36]

The following three questions of political philosophy therefore seem to me to merit particular consideration.

First, has there not in all likelihood been something radically mis-taken in the conceptualization of the first three attempts to create 'lasting and universal peace'?

Second, is it possible that their fault lies in not having been able fully to realize the 'centralist' and 'globalist' objective of a world government which, following the 'domestic analogy', has been the particular aim of the founders of the United Nations? Or, by contrast, is it the very attempt to overcome at international level the statist structure and inherently anarchic fragmentation of power which cannot be successful so long as it is exercised in accordance with the cosmopolitan model of the Holy Alliance?

Third, more basically still, can it be that the quest for lasting and universal peace amounts to no more than a utopian aspiration which cannot fail to founder on the rocks of real-life political forces? Is it the case that aggression and war, as certain anthropologists maintain, go so deep into the roots of *homo sapiens* that they have to be considered wholly innate instincts and even, in the final analysis, evolutionary necessities? Was the failure of the Holy Alliance, the League of Nations and the United Nations therefore inevitable and their inability to maintain peace a matter which went far beyond the theoretical or practical limitations of these organizations? Can any cosmopolitan project ever be anything other than an inherently hegemonic and violent undertaking?

Notes

1 The term *Cosmopolis* is employed here in accordance with the meaning given to it by Stephen Toulmin in his essay *Cosmopolis: The Hidden Agenda of Modernity*, New York: The Free Press, 1990. According to Toulmin one of the most characteristic expressions of the Enlightenment (and of Newtonian scientism) was the effort to build a new Cosmopolis. In origin the term *Cosmopolis* belongs to Stoic philosophy, where it denoted the idea of a close correlation between the harmony of the universe (*cosmos*) and the political order of a human community (*polis*). It should be noted that the adjectival form 'cosmopolitan' has been adopted for the purposes of the present work rather than the less wieldy 'cosmopolitical' indicated by Toulmin (p. 134).

2 B. V. A. Röling, 'Are Grotius' Ideas Obsolete?', in H. Bull, B. Kingsbury and A. Roberts (eds), *Hugo Grotius and International Relations*, Oxford: Oxford University Press, 1990, pp. 292–3.

3 See: G. Modelski, 'Long Cycles of World Leadership', in W. R. Thompson (ed.), *Contending Approaches to World System Analysis*, Beverly Hills: Sage Publications, 1983; R. Gilpin, *War and Change in World Politics*, Cambridge: Cambridge University Press, 1981; I. Wallerstein, *The Modern World System, II*, New York: Academic Press, 1980.

4 W. R. Thompson, *On Global War: Historical-Structural Approaches to World Politics*, Columbia (SC): University of South Carolina Press, 1988, p. 5.

5 R. Väyrynen, 'Global Power Dynamics and Collective Violence', in R. Väyrynen, D. Senghaas and C. Schmidt (eds), *The Quest for Peace*, London: Sage Publications, 1987, pp. 81ff.

6 For an important exception cf. H. J. Morgenthau, *Politics Among Nations*, New York: Knopf, 1960, pp. 456–77; on system analysis cf. Väyrynen, 'Global Power Dynamics', pp. 80–96.

7 I. Clark, *The Hierarchy of States*, Cambridge: Cambridge University Press, 1989, pp. 219–20.

8 L. Gross, 'The Peace of Westphalia 1648–1948', *American Journal of International Law*, 42 (1948), 1, pp. 20–41; R. A. Falk, 'The Interplay of Westphalia and Charter Conceptions of International Legal Order', in C. A. Blach and R. A. Falk (eds), *The Future of International Legal Order*, I, Princeton: Princeton University Press, 1969, pp. 32–70.

9 G. W. F. Hegel, *Grundlinien der Philosophie des Rechts* (1821), ed. E. Gans, Stuttgart: Friedrich Frommann Verlag, 1964, pp. 434–5; Engl. trans., *Elements of the Philosophy of Right* (addition to paragraph 324), ed. A. W. Wood, Cambridge: Cambridge University Press, 1991, p. 362. Norberto

Bobbio criticizes Hegel for deriding Kant's project as if it were the dream of a visionary (cf. N. Bobbio, *Il terzo assente*, Turin: Edizioni Sonda, 1989, p. 104). In fact Hegel derides Kant for the opposite reason, that his project seems to have been realized by the Holy Alliance: 'Thus, Kant proposed a league of sovereigns to settle disputes between states, and the Holy Alliance was meant to be an institution more or less of this kind.' On Kantian pacifism see, among a few others, W. B. Gallie, *Philosophers of Peace and War: Kant, Clausewitz, Marx, Engels and Tolstoy*, Cambridge: Cambridge University Press, 1978, pp. 8–36; M. Doyle, 'Kant, Liberal Legacies, and Foreign Affairs', *Philosophy and Public Affairs*, 12 (1983), 2, pp. 230ff; A J. Hurrell, 'Kant and the Kantian Paradigm in International Relations', *Review of International Studies*, 16 (1990), 3, pp. 183–205; G. Marini, 'Kants Idee einer Weltrepublik', in P. J. M. von Tongeren et al. (eds), *Eros and Eris*, Dordrecht: Kluwer Academic Publishers, 1992, pp. 133–46; T. Donaldson, 'Kant's Global Rationalism', in T. Nardin and D. R. Mapel (eds), *Traditions of International Ethics*, Cambridge: Cambridge University Press, 1992, pp. 136–57.

10 From 1825 to the institution of the League of Nations in 1920 regulation of the relationships between the European states was committed to the so-called 'Concert of Europe', that is to single international conferences summoned *ad hoc* – e.g. in Geneva (1864 and 1906), The Hague (1899 and 1907) and London (1908 and 1909) – and to the Permanent Court of Arbitration.

11 H. J. Morgenthau, *Politics among Nations*, p. 464; F. H. Hinsley, *Power and the Pursuit of Peace*, Cambridge: Cambridge University Press, 1978, pp. 195–212, 213–8.

12 In 1821, for instance, a Russian proposal for collective armed intervention in support of the Greek nationalistic uprising against the Ottoman empire was turned down by the British Foreign Minister (and, of course, by Metternich).

13 Actually, article 15 of paragraph 10 of the Covenant of the League of Nations introduced a second exception to unanimity, namely when the controversy was transmitted to the Assembly from the Council. In this case a majority of the members of the Assembly sufficed, provided that this majority included the representatives of the states which were also members of the Council. This exception, at least formally, made somewhat more effective the interventive power of the Assembly. See the Covenant in appendix to F. S. Northedge, *The League of Nations: Its Life and Times 1920–1946*, New York: Holmes & Meier, 1986, pp. 317–27.

14 Initially the non-permanent members were only four, but later reached the number of eleven, with the result that, from 1922 on, a large majority of the Council was composed of non-permanent members. At its greatest state of expansion the League of Nations included seventy states.

15 A. Cassese, *Il diritto internazionale nel mondo contemporaneo*, Bologna: Il Mulino, 1984; Engl. trans. *International Law in a Divided World*, Oxford: Oxford University Press, 1986, p. 61.

16 Hinsley, *Power and the Pursuit of Peace*, pp. 309–22.

17 B. Conforti, *Le Nazioni Unite*, Padua: Cedam, 1994, pp. 1–6; see also R. C. Hilderbrand, *Dumbarton Oaks: The Origins of the United Nations and the Search for Postwar Security*, Chapel Hill: University of North Carolina Press, 1990; R. B. Russell, *A History of the United Nations Charter: The Role of the*

United States 1940–1945, Washington (DC): The Brookings Institution, 1958; see in particular the appendix to this broad historical and documentary reconstruction which contains the text of the 'United States Tentative Proposals for a General International Organization' (pp. 995–1006), the text of the 'Dumbarton Oaks Proposals for the Establishment of a General International Organization' (pp. 1019–28) and a telling 'Guide to Evolution of Charter Articles' (pp. 1067–72).

18 See article 51 of the Charter of the United Nations which, contrary to the intentions expressed at Dumbarton Oaks, recognizes the 'inherent right of individual or collective self-defence if an armed attack occurs against a Member of the United Nations, until the Security Council has taken the measures necessary to maintain international peace or security'.

19 Within a few weeks of this the Second World War finally came to an end, after the atomic bombardment of Hiroshima and Nagasaki by the United States on 6 and 10 August 1945. Precisely between these dates, on 8 August, the victorious powers signed in London their agreement for the constitution of the International Military Tribunal of Nuremberg in order to prosecute German war criminals.

20 Article 12 states that 'While the Security Council is exercising in respect of any dispute or situation the functions assigned to it in the present Charter, the General Assembly shall not make any recommendation with regard to that dispute or situation unless the Security Council so requests.'

21 See in particular articles 42, 43, 45, 46 and 47.

22 That is, the United States, Soviet Union, United Kingdom, France and China. The ten non-permanent members are designated by the General Assembly every two years. From 1945 to 1965, however, the members of the Security Council numbered eleven, the non-permanent members being six and the qualified majority necessary for the deliberations being seven. During that time, therefore, the five permanent members needed to win the agreement of only two non-permanent members in order to reach the number required for the majority.

23 Morgenthau, *Politics among Nations*, p. 480: 'The United Nations is an international government of the great powers which resembles in its constitutional arrangements the Holy Alliance and in its pretense the League of Nations.'

24 Morgenthau, *Politics among Nations*, p. 480.

25 Clark, *The Hierarchy of States*, pp. 217–18.

26 The financing mechanism of the United Nations poses serious problems in many respects. The fact that eight big or middle powers contribute almost three-quarters of the budget – United States (25%), Japan (10.8%), Russia (10.2%), Germany (8.2%), France (6.4%), United Kingdom (4.9%), Italy (3.8%) and Canada (3.1%) – whereas the other 151 members contribute a little more than 27%, provides the eight financially hegemonic states with an additional power of veto against any unwelcome initiative. The budget of the United Nations for the financial year 1992–3 was US$2.363 billion.

27 The United States has used the power of veto to protect in particular the state of Israel, which has often been accused and sometimes even formally censured on account of its numerous violations of the UN Charter.

28 The veto has been exercised against the measures that the Security Council could take on the basis of article 94 of the Charter. 'In fact none of the Big Five in the Security Council has been willing to submit its claims to use force

to the normative discipline of international accountability, seeking to the greatest extent possible to avoid even a debate as to its propriety under the UN Charter' (R. A. Falk, S. S. Kim and S. H. Mendlovitz (eds), *The United Nations and a Just World Order*, Boulder–San Francisco–Oxford: Westview Press, 1991, p. 3).

29 Falk, Kim and Mendlovitz (eds), *The United Nations and a Just World Order*, p. xi. On the normative functions of the General Assembly see G. Arangio-Ruiz, *The Normative Role of the General Assembly of the United Nations and the Declaration of Principles of Friendly Relations*, Leyden: A. W. Sijthoff, 1972.

30 These expenses are measured in US dollars, with reference to their average value in 1988. Global military spending slightly decreased in 1989 ($910 billion) and fell by about 6 per cent in 1990 (to a little over $850 billion).

31 Northedge, *The League of Nations*, pp. 44–5.

32 On the domestic analogy, see H. Suganami, *The Domestic Analogy and World Order Proposals*, Cambridge: Cambridge University Press, 1989. On domestic analogy in the establishment of the United Nations see particularly pp. 114–28. This argument adopts the view that the creation of order between states parallels its development within them.

33 See for instance article 55 of the UN Charter and article 23 of the Covenant.

34 Falk, Kim and Mendlovitz (eds), *The United Nations and a Just World Order*, p. 3.

35 For a survey of the history of internationalist theories, see Hinsley, *Power and the Pursuit of Peace*, pp. 13–149.

36 M. Wight, 'Why is there no International Theory?', in H. Butterfield and M. Wight (eds), *Diplomatic Investigations*, London: George Allen & Unwin, 1969, pp. 17–34.

2 The Gulf War: The First Cosmopolitan War

> The United Nations' failure in relation to the Gulf War is tragic and far-reaching.
>
> R. A. Falk, 'Reflections on the Gulf War'

> The military interventions of the United Nations are without exception mistaken: where they are not useless, they do damage.
>
> Hans Georg Gadamer, *Interview*

The United States Wins the Fourth World War

The year 1987 saw the emergence of *perestroika* in the Soviet Union and the establishment of Mikhail Gorbachev and Edward Shevardnadze as world figures. From this point there began to take shape what the new UN Secretary General, Javier Pérez de Cuéllar, claimed to be able to call 'the growing commonality factor in international affairs'.[1]

This plunge into international affairs on the part of the Soviet Union has not ended without embarrassment to the United States, and it is worth tracing how this process has occurred. In place of the traditional Soviet distrust of the United Nations, a diplomatic offensive was launched which heralded recognition of the value of such concepts as 'global interdependence' and a 'comprehensive security system'.[2] In his speech to the 42nd session of the UN General Assembly, Edward Shevardnadze went as far as proposing the setting-up of a naval peacekeeping force and the establishment of a permanent military unit under the control of the Security Council, to be composed of troops furnished by each of the member states in rotation.

Such enthusiastic Soviet initiatives in these directions gained impetus in the short term from the cautious support they received from the United States and the energy of the new Secretary General. For a while an era of international co-operation appeared to have arrived and, for the first time since its inception, the United Nations seemed capable of fulfilling the global role assigned to it by the great powers in 1945. With the causes of antagonism between the two superpowers removed, the time seemed ripe for an expansion of the existing functions of the Security Council as an organ of international government dedicated to the service of peace. In July 1987 an event occurred which had been completely without precedent in the history of the United Nations: an important resolution of the Security Council, which dealt with the Iran–Iraq war, was presented to the Council and received unanimous approval from all five permanent members.

The practical results of this were by any standard impressive, even if they are viewed for the most part as natural consequences of the ending of the Cold War. It may be recalled that the constitution of the United Nations is so framed that agreement between the largest powers is a condition which is *de facto*, if not *de jure*, not only necessary but also sufficient for its functioning. The years 1988 and 1989 saw a remarkable series of events: under United Nations auspices Soviet withdrawal from Afghanistan was facilitated, the Iran–Iraq war was concluded, peace negotiations were initiated in Cambodia, and conditions were created which were to lead to the independence of Namibia. In 1988 the United Nations was awarded the Nobel Prize for Peace.

In 1990, however, after the 'democratic revolution' which freed the countries of Eastern Europe from Soviet domination and led within a short time to the reunification of Germany, the situation quickly changed. The United States's support of the United Nations became progressively more qualified and selective in that the Soviet proposals for strengthening the military functions of the Security Council were allowed to lapse, and only very limited controls on nuclear armaments were accepted. More significantly, the traditional political hegemony of the United States in the Middle East and Central America underwent no change at all.[3]

It became increasingly clear at this point that the end of the Cold War had resulted also in the end of bipolarity. The Soviet Union was in the process of breaking down not only as a great power but even as a political entity. Not without certain elements of pathos or without arousing mixed feelings amongst the international community, Mikhail Gorbachev and Edward Shevardnadze lost their primacy on the world stage as, together with them, did the Soviet Union itself. The new-found internationalist fervour of the Soviet Union turned out to have been in the end no more than the other face of the imminent collapse of its empire.

The United States and its western allies could therefore congratulate themselves on having won, thanks to economic and technological superiority and without having fired a single shell, what might well be called the third world war – or, if the Napoleonic wars are rightfully included, the fourth. On 7 July 1990 the decision was taken in Moscow to dismantle the military structure of the Warsaw Pact. The Soviet Union had surrendered unconditionally.

'Global Security' and the 'New World Order'

In chapter 1 it was seen how on three occasions over the past two centuries those powers which had triumphed in large-scale conflicts subsequently devised cosmopolitan schemes to ensure lasting and universal peace. The close of the Cold War has proved no exception to this practice. For at that point the United States and its victorious western allies conceived the idea of a 'New World Order' and launched a new strategy for universal peace.

Naturally the need has not presented itself in this case, as it did with the League of Nations and the United Nations, for the wholesale construction of an international organization. Instead it has been more a matter of reworking the existing model. For, despite the prolonged death-pains of the institution itself, the organizational structure of the United Nations has survived the Cold War intact and even, towards the end of the war, rediscovered a certain vitality. The task facing the victors this time has therefore been one of reinterpreting the role of the United Nations and other international organizations in the light of the post-war situation. This situation is one in which, despite its current economic problems, the United States has emerged as the only power able to play an extended strategic role and, through its military might, capable of occupying a commanding position in relation to the whole of the rest of the world.[4]

It has become the case, therefore, that – for all the great and perhaps even growing difficulty of the task – the job of guaranteeing the world lasting and universal peace lies now solely in the hands of the United States. This is a situation totally without modern precedent. From at least the time of the Peace of Westphalia no single state – even Great Britain, whose victory over France extended broadly into the last years of the League of Nations – has found itself in so untrammelled a position of world hegemony. At the centre of the planetary system of the Cosmopolis there now shines no more than a single star. The cosmopolitan model of the Holy Alliance, conceived and painfully built up as a means to guarantee peace on the basis of agreement between at least two superpowers, is therefore unquestionably bound to undergo dramatic functional alterations. Inevitably now, the scheme of universal peace will tend to coincide with the strategy for preservation of the *status quo* which the victorious superpower considers best for the protection of its own particular 'vital interests' *qua* single superpower. And, clearly, it will be as part of this strategy rather than in contention with it that the emerging role of the United Nations will lie. The United Nations was of course conceived, in the same way as the Holy Alliance and the League of Nations had been before it, as just such a means by which victorious powers could be assured coercive control over the world order.

On 2 August 1990, in a speech delivered at Aspen, Colorado, President Bush – as previously Woodrow Wilson had with his Fourteen Points in 1918, and as F. D. Roosevelt and Winston Churchill had with the Atlantic Charter in 1941 – outlined a new scheme for lasting and universal peace. This scheme was further elaborated in August 1991, i.e. a few months after the conclusion of the Gulf War, in the directive entitled *National Security Strategy of the United States*[5] and, at the beginning of 1992, the strategic lines traced by the President were developed in detail in the significant document *Defense Planning Guidance*, produced by staff drawn from the State Department and the Pentagon under the chairmanship of the Under-Secretary of Defense, Paul Wolfowitz.[6] In the meantime an extensive amount of specialist literature filled out the strategic and military implications of the notion of 'global security' which lay at the centre of these documents. In a world no longer divided by ideological conflict but instead ever more interdependent, it was argued, threats to peace do not disappear but become more diffuse and insidious. To combat these, new forms are needed of the concentration and application of international power.[7]

In essence the strategic pointers contained in these documents may be identified as the following.

First, the collapse of the Soviet Union and the ending of the Cold War have brought about a new era in which the global nuclear threat has finally been removed. The United States has within its grasp the 'extraordinary opportunity' to bring about a fair and peaceful international system, based on the western values of freedom and democracy. The only power capable of guaranteeing such world order and security in the post-nuclear age is the United States.

Second, construction of the New World Order should take place on the basis of a 'global' security system which takes account of the growing economic, technological and information-based interdependence of the planet. (In this respect the new US strategy paradoxically appears to owe not a little to the conceptual categories employed by the Soviet Union in its period of *perestroika*.) Such a 'global security' system demands close co-operation between the countries of the three great industrial areas of the world – North America, Europe (headed by Germany) and Japan – beneath the overarching political and military leadership of the United States.

Third, organization of a 'global security' system means that drastic alteration is necessary to the strategy of NATO (as well as to that of the Western European Union and the Conference for Security and Cooperation in Europe).[8] Restrictions on the traditional geographical ambit of the Atlantic alliance should be loosened so as to take account of the increasing dangers of international anarchy arising from a multiplicity of regional areas, especially from the so-called Third World. Here in particular lies the most serious potential source of threats, not solely of a military nature, to collective security and peace as a result of the many possible causes of conflict it contains. Increasing economic disparity between different Third World countries, aggravated nation-alistic interests, religious intolerance, racial hatred, demographic pressure, climatic variations on a scale potentially leading to environmental disaster are all factors capable of threatening the security of the world community and in particular the interests of the industrialized nations.[9]

Fourth, as a result of the increased complexity and interdependence of international factors, the vital interests of the industrial nations have developed greater vulnerability. These interests include regular and unimpeded access to sources of energy (above all oil), the ready supply of raw materials, the stability of world markets (especially the world financial market) and the freedom and security of commerce by air and sea. At a further level they extend also to the repression of international political terrorism and to a check on the proliferation of biological, chemical and nuclear weapons. In respect of the last, danger is already sufficiently posed by Third World countries such as Iraq, Iran, India, Pakistan and North Korea.

Fifth, in order to achieve concrete realization of the aims of the new strategy, the great industrial powers will have to be strong-minded enough to set aside the old principle of non-interference in the internal affairs of sovereign states. They will need to exercise, and to claim *de facto* legitimation of, the duty they have to carry out 'humanitarian intervention' in all cases where they judge intervention to be necessary to resolve crises within individual states.

From the viewpoint of this strategy, the Gulf War could readily be interpreted as the first opportunity for the United States to realize the conditions of 'permanent peace'. Seen thus, the war became 'the crucible of the New World Order'. The crisis in the Persian Gulf found a world community ready as never before to organize collective intervention in order to repress by force an act of aggression against a member of the United Nations. For the first time in its history, declared the United States President, the United Nations had fulfilled the role originally envisaged for it by its founding fathers.

The Gulf War: A Global War

The difficulty of giving actual fulfilment to the peace guarantee promised by international 'global security' – the linchpin of the American reworking of the cosmopolitan model of the Holy Alliance – became very rapidly apparent. On 2 August 1990 the Iraqi invasion of Kuwait took place, and military occupation of the country began. Between August and November the UN Security Council passed a series of resolutions which began with condemnation of the Iraqi aggression and demanded that sovereignty be restored to Kuwait, moved on to the imposition of an embargo, and ended on 29 November with the passing of resolution 678. By this the Council authorized member states, provided Iraq failed to comply with the preceding resolutions by 15 January, to take all necessary measures to reinstate Kuwaiti sovereignty and to restore peace and security to the area.[10]

Following the expiry of the ultimatum, Operation 'Desert Storm' was unleashed on 17 January and lasted six weeks, until the signing of a cease-fire by Iraq and the United States took place on 28 February. The armed conflict ended with the defeat of Iraq, liberation of Kuwait, restoration of the semi-feudal regime of the Emir, Jaber al-Ahmed al-Sabah, and a continued military presence of the United States in the Middle Eastern zone estimated at about a hundred thousand personnel.[11]

The war had involved over half a million men and women of the American forces and about 160,000 combatants from some twenty-seven allied countries, all of which formed the largest military expedition in the history of the world.[12] It has been calculated that the Allies used a greater quantity of explosives in the forty-two days of 'Desert Storm' than were used in the whole of the Second World War.[13] The loss of human life incurred in the war has been impossible to ascertain with any accuracy, since no authority in Iraq or in the West has been responsible for compiling total figures. All that is known for certain is that the losses sustained by the United States forces amounted to 148 dead, 37 of them the victims of 'friendly fire'. Credible evaluations of Iraqi losses put the corresponding figure in excess of 220,000, including civilian casualties.[14]

The destructive power of the weapons used in the conflict has given rise to the observation that the technological sophistication of present-day 'conventional' arms has shown itself to be so effective and 'clean' as to cause the future use, perhaps even the manufacture, of nuclear weapons to be superfluous. Stockpiling of such weapons has been shown to be dangerously disproportionate even to the needs of a global war, whose likelihood, at least for the near future, seems to have been in any case reduced. The very distinction between conventional and non-conventional armaments seems to a large degree to have lost its traditional military significance[15] and even, assuming it ever had one, its moral one also. Ramsey Clark, Attorney General from 1961 to 1968, has stated that the use by his country of conventional weapons in the Gulf War exceeded the bounds of war crimes and crimes against humanity established by the international conventions and by the rules of the Nuremberg Tribunal.[16]

It is known that fuel-air explosives, together with cluster bombs, were used on the final night of the land offensive. By this point in the war, defeat of the Iraqi army had largely been achieved, Radio Baghdad had announced its country's future adherence to resolution 660, and the process of withdrawal of troops from Kuwait had already begun. On the infamous 'Highway of Death', the road which joins Kuwait City with Bassora, a logjam of vehicles over more than ten kilometres in length was annihilated in the course of that night by a prolonged series of attacks from the air.[17] Once again the enormous disparity in military technology between the two sides was demonstrated, and the absurdly disproportionate losses find a parallel only in the atomic bombing of Hiroshima and Nagasaki.

Two further aspects lend credence to the idea that what took place in the Gulf was the first unsimulated experiment in what one US general has termed the 'warfare of the future'. The first of these is the destruction of the environment which was caused in varying degrees by the exceptional amount of explosive – in some cases highly toxic and even radioactive – which was detonated,[18] by the power of the sophisticated weaponry and by the crude oil which was either set alight or spilt into the waters of the Persian Gulf.[19] Experts calculate that the pollution which took place of earth, water, air, sea and the upper atmosphere cannot avoid, in both the short and the long run, causing further severe damage to human, plant and animal life not only in terms of the regional ecosystem but also on a wider planetary level. The ecological disaster has with some justice been compared by T. M. Hawley to those which took place earlier at Bhopal and Chernobyl, the difference being that in this case it was non-accidental.[20]

The second aspect is the televisual. So great was the quantity of highly spectacular information transmitted around the world that the Gulf War was unquestionably the most 'communicated' event so far in human history. But it was accompanied at the same time by the strictest secrecy surrounding the military operations and a severe form of censorship which on more than one occasion drew protest from the news and television journalists of the western countries. Information, both in quantity and quality, was subordinated to the logic itself of the war, and a well-defined strategy of politico-military communication was followed.[21] Opportunities for the reporting and description of death, suffering and destruction were reduced to the minimum, while other aspects – often those best tailored for television – were instead given emphasis, such as the sophistication and precision of the weaponry, the professionalism of the fighting forces, the efficiency of the planning and organization. In some cases the conduct itself of military operations was adapted so as to serve best the demands of media presentation.[22]

In this sense too – over and beyond, as we shall see, its compliance with the strategic model of 'global security' – the Gulf War may be said to have been, in the precise technical meaning of the term, a 'global war'.[23] Hundreds of millions of people throughout the world were, by the means of television, drawn into, and fascinated by, the spectacle of a 'live' war. None of them, however, were in a position to assess or control the credibility of the flood of information which, coming as it did with such speed, continuity and urgency, operated even at a subliminal level. On at least a cognitive level, no one was left untouched by the violence of the war. There is a certain truth in the contention of Jean Baudrillard that the Gulf War in some sense never really existed as such, but was more a figment created by the international television network.[24]

A Global Cosmopolitan War

The Gulf War, perhaps more than most modern wars, may reasonably be called – to adopt the terminology of the preamble to the United Nations Charter – a 'scourge'. It brought about, in the words of the official report to the UN Secretary General, 'an almost apocalyptic devastation which has returned Iraq to preindustrial conditions'.[25] It was a scourge which, as ever in the past, international institutions were powerless to prevent, but which on the other hand, and for the first time in history, they formally legitimized and concerted as a cosmopolitan action. What, then, has been the response of those concerned with the legal and philosophical aspects of the war?

Reactions to the Gulf War have been noticeable for the extent to which they have crossed established party lines between what has long been thought of in western public opinion as 'left' and 'right', as well as the infinitely less transparent divisions which continue to separate conservative and more progressive positions. Many of the most authoritative 'masters' of western thought, ranging from Habermas to Lyotard, and from Dahrendorf to Bobbio, have maintained that the war was, if not just, then certainly 'justified'.[26] Two important and contrasting exceptions stand out: that of the Pope, who condemned the immorality of the war, and that of Michael Walzer, who gave endorsement to the war, as being 'just' in the fullest ethical sense of the term.[27] A large majority of western public opinion accepted the war as both necessary and inevitable, and, in this, legitimation of the war by the UN Security Council, which was largely unanimous in its deliberations, exercised an enormous influence. Fundamental disagreement in the West was expressed only by small minorities representing pacifist, ecological or radical-democratic views.

What, then, were the arguments on each side? For the present I shall put to one side the judgement of experts on the ethics of international relations and the opinion of adherents of the theory of the just war, since these will form part of the subject matter of the next chapter. Nor will my discussion be extended to include the arguments of those who have sought to assign general political causes to the war, seeing it as a secular-democratic crusade against Islamic fundamentalism[28] or, at the opposite extreme, as an exercise in imperialism whereby the United States deliberately provoked war in order to consolidate its hegemony in the Gulf and thus ensure continued protection of access to the immense oil reserves of the region.[29]

More important from the point of view of the present study are the opinions of those who have assessed the war's significance in relation to the international institutions which bore responsibility at the time for the maintenance of peace. Particular interest attaches to the arguments of those who have given specific attention to the crucial factor that the United States is at present the only world power which is able to exercise the function of guaranteeing world peace. The essential question is whether, confronted with the *fait accompli* of the invasion of Kuwait, the international institutions acted correctly not only in helping to restore sovereignty to the aggrieved state but also in moving to prevent the outbreak of a war of considerably larger proportions.

A subsidiary question is whether the task or the duty fell to the United Nations to give – or perhaps even whether the duty fell to them not to give – formal authorization to the armed conflict as a war of 'collective self-defence'. The question arises even if, hypothetically, the war appeared in the end to have been inevitable since it accorded with the judgement of the most powerful world nation. Nor should the danger be underestimated of the military enterprise which was authorized, given that the United States came to the point of threatening, via diplomatic channels, to launch a nuclear attack[30] and that this solution received the backing of close on half of the American public.[31]

It is for these reasons that I shall give detailed consideration here to the positions taken in particular by the Italian political philosopher Norberto Bobbio and the American international relations theorist Richard Falk. Both authors speak with equal academic authority and are respected also for the level of their civil involvement and, not least, their militant pacifism. Their evaluations of the Gulf War are all the more interesting as being expressed in terms of theories developed over the course of many years and disseminated through a large number of publications and contributions on many different levels, including, in Falk's case, the establishment of a number of international concerns.[32]

Bobbio's 'institutional pacifism' and Falk's 'global centralism' both belong to what I propose to call here the 'cosmopolitan paradigm' in the philosophy of international institutions. Both maintain that a fairer and more peaceful world order will result only from the overcoming of 'statist' anarchy and from the granting of effective powers of intervention to a central authority of supranational character. In their opinion it is only by crossing this threshold of rationality that the human race will be able to remove the threat of self-destruction. Both term themselves realists and both maintain that the United Nations represents an anticipation – and may perhaps even be the progenitor – of the 'central institutions' which appear in their projections.

For all their common theoretical basis, however, Bobbio and Falk have taken opposite positions on the Gulf War. For Bobbio the fact that this was the first war to be 'authorized' by an international institution represents in the final analysis 'a step forward in the process of the formation of a common power set over and above the nation states',[33] while, for Falk, this very authorization and legitimation of the war signals 'a tragic failure on the part of the United Nations'.[34]

Norberto Bobbio's Cosmopolitan Pacifism

Bobbio's thought has its roots far back in Hobbes and Kant. His interpretation and development of Hobbes's contractualism receives a Kantian slant from the universal and cosmopolitan value which he attaches to it, while his interpretation of Kant's federalism contains Hobbesian elements through his view of it as the surmounting of nation state sovereignty and the constituting of a 'world state'.[35]

Adopting without reservation the 'domestic analogy' model, Bobbio employs such central categories of Hobbesian political philosophy as the notions of *pactum societatis* and *pactum subjectionis*. For Hobbes, of course, these general categories served to represent the passage of humankind from the natural condition, dominated by fear and unregulated conflictuality, to the secure and peaceful political society in which power is exercised by the Leviathan state. In practice, Hobbes's contractualism can be seen, from the viewpoint of political history, to have formed a response to a specific development in seventeenth-century English history, the emergence of one of the first forms of the modern state from the remnants of feudalism and medieval power. Hobbes's position at the birth of the industrial revolution enabled him to replace the universalism of the theological conception of power with a defence of absolute and sovereign power exercised within the territorial boundaries of the nation state.

Bobbio applies Hobbes's contractualism normatively to the relations between states, and argues that, in order to move from a situation of international anarchy and war to an ordered and peaceful political system, it is necessary for the individual states to subscribe both to a *pactum societatis* and to a *pactum subjectionis*. These pacts he figuratively understands as consensual procedures whereby states confer on a 'third party' the power of coercive control over their relations and potential disagreements, thus guaranteeing peace between nations. The best and ultimate remedy is, for him, the 'concentration of power in a new and supreme body' – i.e., the institution of a 'superstate' or 'world state' as holder of a legal monopoly of international force.[36]

From Kant's *Zum ewigen Frieden* Bobbio draws a further prescription: that the states which intend to create a federation devoted to peace and, out of this, the world state should all be, in the Kantian sense of the term, 'republics'. They should be, if not democracies in the full sense, at least states which are constitutionally committed to the recognition and protection of the fundamental freedoms of their citizens. It is this which, in Bobbio's view, ensures that the power of the international Leviathan would not be oppressive, since the international system would itself assume the nature of an 'international democracy', capable of protecting human rights outside the boundaries of the individual constituent states and overriding also the claims of these states to absolute sovereignty. Peace and democracy are inextricably intertwined: whereas despotism may be seen as the continuation of war within the state, international democracy provides the means of expanding and strengthening peace beyond the bounds of the individual states.[37]

In summary, Bobbio's scheme of cosmopolitan pacifism involves a progression through the following four stages.

First, a preliminary negative treaty of non-aggression between the states proposing to set up a permanent association (first *pactum societatis*).

Second, a second positive treaty by which the states agree to a series of common rules for the resolving of disputes, avoiding thereby recourse to combat (second *pactum societatis*).

Third, submission to a common power capable of ensuring adherence to the two previously agreed treaties by eventual recourse to the use of force (*pactum subjectionis*).

Fourth, recognition and protection of fundamental rights of civil and political freedom, as a means of preventing the consensually established power becoming despotic.[38]

Thus, in Bobbio's view, the establishment of the League of Nations and, even more so, of the United Nations has finally set the history of international relations on the path of institutional pacifism, rendering obsolete the two traditional options of the past, anarchy and imperially imposed peace. Both international institutions are therefore seen by him as the result of a genuine *pactum societatis*, even if this has not been followed by the necessary *pactum subjectionis* in the form of submission of the contracting states to a common power endowed with the exclusive right to the exercise of coercive measures. The United Nations,

> while having taken a step beyond the League of Nations, which was no more than an elementary association of States, has not brought about the birth of a superstate, i.e. that form of coexistence whose principal characteristics are sovereign power and the monopoly of legitimized force. The nations which were then united and all those which have subsequently become united have remained sovereign States and have not ceded a monopoly of force to any superior entity.[39]

Even so, Bobbio argues, an 'enormous step forward' has taken place over and beyond the League of Nations, by virtue both of the effective universality of the treaty which brought it into being and of the granting to the Security Council, through articles 42 and 43 of the Charter, of the power to take in hand all necessary action, including military action, to ensure the restoration of peace.[40] Less tangibly, but no less importantly, he would also add to these two elements the 'democratic inspiration' of the United Nations, since the authority of the consensual international organizations which have sprung up is circumscribed by their recognition of human rights and they are consequently denied the unlimited power of autocratic governments. (Somewhat surprisingly Bobbio's reference here is to the Universal Declaration of Human Rights, whose influence has arguably done little in practice to restrict the authority of any of the organizations, and certainly not that of the Security Council.) It is a matter of considerable significance, his argument continues, that there is found within the United Nations 'the characteristic institution of every democratic society, the assembly in which all the contracting parties are represented on an equal footing and in which the basis of decision is the majority vote'.[41]

For Bobbio, therefore, the process of democratization will remain incomplete until the international organizations show a true combination of the old principle of the sovereignty of states (including their precarious balance) and the new movement towards the creation of a 'strong common power'. At present the old and the new do coexist – the old, however, having lost legitimacy with respect both to the letter and the spirit of the United Nations constitution and the new having failed to achieve either full realization or full efficacy[42] – but this coexistence adds up to no more than the parallel, and frequently opposed, existence of two separate systems.[43]

This is the theoretical background to – and, in my opinion, the basis for assessment of – the position taken by Bobbio on the Gulf War. From the legal point of view, he has argued, this was an exemplary case of a war which was 'just' in the Aristotelian sense of being 'in accordance with law' or 'legal'.[44] A just war denotes the 'legitimate use of force'. Thus, once aggression had taken place against a sovereign state in outright violation of international law, the United Nations had the duty to react to the aggression by resorting in its turn to the use of military force. This force was not, he acknowledges, exercised directly by the United Nations under the command and control of the Security Council, as had been envisaged by Chapter VII of the Charter, but that consideration is far outweighed in this case by the fact that

> the response to the violation of international law did not come under the traditional category of the right to self-defence, as has always in effect been the case in the past, but was, as the UN Secretary General stated publicly, 'authorized'. This meant that its justification came from an authority higher than the individual states, and was such as can be called 'legal' in the sense that it was in accordance with the constitutional law of the supreme body of the United Nations. This fact could well represent a step forward in the process of the formation of a common power above the nation states, and consequently in the transformation of the international system, one stage consisting of the United Nations itself, despite its failure so far to reach its full potential.[45]

Although the Gulf War may not 'correspond to the ideal model of institutional pacifism',[46] Bobbio argues that the Security Council's authorization of the use of force is to be considered as a 'step towards a step', because, following the reduction of conflict between the great powers, 'the exercise of that primary form of common power, feasible even now under the potentially anarchic system of nation states, has finally become possible through the agency of the imperfect yet perfectible institution of the first truly universal international organization'.[47]

There is no doubt to be entertained, in my opinion, about the rigorous coherence of Bobbio's theory of cosmopolitan pacifism or about its application to the Gulf War. Moreover, it should be recognized that Bobbio has never played down his misgivings as to the efficacy of the war. Given the extent of the casualties, the physical destruction and danger of escalation which the duration of the war continually entailed, he expressed serious doubts towards the end on both its advantageousness and its unavoidability.[48]

But it is clear that from Bobbio's cosmopolitan point of view there are no pacifist alternatives to his 'institutional pacifism'. All other critiques of war end, in his opinion, either in the dangerous naivety of radical pacifism, which sees all wars as unjust, or in the sterile ideological contradistinctions which seem to do no more than to transfer to a theoretical level the arguments which already divide the warring parties. Bobbio's entire theoretical construct, however, stands or falls, in my opinion, with each of the following four assumptions (the first two being implicit, the third and fourth explicit).

First, that, in terms of methodology, the 'domestic analogy' model provides trustworthy lines of argumentation for the construction of a theory of international relations and, in particular, the construction of a theory of peacemaking and peacekeeping.

Second, that concentration in the hands of a supreme international authority (the 'third' party set over others) of military force, at present anarchically split up in furtherance of the principle of nation state sovereignty, is the *only* way to construct a secure and peaceful international system.

Third, that the formation of the United Nations represents an 'enormous step forward' in this direction beyond all previous international organizations, and especially beyond the League of Nations, in that the United Nations is the product of a universal agreement, is funded on democratic principles and entrusts coercive power to a superior entity.

Fourth, that the United Nations is capable of further improvement in terms both of its democratic content and of its ability to apply force effectively, these two aspects containing no mutual incompatibility.

Richard Falk's Global Centralism

Richard Falk is a fervent proponent of a form of pacifism which it would not be misplaced to term institutional (in the Bobbian sense) and cosmopolitan. Unlike Bobbio, however, he goes beyond plain delineation of a scheme of institutional transition from war and anarchy to a state of peace. Since the early 1970s Falk has produced a constant flow of concrete proposals which he believes to be necessary to bring about the 'structural change' from the system of sovereign states, which dates back to the Peace of Westphalia, to a Just World Order.[49] This approach may be seen, for example, in *A Study of Future Worlds* (1975), where he set out his aim of a 'central guidance system' complete with an outline analysis of its institutional structuring, and then attempted to indicate the tactics and strategies which would be needed to produce the broad political mobilization required for realization of the scheme.[50]

In more recent works Falk has attempted to explore more closely the normative gap which exists between his centralizing and globalistic stance[51] and what he calls the 'patterns of statist imperatives', i.e. the objectives myopically, in his opinion, pursued by individual states with a view only to narrow short-term results. Among 'statist imperatives' he includes the race run by nation states towards economic growth measured purely in terms of gross domestic product, economic and technological competition between states, diversion of international institutions to the service of internal goals, political barriers against movement of people between countries, the refusal to pursue effective international demographic policies.[52]

Elsewhere Falk has been at pains to stress the close link between the objectives of his centralizing globalism and the expansion of democracy at international level, highlighting the need for international protection of human rights and popular self-determination, which embraces political independence, territorial integrity, economic autonomy and environmental protection.[53]

In the wake of the Gulf War, Falk has again outlined, with all the force of his apparently inexhaustible normative impetus, a wide-ranging project along globalistic and pacific lines. His argument in *Positive Prescriptions for the Near Future* is that the crisis in the Gulf, following the end of the Cold War and the democratic revolution of 1989, has introduced a fresh period of unforeseen change in international affairs. Even in this new 'geopolitical phase' both the analysis and the prescription provided by 'value-oriented globalism' retain their value. Indeed, one of the positive aspects of the new situation is 'the widening of *the horizon of plausible aspirations* to include far more ambitious extensions of law and institutions in relation to the governance of international political and economic life'.[54]

This prospect encourages him to see 'global constitutionalism' as a vehicle leading to a 'transnational democracy' which will be rooted in the efficacy of international law and the protection of human rights and which will have as its objectives peace and the ecological balance of the planet. The social basis of the new constitutional and democratic structure is now seen by him, with a much more Lockian than Hobbesian approach, as developing out of the 'global civil society' which is emerging from the network of spontaneous transnational initiatives, especially those devoted to ecological globalism.[55] Such optimism is, however, accompanied by a severely critical evaluation of the ability of the United Nations to match up to its prescribed functions. The United Nations is, he claims,

> weak and dependent; it lacks a sufficiently secure financial and political base to be capable of upholding its Charter against even the most flagrant violations, it is unable to challenge uses of force by leading states, and it is often ineffectual in relation to local and regional war, as well as against patterns of human rights and environmental abuse. Furthermore, international institutions remain overwhelmingly statist in outlook and operation; they tend to be dominated by a few rich and powerful members who use these arenas to promote their interests, regardless of normative factors, and who retain a military option to be used as a matter of discretion.[56]

Surprisingly, however, in view of this, Falk argues that global constitutionalism can draw support not only from the development of an increasingly broad view of the rights and duties of individual states and the growing influence of such international voluntary organizations as Amnesty International, America Watch and Greenpeace, but also from the

> nucleus of central institutions that had initially been under the general auspices of the League of Nations but subsequently continued and expanded within the framework of the United Nations. The United Nations has within its framework and organic law (the UN Charter) the capacity for almost limitless further expansion of function and authority; its role is dependent almost entirely on the political will of its members, especially of the most influential states, and their political will is a reflection of the exertion of democratic influences.[57]

Falk has also applied his political theory of pacific globalism and cosmopolitanism to the actions of the Security Council and the United States in the Gulf War. He argues on the one hand that the Iraqi invasion of Kuwait represented a challenge – which was successfully met – to the will and ability of the United Nations to respond effectively to aggression in the name of collective security. For the first time in the history of modern international institutions a prompt and effective response was given which demonstrated a high degree of consensus. The United States 'displayed the initiative and muscle to confront Iraq with effective challenge and to mobilize a common front within the Security Council behind the demand that Iraq withdraw unconditionally from Kuwait'.[58]

But he also argues on the other hand that the effect of resolution 678 was for the United Nations to give official backing to a war which it was not in a position to keep under control and whose objectives by far exceeded the simple restoration of sovereignty to the aggrieved country. The practical problems of halting Iraq's advance and liberating Kuwait would have been better handled by employing the military might of the United States under the strict supervision of the Security Council, as is in fact demanded by Chapter VII of the Charter. This would have led to a tight restraint on the numbers of foreign troops in the area and control over the objectives and methods of the war.[59]

By the time, however, of the massing of troops in Saudi Arabia – a decision taken unilaterally by the government of the United States on 8 November – it had already become clear that a vast offensive action had begun against Iraq which had complete independence from any decisions which might possibly be taken by the Security Council. In fact the Security Council, having abandoned the path of economic sanctions without having first shown – as it had a duty to do – that such measures were impracticable, authorized recourse to military intervention under heavy pressure from the movement by the United States government towards the 'New World Order'.[60] The Gulf War represented therefore not the success of the United Nations but the tragic inability of the Security Council to match up to its international commitments. Instead of organizing and controlling an operation of international policing, it authorized the greatest world power to wage unlimited war on Iraq.

The hesitancy in Falk's position arises, to my mind, from his liberal-minded but scarcely realistic interpretation of the United Nations Charter, which he takes as a foundation by which to judge the actions of the Security Council and the United States government. Like Bobbio, he does not submit either the formal or the actual constitution of the United Nations to theoretical critique. Instead, again like Bobbio, he goes no further than deploring the inadequate enforcement of articles 43–7 by which control of military operations is granted to the Security Council, assisted by a Military Staff Committee composed of the Chiefs of Staff of the five permanent members.

Falk therefore legitimizes the constitutional structure of the United

Nations from the viewpoint of his globalistic and centralistic pacifism and enthusiastically endorses both the conduct of the United States up to 8 November and the action of the Security Council up to the ultimatum of 29 November. Until the end of November, then, the Security Council and government of the United States were in a position to act in the service of collective security and world peace. But from that moment onwards, he argues, they abided by neither the spirit nor the letter of the United Nations Charter, but operated 'unconstitutionally'.

In fact it might well be more accurate, in my opinion, to say that the Security Council and the United States never abided, either before or after 29 November, by the principles of Falk's globalistic pacifism. These are principles which bear no relation either to those which informed the minds of the founding fathers of the United Nations or to the not entirely dissimilar ones which have so far lain behind the foreign policy of the United States.

The objections to be made against Falk are as follows. First, the Charter of the United Nations, as elaborated at Dumbarton Oaks and at Yalta by Roosevelt, Churchill and Stalin, gives the Security Council discretionary powers which are in practice boundless and subject to no accountability. In particular the Security Council is not compelled, as Falk believes it is, to exhaust all peaceful means before embarking on violence. Article 42 gives it absolute power to decide if and when a case has arisen for the 'taking of all necessary action to restore peace and international security'.[61] Nor is it possible to find any normative element in the Charter which allows the Security Council a selective use of the methods of war – a kind of *jus in bello* which permits the distinction (in absolute terms a questionable concept in any case) between an outright act of war, which would be forbidden, and an international policing operation, which would fall within the competence of the institution.

Second, for all the universalizing rhetoric of the preamble to its Charter, the constitutional basis of the United Nations is built, as has been seen in the preceding chapter, wholly along the lines of the hierarchical model of the Holy Alliance. Thus the task of maintaining or of re-establishing peace is effectively entrusted solely to the permanent members of the Security Council, while the strategic direction of its operations of war is delegated, as a matter of law, to their military high commands.

It is therefore inconceivable, even without the power of veto, that the United Nations could undertake a military operation not so much against one of the permanent members of the Council (would that same member be responsible for directing the strategy of the operation?) as against some other country without using the military forces of the permanent members and under the control of some authority other than that of the Chiefs of Staff of the permanent members. The belief that the Security Council has at its disposal a power, wishfully symbolized by the figure of the Secretary General,[62] which exists separately from and superior to the military organizations (and nuclear arsenals) of the great powers is nothing other than a pure mirage. It is consequently a matter of equal illusion to think that the Security Council, once having given authority for the conduct of the war to the American superpower, was in any sense in a position to control the handling of military operations or to lay down conditions during the general course of the conflict, still less on the battlefield itself.

In this context the failure of articles 43–7 to be applied, which has been seen by some jurists as a reason for declaring the intervention against Iraq to be illegal, is shown to be a technical flaw of little relevance, especially since the great majority of legal experts maintain that the normative construct of which they form a part has long fallen into disuse.[63] The reality is that the United States, the sole superpower now standing at the head of the international hierarchy, obtained authorization from the other four permanent members of the Security Council to carry out the war against Iraq. These other members either voluntarily accepted the strategic command of General Schwarzkopf or, in the case of the Soviet Union and China, declined to take part in the military operations which they had *de jure* or *de facto* authorized.[64] As for the ten non-permanent members of the Council – Canada, Columbia, Cuba, Ethiopia, Finland, The Ivory Coast, Malaysia, Romania, Yemen, Zaire – they voted unanimously, except for intermittent abstentions from Cuba and Yemen and the vote of these two countries against resolution 678, in favour of the resolutions calling first for sanctions and subsequently for military action against Iraq. The assent of many of these countries, Ramsey Clark has argued, was obtained by the United States's use of the natural means of persuasion open to a great power, the promise of patently advantageous economic and financial favours.[65]

Third, the Security Council's discretionary power in taking decisions and freedom from accountability is further underlined by the right of veto which gives the permanent members the ability to protect not only themselves but also their particular allies. Exercise of this veto has given rise over the years to the fundamentally illegal practice of operating double standards in applying sanctions against, and even in deciding whether or not to take into consideration, violations of international order. Evidence of this is readily to be seen in the privileged treatment accorded to the state of Israel, despite its many acts of aggression against sovereign states (Egypt, Lebanon, Tunisia) and its constant disregard of United Nations resolutions requiring it to cease occupation of the West Bank, the eastern area of Jerusalem and the Gaza Strip. Similar violations of international order which have been committed by China, Indonesia and Syria have also failed to provoke intervention from the Security Council.

Fourth, there is little realism, finally, in the expectation that the greatest world power should undertake a war of the proportions, danger and cost of the Gulf War purely in order to re-establish world order and to guarantee peace. It is far more realistic to believe that the United States government expects its reaction to violations of world order to coincide with its own need for selective re-establishment of the *status quo* whenever – and, of course, only when – its 'vital interests' are at issue.[66] It comes as no surprise, then, to find that the strategy of 'global security' proved capable of accommodating United States interests in the Gulf region. Such an objective was, furthermore, the inevitable outcome of some two centuries of United States political involvement in the Middle East, as has been shown by Michael A. Palmer's painstaking and balanced study, *Guardians of the Gulf*.[67] This involvement was formally confirmed in 1980 by the 'Carter doctrine', also endorsed by successive Presidents, which declared the free traffic of oil in the Gulf to be a 'vital interest' of the United States.[68] Iraq, whose armaments gave it the status of fourth-largest military power in the world, already formed a disquieting presence in itself. Its invasion of Kuwait could have, therefore, only one outcome: military intervention by the United States in order to curtail Iraqi military power and to strengthen its own presence in the region. Thus United States diplomacy scored the notable success of converting a war which was for other reasons inevitable into one which was authorized by the United Nations (and hence also by the United States Congress) and which was presented on the televisions of the world as an operation of international policing carried out to ensure the protection of cosmopolitan interests. It is legitimate, however, to add to this that the explicit terms of the constitution of the United Nations very easily laid it open to use by the United States as the instrument of its own diplomacy.

Towards Reform of the United Nations? Autocratic Cosmopolitanism and Democratic Cosmopolitanism

Amongst supporters and detractors alike of military intervention against Iraq a new awareness of the inherent potential of the United Nations in the areas not only of peacemaking but also of humanitarian intervention and world growth was aroused by the Gulf War. The expectation has now arisen that, after forty years of institutional flaccidity, the pivotal role played by the United Nations in the Gulf crisis may prove capable of initiating a period of activity and renewal. This expectation received increased impetus in the period immediately succeeding the war from the interventionist activities of the United States: acting with the implicit authorization or tacit consent of the Security Council, the United States undertook a series of humanitarian missions in northern and in central Iraq.

Throughout the years 1992–4 the politics of 'humanitarian intervention' became established and developed their own form of legitimacy outside any normative frame of reference, including even the United Nations Charter.[69] The intervention by the United States and several other powers in Somalia, motivated in the first instance by the need to ensure the free flow of food and medical supplies, changed rapidly into a bloody military conflict whose objectives became increasingly distant from the institutional remit of the United Nations, and in all likelihood bore more in common with the interests of a number of powerful oil companies. Later in 1993–4, the prospect of 'humanitarian' intervention in the territories of the former Yugoslavia suffered from many of the same signs of uncertainty and controversy. Particularly questionable in this context was the involvement of NATO forces, as if this organization formed a military wing of the United Nations rather than a politico-military structure formally constituted for the defence of western political interests of varying degrees of legitimacy.

For sympathizers of the armed intervention against Iraq – who have still more reason to approve of the new phase of humanitarian intervention – the United Nations has regained full credibility as an authority which stands above other parties and is able to use force to guarantee respect for international order. For them the long process of institutional evolution towards 'world government' is now within sight of realization. The Gulf War has revealed significant ground to have been crossed in the intermediate phase of the transition from an unstable balance between states to a situation of stable collective security. A further and decisive step forwards would now be provided by an international agreement restoring to the Security Council all the power originally assigned to it by the Charter and subsequently negated by the Cold War.

Opponents of armed intervention, on the other hand, believe that the Gulf crisis and the events which succeeded it have shown that the United Nations, for all the high-reaching intentions behind its existence and the important means at its disposal, is still far too exposed to the influence of the great powers. The handling of the Gulf War dramatically symbolizes a movement from a situation of bipolar equilibrium to one of absolute hegemony. The institutional mechanisms of the Security

Council may well have been rescued by the War from decades of paralysis, but they have in the end been subordinated to the geopolitical objectives of the United States instead of being placed, as was both possible and morally desirable, at the service of world needs. As a result of this false – if not retrogressive – step, the goal of international democracy remains as far removed as ever. The pressing need, now that the United Nations has given proof of the extent of its potential, is that of bringing about democratic reform within the organization itself. For it is only a democratic world government which will prove capable of meeting the challenge of the movements towards globalization in such spheres as ecology, demography, financial systems and information technology, while at the same time being able to control the explosion of nationalistic and ethnic sectional interests.

In terms of political theory, both defenders and critics of the Gulf War have seen the event as providing a basis for their proposals for the reform of the United Nations. This has given further expansion to the already considerable tradition of reformist literature,[70] which ranges from the radical restructuring envisaged in 1960 by Clark and Sohn in their famous but now dated *World Peace through World Law*[71] to the more cautious elaborations of Marc Nerfin, Maurice Bertrand, Pierre de Senarclens, Saul H. Mendlovitz and Richard Falk himself.[72]

The latest proposals for the reform of the United Nations have in view two distinct, but markedly polarized, objectives which admit of little overlap with one another. The first, which comes under the heading of what may be called 'autocratic cosmopolitanism', is reinforcement of the United Nations' authority and power to coerce. The second, which may be characterized as 'democratic cosmopolitanism', is the democratization of the institution itself, a negation or at least a scaling-down of the arrangements set in place at Dumbarton Oaks and Yalta.

The main aim of autocratic cosmopolitanism is to strengthen further the authority of the Security Council, traditionally viewed as the sole decision-taking body in the United Nations. A secondary aim is the development of a deeper and broader capacity for military intervention. Problems such as the representativeness of the various elements of which the United Nations is composed or the democratic nature of their procedures are either marginalized or ignored. Consideration is given especially to the following four points.

First, an increase in the number of permanent members of the Security Council. One example of this is President Clinton's proposal, advanced in the interests of 'global security', that Germany and Japan should be permanently admitted to membership of the Council, with the right of veto included. Others have suggested the assignment of a permanent seat to the European Community, or to each continental area (Europe, Africa, Asia, Latin America etc.), or to 'demographic powers' such as India or Brazil, or even, more generally, to the Third World, a proposal apparently favoured by the current Secretary General, Boutros Boutros-Ghali.

Second, the organization of a permanent military force, controlled by a Military Staff Committee of the United Nations, to act as an international police force with an extensive remit in the areas of prevention and humanitarian intervention. The aim, in effect, is to set up a 'humanitarian rapid intervention force', equipped to intervene on occasions of civil war, ethnic conflict, violation of minority rights or the inability of local governments to restore internal political order. This objective, which accords entirely with the strategy of 'global security', has received considerable support from the current democratic administration in the United States.[73]

Third, the attribution to the Secretary General of greater powers and autonomy, a move which appears to have been called for by, amongst others, the present holder of that office.

Fourth, the reorganization of the financing and general administration of the United Nations, with the aims of freeing the organization from continual financial restraint and giving it greater financial autonomy. The idea has been advanced of imposing compulsory progressive taxation on all states.

The proposals for reform which look instead towards the transformation of the United Nations into a democratic assembly devoted, over and beyond the promotion of peace, to the protection of popular and individual rights may be summarized under the following five headings.

First, the abolition (or reduction) of the power of veto of the five great powers, perhaps in connection with an expansion of the Security Council to take into account demographic, economic and military developments.[74]

Second, the creation of a new assembly, either parallel to the General Assembly or to take its place, elected by universal suffrage. Unlike the present assembly, where the governments of the states are represented according to the formula of 'one state, one vote', the new assembly should be representative not only of peoples but also of voluntary associations (the so-called non-governmental international organizations). The establishment of yet a third chamber has been proposed by Marc Nerfin, to accommodate representatives of the economic institutions and companies of the world. Other proposals pursue quite simply the idea of the abolition of the Security Council and the complete reorganization of the United Nations through the application to world society of the classic principles of representative democracy.

Third, strengthening of the administration of international justice through reform of the International Court of Justice, so as to make compulsory its jurisdiction over disputes between states and to recognize the ability of peoples, associations and individuals to initiate proceedings.[75] Although little acknowledged by its proponents, this proposal entails the institution of an extensive international judicial police force, backed up by effective military resources. In addition, if the jurisdiction of the Court is not to fall short of the weight of the great powers, the international judicial police force must itself, as has at times been recognized in the past,[76] possess a nuclear capability.

Fourth, reform of financial and tariff organizations, especially the IMF, World Bank and GATT, which would free them from subservience to the politics of western economic and financial interests and place them at the service of countries with the potential for growth. The promoters of the *Human Development Report 1992* have proposed in particular that a 'Development Security Council' should be constituted, alongside the current Security Council, comprising twenty-two members and charged with addressing problems such as the fight against poverty, the international price of goods, drug trafficking and ecological equilibrium.[77]

Fifth, and least easily, the United Nations should be enabled to exercise general control over the production of, and trade in, arms so as to bring about a gradual general disarmament, retaining for itself only limited functions of international policing.[78]

Cosmopolitan Pacifism and Globalism

The questions of political philosophy which I formulated at the end of the preceding chapter have so far therefore failed to receive an answer. Neither Bobbio's cosmopolitan pacifism nor Falk's global constitutionalism nor the more radical demands of the reformers – both autocratic and democratic cosmopolitans – of international institutions address what appear to be significant problems. The cosmopolitan scheme of a more effective 'world government' – whether it is to be realized by reinforcement of the central organs of the international institutions or by extending the competence of these bodies to the realm of individual states or, more radically, by reforming them from within along democratic lines – seems to be an objective shared by all. Even those who somewhat unrealistically go further and propose abolition of the Security Council, without taking into account that this would inevitably lead to abolition of the United Nations *tout court*, do so not through criticism of the model of the Holy Alliance or of the cosmopolitan paradigm, but in pursuit of a radical democratism which naively extends to international institutions the representative scheme of European liberalism.

The effect of the Gulf War and of the interventionist policies which have been pursued thereafter should, however, have been to give all the more justification and point to the questions which were posed earlier in this book. For, from the point of view of political theory, the chief lesson of the war and its succeeding events is that the entire structure of the existing international institutions which are devoted to the maintaining of peace lends itself in reality to a very different end: the diplomatic preparation for, and formal legalization and legitimation of, war.

The basic moral to be drawn is not, therefore, that the United States and its western allies are even now prepared, despite the ending of the ideological differences which have divided the world, to continue to carry out forceful intervention and to engage in large-scale military conflicts to ensure the preservation of their own vital interests. As circumstances stand, so much is obvious. Nor is it a matter of particular seriousness that the United States's commitment to conduct the Gulf War and successive 'humanitarian interventions' under the umbrella of the United Nations exceeded all precedent. In all probability it was the strategic circumstances of 'global security' which made, for both internal and international purposes, ideological and ethical legitimation of the war so important. (The Security Council's authorization and the low level of loss of human life were the two elements which enabled the US government both to set the war in train and subsequently to bring it to its end without either Congress or internal public opinion questioning its legal and ethical basis.)[79]

Far more important, to my mind, from the theoretical point of view is that the United States obtained the legitimation it needed, together with the agreement of practically all permanent and non-permanent members of the Security Council, not through any non-standard application of the formal rules and actual constitution of the United Nations, but through an application of those rules which was in all essential features legal and correct.

How could this ever have been?

There is thus an important additional reason for posing once more the questions with which the preceding chapter concluded: is there something essentially mistaken in the first four projects for stable and universal peace which have so far been seen, from the Holy Alliance to the New World Order? Is the cosmopolitan attempt to overcome the 'statist' fragmentation of international power through a military-political structure and a highly centralized jurisdiction really the primary means by which to contain international aggression and to reduce the force of its destructive effects?

Bobbio, as has been seen, fails to take into account any possible methodological fallacy in the 'domestic analogy'. He takes it for granted that international institutions are evolving towards a globalistic end-position which will result in a stable, peaceful and democratic international order. He appears to find so little wrong with the model of the Holy Alliance that he is able to see even such a scourge as the Gulf War not as a tragic failing but as an initial realization of the new order.

Compared with Bobbio's cosmopolitan pacifism, Falk's more complex 'global constitutionalism' admits of subtler distinctions. His strong opposition to the Gulf War arises from his belief that the actions of the Security Council violated the UN Charter. His severe criticism of the principal international agents has not gone so far, however, as to raise the question of the basic structure of the institutions, nor has it led him to any self-critical reflection on the aim of globalism and institutional centralism. In his more recent writings he has added still further to this aim with the idea of an emerging 'global civil society' in which the establishment of an 'increased central guidance' should be firmly rooted.[80]

As will by now have become clear, my own view is that the western tradition of institutional pacifism and political cosmopolitanism – from Émeric Crucé to William Penn, l'abbé de Saint-Pierre, Kant and finally to Bobbio and Falk – should be revised in the light of a broad and consistent political philosophy of peacemaking. Such a philosophy should not fail to take notice of basic questions concerning the biological, psychological and sociological conditions of violence and war. The problem of containing human aggression cannot be simply conceived of as a matter of institutional engineering. The discussion must be widened to include at least the normative aspects of ethics and law, as I shall attempt to do in the succeeding two chapters. In the final chapter I shall resume more directly the discussion of political institutions which I have so far advanced in these pages.

Notes

1 Falk, Kim and Mendlovitz (eds), *The United Nations and a Just World Order*, p. 1.
2 M. Gorbachev, *Realities and Guarantees for a Secure World*, Moscow: Novosti Press Agency Publishing House, 1987, pp. 3–16, republished in Falk, Kim and Mendlovitz (eds), *The United Nations and a Just World Order*, pp. 188–97.
3 Falk, Kim and Mendlovitz (eds), *The United Nations and a Just World Order*, p. 79.
4 Throughout the Cold War the United States permanently stationed abroad in thirty-five different countries half a million soldiers and an only slightly smaller number of Pentagon civil servants, assigned to almost four hundred military bases and hundreds of other installations of minor importance.

After the dissolution of the Warsaw Pact, many of these bases have become superfluous, but it is greatly to be doubted whether the 'advanced presence' of the United States in the world will also be reduced. At the beginning of the 1990s the United States's naval force included fifteen aircraft carriers and more than five hundred warships.

5 Published by the White House in August 1991; see: The President of the United States, *National Security Strategy of the United States*, Washington: The White House, 1991.

6 Under the title *Defense Planning Guidance for the Fiscal Years 1994–1999* this document was published in the *New York Times*, 8 March 1992. After the furore caused by its publication, the text was further modified by Paul Wolfowitz (cf. *New York Times*, 26 May 1992).

7 Compare, among many others, P. Wolfowitz, 'An American Perspective', in E. Grove (ed.), *Global Security: North American, European and Japanese Interdependence in the 1990s*, London: Brassey's, 1991, pp. 19–28; R. Art, 'A Defensible Defense: America's Grand Strategy after the Cold War', *International Security*, 15 (1991), 1, pp. 5–53; J. L. Gaddis, 'Toward the Post-Cold War World', *Foreign Affairs*, 70 (1991), 2, pp. 102–22; see in addition R. F. Helms II and R. H. Dorff (eds), *The Persian Gulf Crisis: Power in the Post-Cold War World*, Westport–London: Praeger, 1993. For a much more prudent approach to the question of 'collective security' in the post-Cold-War era, see T. G. Weiss (ed.), *Collective Security in a Changing World*, Boulder–London: Lynne Rienner Publishers, 1993.

8 On the complex and sometimes ambiguous connections between the new NATO strategy and the tasks attributed to WEU and CSCE compare D. Gallo, 'Il Nuovo Ordine Internazionale fra predominio degli Stati Uniti, debolezza dell'ONU e militarizzazione delle istituzioni europee', in U. Allegretti, M. Dinucci and D. Gallo, *La strategia dell'impero*, S. Domenico di Fiesole: ECP, 1992, pp. 77–89.

9 See also the statement of the NATO Secretary General, Manfred Wörner, *Global Security: The Challenge for NATO*, in Grove, *Global Security*, pp. 100–5.

10 For the whole series of the fourteen resolutions (660–70, 674, 677–8), see: United Nations, *United Nations Security Council Resolutions Relating to the Crisis in the Gulf*, UN Department of Public Information, DPC/1104, November 1990; Add. 1, December 1990.

11 Not including the United States military installations in Morocco, Tunisia, Sudan, Somalia, Kenya and other countries of northern and eastern Africa, or those allocated in Pakistan and Qatar.

12 The most important military contribution was provided by the western powers: Britain, France and, to a much smaller degree, Italy. All these forces operated under the command of the US general, Norman Schwarzkopf, although each flew its own national flag. Unlike the position in Korea, no use was made of the United Nations flag. More than 100,000 bombings were carried out by the Allies – one every thirty seconds – and over 80,000 tons of bombs were dropped on Iraqi territory, not including missiles launched from land, air or sea; cf. R. Clark, *The Fire this Time*, New York: Thunder's Mouth Press, 1992, pp. 38–42, 59–84.

13 See J. Balzar, 'Marines Feel Pity as B-52s Pound Iraqis', *Los Angeles Times*, 5 February 1991.

14 But no one is in a position to say how many Iraqi soldiers were buried, often

still alive, by the advance of the Allied armour which literally bulldozed its way through the enemy bunkers and trenches dug in the sand. (On this see J. Adams, 'Iraqi Toll Could Be 200,000 Dead', London *Times*, 3 March 1991; P. Sloyan, 'Buried Alive', *Newsday*, 12 September 1991.) Civilian casualties, both as a direct and an indirect consequence of the bombings and as a result of the sanctions applied before and after the war, have been put at not less than 100,000, made up of Kurds, Iraqis and Shi'ites, many of them children; compare Clark, *The Fire this Time*, pp. 59–84; Clark's evaluation is based on data provided by UNICEF, in addition to his direct experience.

15 One major new component of the US military arsenal – apart from napalm bombs, cluster bombs and GBU-28 superbombs – was formed by fuel-air explosives (FAE). These may be classed as quasi-nuclear devices because, except for emitting radiation, the effects they produce are the same as those of a minor nuclear explosion. From each explosive a cloud of highly volatile vapours is released which mixes rapidly with the air and explodes. The resulting shock wave and total combustion of oxygen together destroy all forms of life within an area of some 350 metres in diameter. Jeffrey Smith, correspondent of the *Washington Post*, has written that the entire Iraqi front was subjected to intensive bombardments with BLU-82 bombs, containing fuel-air explosives (see: *Washington Post*, 23 February 1991). According to *Soldier of Fortune* (July 1992) at least eleven BLU-82 bombs were released between 7 February and the beginning of the big land assault. Compare also A. Whitley, 'Kuwait: The Last Forty-eight Hours', *New York Review of Books*, 30 May 1991, pp. 17–18.

16 Clark, *The Fire this Time*, pp. 38–84, 163–82. The international legal norms on which accusations of 'war crimes' are normally based are, besides the old rules dictated by the Hague Conventions of 1899 and of 1907, the Geneva Protocol of 1925 and the successive Conventions of 1949 and of 1977. As is well known, these conventions prohibit the use of fragmentation weapons, of incendiary weapons, of 'explosive traps' and similar devices. More generally these conventions prohibit the use of arms which can cause 'unnecessary suffering' and they forbid in any case the killing or injuring of enemies who have in fact surrendered. As far as so-called 'crimes against humanity' are concerned, the relevant normative text is the Nuremberg rules. See I. Detter De Lupis, *The Law of War*, Cambridge: Cambridge University Press, 1987; Cassese, *Il diritto internazionale nel mondo contemporaneo*, Engl. trans., pp. 253–86.

17 The jam consisted mainly of lorries, buses, ambulances and hundreds of small cars in disordered flight. Thousands of civilians, many of whom were Palestinians, Sudanese and Egyptians, were killed in an entirely defenceless position. The news and documentation of the slaughter were initially provided by British sources (BBC and *The Times*) and were then reported, among others, by *Newsweek* (11 March 1991). According to these sources no journalist or photographer was admitted to the 'apocalyptic spectacle of the slaughter' – as it was so defined by the American major Bob Williams – before thousands of burnt corpses had been buried in the course of three days; see also S. Sackur, *On the Basra Road*, London: London Review of Books, 1991; K. Royce and T. Phelps, 'Pullback a Bloody Mismatch', *Newsday*, 31 May 1991.

18 See N. Cohen, 'Radioactive Waste Left in Gulf by Allies', London *Independent*, 10 November 1991.

19 See T. M. Hawley, *Against the Fires of Hell: The Environmental Disaster of the Gulf War*, New York–San Diego–London: Harcourt Brace Jovanovich, 1992.
20 Hawley, *Against the Fires of Hell*, p. 184.
21 See P. M. Taylor, *War and the Media: Propaganda and Persuasion in the Gulf War*, Manchester: Manchester University Press, 1993; H. Mowlana, G. Gerbner and H. I. Schiller (eds), *Triumph of the Image: The Media's War in the Persian Gulf*, Boulder–San Francisco–Oxford: Westview Press, 1992; H. Smith, *The Media and the Gulf War*, Washington (DC): Seven Locks Press, 1992; more generally: D. Wolton, *War Game: L'information et la guerre*, Paris: Flammarion, 1991.
22 It has been observed that the timing of military operations was in some cases decided by the Allies in order to coincide with the timing of satellite TV transmissions, as is commonly the case with important sporting events.
23 I use the notion of 'global war' (or 'hegemonic war') in the sense elaborated by system analysts, and especially by William R. Thompson: 'global wars are wars fought to decide who will provide systemic leadership, whose rules will govern, whose policies will shape systemic allocation processes, and whose sense or vision of order will prevail' (*On Global War: Historical-Structural Approaches to World Politics*, p. 7); cf. also Väyrynen, 'Global Power Dynamics and Collective Violence', pp. 80–6.
24 See J. Baudrillard, *La Guerre du Golfe n'a pas eu lieu*, Paris: Galilée, 1991; for a 'realist' critique against Baudrillard see C. Norris, *Uncritical Theory: Postmodernism, Intellectuals and the Gulf War*, Amherst: The University of Massachusetts Press, 1992.
25 Quoted in R. A. Falk, 'Reflections on the Gulf War Experience: Force and War in the United Nations System', *Juridisk Tidskrift*, 3 (1991), 1, p. 192.
26 Habermas has made a scholastic distinction between the metaphysical character of the notion of a 'just war' (not to be used) and the accurate notion of a 'justified war'. He finds the war of the western powers against Iraq to have been totally 'justified' because it was necessary to defend the violated international legal order and, above all, to destroy the Iraqi chemical arsenals which posed an unbearable threat to Israel. But the strongest argument in favour of armed intervention in the Gulf was, according to Habermas, 'the circumstance that the United States and their allies had the opportunity for playing, even if in a substitutive and temporary way, the neutral role of an international police force which is the (today unrealized) task of the United Nations'; cf. J. Habermas, 'Der Golf-Krieg als Katalysator einer neuen deutschen Normalität?', in J. Habermas, *Vergangenheit als Zukunft*, ed. M. Haller, Zürich: Pendo-Verlag, 1990, pp. 19ff.
27 Michael Walzer in an interview with Gianni Riotta declared that 'judging the war from an ethical point of view, it is impossible to imagine a nobler cause or a more infamous enemy'; cf. 'La sinistra conservatrice', *Micromega*, 6 (1991), 2, p. 35. Walzer has also devoted the preface to the second edition of his *Just and Unjust Wars* (New York: Basic Books, 1992, pp. xi-xxiii) to the justification of the Gulf War. For moral justification of the war expressed in the classical terms of the theory of the 'just war', see J. T. Johnson and G. Weigel, *Just War and the Gulf War*, Washington (DC): Ethics and Public Policy Center, 1991, pp. 3–42.

28 The Italian journal *Micromega*, published by a group of socialist intellectuals, wrote that 'the supporters of the coalition headed by Bush struggled to defend a weak people from the imperialistic project of a sanguinary dictator'. Accusing the Italian pacifist movement of sharing anti-semitic and anti-Israeli sentiments deriving from Nazism, *Micromega* maintained that western intervention in the Gulf set the lay ideals of democratic liberalism against the fundamentalism and integralism which dominated a large portion of the Islamic and Catholic worlds; cf. the editorial preface in *Micromega*, 6 (1991), 2, pp. 4–7.

29 Thus, rather than defending the *status quo*, the victorious superpower has resumed without delay the military initiative in order to gain further 'imperial' profits. This thesis has been maintained by, amongst others, Ramsey Clark (*The Fire this Time*, pp. 3–37). The thesis holds that the United States went to war with Iraq in order to obtain, immediately after the collapse of the Soviet Union's influence, a hegemonic presence in the Gulf region. Michael Palmer, in his accurate reconstruction of the political-diplomatic developments in the area over the two years before August 1990, rebuts the idea that the United States directly provoked and then induced Iraq to invade Kuwait; compare M. A. Palmer, *Guardians of the Gulf*, New York: The Free Press, 1992, pp. 150–62. See also, in H. Bresheeth and N. Yuval-Davis (eds), *The Gulf War and the New World Order*, London: Zed Books, 1991, particularly the essays of Noam Chomsky (pp. 13–29), Alan Freeman (pp. 153–65) and Haim Bresheeth (pp. 243–56).

30 Falk, 'Reflections on the Gulf War Experience', p. 187.

31 A Gallup poll, published 10 February 1991, showed that 45 per cent of United States citizens were in favour of the use of nuclear arms in order to bring the war to a rapid conclusion; cf. V. Zucconi, 'Ma perché non usiamo l'atomica?', *la Repubblica*, 12 February 1991, p. 5.

32 For the more relevant texts of Norberto Bobbio, see: *Il problema della guerra e le vie della pace*, Bologna: Il Mulino, 1984; 'Democrazia e sistema internazionale', in N. Bobbio, *Il futuro della democrazia*, Turin: Einaudi, 1984, pp. 195–220; *Il terzo assente*; *Una guerra giusta?*, Venice: Marsilio, 1991. The following theoretical works may be selected from Richard Falk's wide bibliography: *A Study of Future Worlds*, New York: Free Press, 1975; *A Global Approach to National Policy*, Cambridge (Mass.): Harvard University Press, 1975; *Human Rights and State Sovereignty*, New York: Holmes & Meier, 1981; *The End of World Order: Essays on Normative International Relations*, New York: Holmes & Meier, 1983; *Positive Prescriptions for the Near Future*, Princeton: Center for International Studies, Paper no. 20, 1991; *Explorations at the Edge of Time: The Prospects for World Order*, Philadelphia: Temple University Press, 1992; *On Humane Governance: Towards a New Global Politics*, Cambridge: Polity Press, 1995. Falk has promoted various international pacifist centers, such as the World Order Models Project (WOMP), active since 1968, and the Global Civilization Project (GCP), organized in 1987 in co-operation with the Soviet Political Science Association.

33 Bobbio, *Una guerra giusta?*, p. 23.

34 Falk, 'Reflections on the Gulf War Experience', p. 192.

35 For the discussion between 'cosmopolitan' interpreters (H. Bull, M. Wight, T. Schlereth) and 'statist' interpreters (F. H. Hinsley, W. B. Gallie, I. Clark, P. Riley, H. L. Williams) of Kant's political thought, see A. Hurrell, 'Kant

and the Kantian Paradigm in International Relations', *Review of International Studies*, 16 (1991), 3, pp. 183–205.

36 Bobbio, *Il problema della guerra*, pp. 80–1.

37 Bobbio, *Il terzo assente*, p. 9; *Il problema della guerra*, pp. 13, 150.

38 Cf. Bobbio, *Il terzo assente*, pp. 8–9. In another passage he somewhat contradictorily grants that 'not only present tendencies, but also historical teaching show that the formation of big states has been realized much more often thanks to an imperial power, therefore from above, than through an agreement among single states, therefore from below. The only real alternative to equilibrium peace has always been the so-called hegemonic peace or even, using Raymond Aron's concepts, "the imperial peace"' (ibid., p. 103). On the notion of 'institutional' or 'legal' pacifism and on its distinction both from 'instrumental' and 'finalistic' pacifism see Bobbio, *Il problema della guerra*, pp. 75–86.

39 Bobbio, *Il terzo assente*, pp. 102–3.

40 Bobbio, *Il terzo assente*, p. 193.

41 Bobbio, 'Democrazia e sistema internazionale', p. 207. These statements are partially weakened by his recognizing that in the international system guarantees of human rights stop short, with rare exceptions, at the threshold of the sovereign power of individual states and that, within the United Nations, the Assembly 'is flanked by the Security Council, within which each of the five permanent members has the right of veto concerning non-procedural questions' (ibid., p. 208).

42 Bobbio, *Il terzo assente*, pp. 100–1. Article 43, for example, which envisaged the obligation of member states to put at the disposal of the Security Council the forces necessary to prevent or restrain violations of peace, has failed even to be applied.

43 Bobbio, 'Democrazia e sistema internazionale', pp. 210–11.

44 Bobbio, *Una guerra giusta?*, pp. 11ff.

45 Ibid., pp. 22–3.

46 Bobbio, interview in *l'Unità*, 9 March 1991.

47 Bobbio, *Una guerra giusta?*, p. 23.

48 Ibid., pp. 57, 75ff, 87–90.

49 For a reconstruction of the various stages of his own intellectual and practical activity, see R. A. Falk, 'The World Order Approach: Issues of Perspective, Academic Discipline and Political Commitment', in Falk, *The Promise of World Order: Essays in Normative International Relations*, Philadelphia: Temple University Press, 1987, pp. 1–33.

50 Falk proposed in particular a 'General Assembly', composed of three chambers with differentiated constituencies and a system of checks and balances between them, in order to ensure correspondence of their normative activity with the expectations of world public opinion and its greatest consensus; he did not, however, exclude the possibility that the 'World Security Forces' he had conceived might make use, if necessary, even of nuclear arms in order to impose general disarmament; cf. Falk, *A Study of Future Worlds*, pp. 224–75. Similar theses had been maintained by Richard Falk in a typically utopian style in a previous text, *This Endangered Planet: Prospects and Proposals for Human Survival*, New York: Random House, 1971. For a lucid and severe criticism of the theses advanced by Falk in this text, cf. H. Bull, *The Anarchical Society*, London: Macmillan, 1977, pp.

50   THE GULF WAR: THE FIRST COSMOPOLITAN WAR

302–5. Compare also S. Brown, *The Causes and Prevention of War*, New York: St Martin's Press, 1987, pp. 122–4.
51 Following Richard Falk's lead, I use the term 'globalism' in a very different sense from that somewhat unhelpfully proposed by P. R. Viotti and M. V. Kauppi to denote a quasi-Marxist point of view, based on notions such as 'world capitalist system' and 'dependency relations' within the context of global economic politics (*International Relations Theory: Realism, Pluralism, Globalism*, New York: Macmillan Publishing Company, 1987, pp. 9–10, 399–426).
52 Falk, *A Global Approach to National Policy*, pp. 17–22. Falk is in favour of state policies of demographic control through economic incentives to encourage the limitation of families.
53 Falk, *The Promise of World Order*, pp. 117–36.
54 Falk, *Positive Prescriptions for the Near Future*, p. 2.
55 Ibid., pp. 7–16.
56 Ibid., p. 11.
57 Ibid., p. 8.
58 Falk, 'Reflections on the Gulf War Experience', p. 182.
59 Ibid., pp. 182, 189–90.
60 Ibid., pp. 182, 189.
61 B. Conforti, 'Per rafforzare il sistema sanzionatorio', *Democrazia e diritto*, 32 (1992), 1, pp. 341–5, answers Falk directly: 'Art. 42 clearly states that the Security Council may use force should it "consider that the measures provided for in Article 41 [i.e. non-violent measures] *would be inadequate* or have proved to be inadequate". So, the Council may skip the stage of non-violent measures if it *considers*, in its absolute discretionary power, that those measures are not effective' (ibid., p. 342).
62 The Secretary General and the officials dependent on him are entitled only to delegated or executive functions; compare Conforti, *Le Nazioni Unite*, pp. 201–4.
63 Compare among many other upholders of the thesis of illegality: M. Chemillier-Gendreau, 'La Carta dell'ONU: la lettera e lo spirito', *Democrazia e diritto*, 32 (1992), 1, pp. 304–8; L. Gianformaggio, 'La guerra come negazione del diritto', ibid., pp. 288ff. On the obsolescence of articles 43–7 of the Charter cf. Conforti, *Le Nazioni Unite*, pp. 187–8.
64 The People's Republic of China notably abstained from voting in the matter of resolution 678, which authorized the military intervention against Iraq.
65 Ramsey Clark uses expressions such as 'open bribery, blackmail, and coercion' and refers to circumstances in which United States diplomats offered considerable financial credits to the representatives of some Members of the Security Council: Clark, *The Fire this Time*, pp. 153–5. Andrew Hurrell, in spite of his acute and balanced analysis of the Gulf War, declares *tout court* that: 'the condemnation of the Iraqi invasion and the imposition of economic sanctions by such a wide range of states does provide solid evidence of the universality of international society'; cf. A. Hurrell, 'Collective Security and International Order Revisited', *International Relations*, 11 (1992), 1, pp. 49ff.
66 Or when military intervention is nothing more than a purely symbolic exercise of the role of world supremacy and it is free of any risk, as it was in the case of Somalia.

67 Palmer, *Guardians of the Gulf*, pp. 243–9.
68 As is well known, the Administration of the United States deemed the invasion of Afghanistan by the Soviet Union to constitute 'a grave threat to the free movement of Middle Eastern oil'. President Jimmy Carter openly declared that 'any attempt by any outside force to gain control of the Persian Gulf region will be regarded as an assault on the vital interests of the United States. It will be repelled by use of any means necessary, including military force'; cf. President Jimmy Carter, *State of the Union Address*, 23 January 1980, *Weekly Compilation of Presidential Documents*, 16 (4), pp. 194–203; cf. also C. A. Kupchan, *The Persian Gulf and the West*, Boston: Allen & Unwin, 1987, pp. 4–5, 68–98, 114–15.
69 The only reference which is usually encountered is to article 39 of the Charter, which grants the Security Council a power to take the initiative, using either peaceful or military means, in cases of a 'threat to peace', a 'violation of peace' or an 'act of aggression'. On the broadly discretional nature of this power, and on possible forms of redress, compare G. Gaja, 'Reflexions sur le role du Conseil de Securité dans le nouvel ordre mondial', *Revue Générale de Droit International Public* (1993), 2, pp. 297–320.
70 For a comprehensive bibliography, see J. P. Baratta, *Strengthening the United Nations: A Bibliography on U.N. Reform and World Federalism*, New York–Westport–London: Greenwood Press, 1987; the bibliographical notes in the appendix to Falk, Kim and Mendlovitz (eds), *The United Nations and a Just World Order*, pp. 583–4, are also useful. For an analytical account of reform projects relating to the Security Council up to 1979 see: H. Newcombe, *Reform of the U.N. Security Council*, Dundas (Ontario): Peace Research Reviews, 1979; see also J. Logue (ed.), *United Nations Reform and Restructure*, Villanova (Pa.): Villanova University Press, 1980; D. Steele, *The Reform of the United Nations*, London: Croom Helm, 1987; M. Bertrand, *The Third Generation World Organization*, Dordrecht: Martinus Nijhoff, 1989.
71 See G. Clark and L. B. Sohn, *World Peace through World Law*, Cambridge (Mass.): Harvard University Press, 1960.
72 See M. Nerfin, 'The Future of the United Nations: Some Questions on the Occasion of an Anniversary', *Development Dialogue*, 10 (1985), 1, pp. 1–25; M. Bertrand, *Refaire l'Onu! Un programme pour la paix*, Geneva: Editions Zoé, 1986; P. de Senarclens, *La crise des Nations Unies*, Paris: Presses Universitaires de France, 1988; S. H. Mendlovitz, 'Struggles for a Just World Peace: A Transition Strategy', *Alternatives*, 14 (1989), 3, pp. 363–9; Falk, *Positive Prescriptions for the Near Future*, pp. 19ff.
73 An account of US government opinions on this is provided by D. Binder and B. Crossette, 'As Ethnic Wars Multiply, United States Strives for a Policy', *The New York Times*, 7 February 1993, p. 1; see also P. Lewis, 'United Nations is Developing Control Center to Coordinate Growing Peace-keeping Role', ibid., 28 March 1993, p. 10.
74 Antonio Cassese, for instance, has proposed an attenuation of individual possession of the veto whereby the Security Council's deliberations should be approved by majorities including at least three permanent members.
75 L. Ferrajoli and S. Senese, 'Quattro proposte per la pace', *Democrazia e diritto*, 32 (1992), 1, pp. 253–6. Falk more modestly proposes that the Court of Justice should be provided with the power of binding interpretation and

control of the activities of the other organs of the United Nations; compare
Falk, *Positive Prescriptions for the Near Future*, pp. 19–20.

76 In *World Peace through World Law*, Clark and Sohn proposed, for instance,
the constitution of an international police force of 600,000 voluntary
professional soldiers, which should be equipped, if necessary, with nuclear
arms by an international agency. In the name of the ethical principle of
'limited horror', a similar proposal has been advanced by F. Cerutti, in
'Ethics and Politics in the Nuclear Age: The End of Deterrence?', *Praxis
International*, 12 (1993), 4, pp. 395–6.

77 United Nations Development Programme, *Human Development Report
1992*, New York–Oxford: Oxford University Press, 1992, pp. 10–11.

78 Clark, *The Fire this Time*, pp. 234–7; Ferrajoli and Senese, 'Quattro proposte
per la pace', pp. 247–9.

79 These are likely to be two aspects which Saddam Hussein failed to take into
account when he decided to invade Kuwait. He relied, in all probability, on
the inability of the United States's Administration to obtain the support of
internal public opinion for the war, which appears also to have been the
principal reason for his defeat.

80 For a general critique of Falk's theses cf. Bull, *The Anarchical Society*,
chapters 6, 7, 12 and 13.

3 The Blind Alleys of International Ethics

> The only institutions whose moral opinions command general
> respect and are generally heard as stating the decent opinion
> of humankind are Amnesty International and similar organ-
> izations which are devoid of physical power or armed force.
>
> S. Toulmin, *Cosmopolis*

> Current theories of international morality have been designed
> to perpetuate the supremacy of English-speaking peoples.
>
> E. H. Carr, *The Twenty Years' Crisis 1919–1939*

Institutional Pacifism and Ethical Pacifism

So far the central theme of this work has emerged through consideration
of the problem of peace from the angle of the political institutions
which are charged with its preservation at an international level. This
has involved exposition and discussion of the tenets of 'institutional
pacifism' and 'political globalism', two theoretical positions which
envisage a 'cosmopolitan' reform of international institutions and the
relations which currently obtain between the great military, political
and economic groupings of the world. Neither of these theories,
however, encompasses analysis of the anthropological, psychological
and sociological aspects of human aggression, and both focus narrowly
on the prescriptive dimension of international *political engineering*. In
addition, in line with a generically realist approach, both neglect the
dimensions of ethics and individual morality.[1]

Alongside institutional pacifism there exists in western culture a
theoretical and practical tradition which sees the alternative between
war and peace as being dependent more on choices of a moral nature
than on options of a political-institutional kind. Within this tradition a
division into two distinct branches is discernible. The first – and clearly

more spiritual – of these derives from the evangelical principles expressed in the Sermon on the Mount or in some equivalent ethico-religious precepts of eastern traditions. The second, a direct heir to the argumentational models of Catholic scholasticism, has developed a complex system of rules for the ethical evaluation of behaviour which it considers to be significant from the point of view of war and peace. Ethically significant behaviour, in this conception, covers not only that of individuals but also that of organized groups, political institutions, states and even of superpowers.

Despite their shared roots in spiritual sources and religious traditions, these two branches of ethical pacifism differ greatly on both the theoretical and practical levels. The first embraces the tradition of non-violence, conscientious objection and the various forms of militant pacifism.[2] This tradition arose first in Protestant lands and the English-speaking world, but, from the second half of the nineteenth century on, the introduction of compulsory military service in virtually all European countries acted as a powerful catalyst to its further expansion. In our own century it has won converts even amongst minority groupings in the Catholic world and has found its most complete and elevated expression in Tolstoy's anti-militarism and, *par excellence*, in Gandhi's *satyagraha*.[3]

The second branch concerns the ethics of war and international relations. This is a line of thought which originated in Augustine's critique of radical non-violence, developed into the doctrine of the *justum bellum* in orthodox Catholic thought of the first and second scholastic periods, and, via Alberico Gentili and Hugo Grotius, has contributed to the emergence of modern international law.[4] Today, following an extensive period of relative eclipse, it has given rise, almost entirely in the English-speaking world, to a spate of writing on the subjects of the ethics of international relations, military ethics and 'nuclear ethics'. With the exception of certain authors still linked to the scholastic tradition,[5] this writing no longer relies, even indirectly, on presuppositions of a theological or fideistic kind. The intention of writers such as Michael Walzer, Charles Beitz, Stanley Hoffman and Joseph Nye is that they should be considered as contributors to an area of ethics which is as 'lay' as the political realism which they set out to challenge.[6] In fact, as will be seen, it is in a number of respects doubtful whether such contributions can be properly included at all under the general heading of pacifism, even in the weaker meanings of the term. In Michael Walzer's case, in particular, the doctrine of the 'just war' has received reinterpretation in accordance with a version of military ethics rigorously contradistinguished to any possible form of pacifism.[7]

What contribution is this bipartite tradition able to offer in present terms to a political philosophy of peacemaking? Is the current state of ethical philosophy in a position to outline operative strategies capable of envisaging the expression of human conflictuality in forms other than war and the practices of 'coercive diplomacy'? What help is offered by ethics of international relations towards an understanding of the reasons why over the last two centuries all institutional schemes for 'perpetual peace' have come to nothing? Are the new versions of the 'just war' theory really at all innovative when seen in the context of a tradition which appears to have made no important contribution to the delegitimation of war, to say nothing of its practical limitation? More particularly, is it the case that the ethical viewpoint, with its universalist approach and implicit reference to the idea of the moral unity of humankind, provides arguments in support of the globalistic and cosmopolitan theories? Is the notion of 'world government', in other words, an ethical as well as political category which alludes to a kind of Kantian 'global ethical commonwealth'?[8] These are the questions which I shall attempt to address in the course of the following sections.

Absolute Pacifism and Gandhian Non-violence

This is not the place for a general discussion of the foundations, theoretical coherence and practical effectiveness of absolute pacifism. Instead I will confine myself selectively to a few observations concerning the issues mentioned above. In addition, I will consider pacifism only where it appears as 'active resistance', in the form conceived and put into practice in this century by men of faith such as Mahatma Gandhi and, following in his footsteps, Martin Luther King.[9] This version of pacifism is to my mind interesting in that it has inspired the two most remarkable attempts to turn a moral virtue – mildness – into the instrument of a socio-political revolution. More precisely, it has outlined practical modes of expression of human aggression that are deliberately conflictual but not destructive.

Non-violent revolutionary action does not aim at annihilation of its opponents in a zero sum game, nor does it seek to inflict moral humiliation. Rather, it endeavours to secure assent by the end of a match played in forms which are firmly antagonistic yet tenaciously cooperative. In other words, it is a theoretical alternative to the logic of coercive diplomacy, a pursuit which expressly includes recourse to force among the possible outcomes of diplomatic bargaining.[10]

In order to bring about the construction of peace, advocates of radical non-violence claim, it is necessary to count upon people's moral nature. Mildness is closely linked to other psychological dispositions or moral virtues, such as a restrained attitude where acquisitiveness is concerned, together with empathy, humility, loyalty and sincerity. The problem of peace is a matter of a personal commitment to acting peacefully within the whole range of social relations. In this perspective, a political community can achieve stable peace both within and outside its confines only when individuals have been converted to the practice of non-violence and its related virtues. War, it is argued, even in its most destructive forms, is but the cumulative expression of the violence which courses through the social fabric. Violence leads to further violence, war further war. Only non-violence, which breaks this self-destructive circle, acts as a force opposed to war and is thus capable of stopping armed conflict.

The central point, indeed the strength of the non-violent option, lies in its refusal to respond to violence by means of violence: *vim vi repellere non licet*. A non-violent person will endure violence by counting on the conversion effect that pain suffered with dignity and fortitude will induce in those who have unjustly caused it. The mild character displayed by the non-violent individual is – as it were – thought to have a capacity of spiritual influence: it is held to be transitive and socially effective above and beyond the immediate investment of moral resources required by the heroic deed of non-resistance to aggression.

Thus formulated, the strategy of absolute pacifism is by no means lacking in a deep moral attraction, and it cannot be denied that in some aspects it is endowed with considerable practical plausibility. In comparison with institutional pacifism, it first of all has the positive feature of representing an attempt to give an answer to a pivotal philosophical question: what are the anthropological and psychological reasons for violence? In this regard, institutional pacifism seems to confine itself to an elementary Hobbesian answer: the practice of violence is made possible by the absence of coercive structures regulating and decreasing the aggression of individuals and social groups.[11]

By contrast, the answer offered by absolute pacifism – violence originates from acquisitive and competitive impulses of individuals – brings the political-institutional dimension of violence back to its anthropological and psychological roots. Violence does not come down from heaven, it is argued, nor is it a simple social phenomenon induced by disorderly and conflictual interaction among the expectations of individuals. Rather, violence has deep and intricate roots in the psychology of individuals, in their latent aggressive potentialities. And it is precisely on account of its radical and universal character that violence is so extremely dangerous. Indeed, the whole strategy of non-violence seems to be conceived – as it certainly was in Gandhi's thought – as individual and social therapy aimed at the conscious control of aggression, as a collective practice of asceticism rather than as a mere technique for overcoming the use of force.

Moreover, it is difficult to deny that under certain conditions and in given contexts the non-violent response to aggression and oppression can in any case prove to be an effective and rational answer, even when considered in the framework of the strictest realism. The epic Gandhian undertaking, with its successes gained both in South Africa and India, demonstrates that the non-violent strategy, in association with the techniques of civil disobedience, fiscal revolt and fasting, had a remarkable capacity to mobilize a great offensive against racist and colonial power, a capacity probably superior to that of armed insurrection or recourse to terrorism. From this point of view, the famous 'salt march' of March 1930 represents an exemplary event. The experience of the struggle against racial discrimination led by Martin Luther King in the United States through the adoption of non-violent techniques which drew inspiration from Gandhism – I refer here to the famous bus boycott in Montgomery, Alabama – provides further proof of the potential socio-political efficacy of active pacifism. As is well known, numerous attempts have in fact been made, from Gene Sharp to Johan Galtung, to go beyond the spiritual context of Gandhian thought in order to champion secular and 'rational' strategies of non-military resistance to oppression, or to bring about the defeat of armed intimidation.[12] When viewed from the standpoint of their possible relevance to realistic and pragmatic pacifism, I would argue that these extended versions represent an important theoretical contribution offered by the experience of Gandhian non-violence.

The limitations of absolute pacifism are, however, as evident as the moral loftiness of its challenge to the logic of power and the political system. They are evident in that they depend to a great extent on the loftiness of the challenge itself, on what might well be termed its moral excess. The fault of Gandhian pacifism was to reverse – it may be said – the axiological relation between ends and means: for the endeavour to achieve a people's political independence without bloodshed, by converting millions of people to non-violence, implies setting onself an intermediate target that is actually higher, nobler and infinitely more arduous than the final goal itself. In India, thanks also to a series of contingent circumstances unconnected with the Gandhian enterprise, the aim of national independence was eventually fulfilled with only the minimum of blood spilled. Nevertheless, Gandhism tragically failed, for it was crushed not by the oppressor's violence, but rather by violence breaking out among the oppressed – Hindus and Muslims – violence which was to turn its blows against the Mahatma himself. After the prophet's death, not only did his ideas wield no influence over the political constitution of the new nation, but they were rapidly shelved and forgotten.[13] Today India, besides being stained with the bloodshed of continuous waves of ethnic-religious violence, is one of the few Third World countries to possess a stockpile of nuclear weapons of its own.

On a historical level, the attempt to turn the asceticism of a charismatic leader into a standard of behaviour for huge masses of people, and furthermore within a social context that was driving aggression to hyper-acute levels, was inevitably doomed to failure. On a theoretical level, the fault of Gandhism was to believe that human violence may be curbed not through a long, arduous and still largely unexplored process of cultural, economic and institutional transformation (of which political autonomy is itself probably one of the remote preconditions) but instead through the immediate influential effect of a display of moral heroism. It is clear that such a distortion derives not only from the charismatic presumption of a religious leader with his providence-based concept of history, but also from an idea of aggression as a moral limitation, as selfishness and as sin. What inevitably escapes Gandhian spiritualism is, on the one hand, the biological rootedness of aggression – its evolutionary dimension that stretches back into the mists of time – and, on the other, its functional value within any political system.

The rudimentary Gandhian theory of the state as an impersonal, immoral and oppressive machine,[14] which is therefore to be destroyed, overlooks the consideration that the political system as such is a veritable 'sociological universal', that is to say a social structure in which, from as far back as the dawn of human history, fear, aggression and violence have been inextricably intertwined with safety, protection and co-operation. In chapter 5 I will take up this philosophical-political theme in greater detail. For the present, I shall restrict myself to discussion of the following point.

In the Gandhian framework, as in that of Martin Luther King, mildness endeavours to reach out beyond its status as an individual moral virtue in order to become not merely an instrument of social struggle but also the principle of a stable political organization. The Mahatma's assertions are unequivocal from this point of view, even though they may ultimately appear disheartened and tinged with pessimism.[15] Furthermore, as is natural for a man of faith, he ascribed to the principles of *satyagraha* the universalistic and deontological character of imperative rules which do not differ, as far as their absoluteness is concerned, from the categorical precepts of Kantian ethics. One thinks, for instance, of the severity with which Gandhi recommended the 'supreme law' of non-violence to the Jews persecuted by the Nazis when he invited them to accept martyrdom, in the confident belief that their sufferings would eventually touch Hitler's heart.[16]

Gandhi's ethics, even when concerned with political and economic topics, is a typical ethics of principle: it cannot be equated with consequentialist ethics, or, still less, with the Weberian ethics of 'responsibility'. The idea of a possible differentiation of moral styles according to the diversity of social backgrounds or outcomes to be achieved was totally alien to Gandhi's thought. Nevertheless, he was often in practice compelled to make 'responsible' – sometimes politically moderate – decisions without succeeding in presenting arguments to justify such decisions, thus leaving his closest followers, Nehru first and foremost, intellectually and morally dismayed.[17] For Gandhi, and indeed for radical pacifism in general, the absolute primacy and universality of principles meant that the results of actions that are morally good, from the point of view of both the purpose and the means adopted, cannot but be good. If they are bad, this means either that the purposes were not truly good or that the means were not as good as the purposes.

A modern realist philosophy of politics cannot fail to point out the twofold fallaciousness of this universalism and ethical deontologism: both as regards its lack of normative foundation and also because it is unsuited to being sensibly experienced outside the bounds of a specific 'subsystem', namely that of ethical-religious experience and personal interactions.

First, on the issue of normative justification, i.e. of the demand for compliance, ethical universalism is firmly contradicted by the realist and subjectivist philosophies of values, that is to say by the entire tradition of ethical non-cognitivism, from Hume to Nietzsche, to Weber, to Neurath, to René Girard, to Rorty. Moreover, on the level of empirical research, an imposing mass of sociological literature displays the moral pluralism which has *de facto* gained currency in secularized societies, not only in the West.

Secondly – and here it is appropriate to refer to the tradition of classical political realism traceable from Machiavelli to Pareto, to Weber and Schumpeter – if the ethics of principle takes the precepts of. mildness ('do not react to violence and do not kill'), of sincerity ('do not lie') and of loyalty ('abide by agreements') as categorical imperatives, it may well provide the motive force behind moral heroism at the level of personal interactions, but is not compatible with the functional code of even the least differentiated and complex political system. The universalistic and impartial character of categorical ethics clashes with the particular and partial nature of the criteria of exclusion and hierarchical subordination on which the 'protective' function of any political order, whether ancient or modern, is founded.[18]

Finally, the social transitivity of the moral influence on which absolute pacifism counts in order to accomplish its political ends appears doomed to come to a halt when faced with such structures as the division of labour and functional differentiation within non-elementary societies. In differentiated societies social complexity manifests itself as a process of growing semantic discontinuity among the languages, types of knowledge and values encompassed within any given social subsystem. The import of an experience encountered within a specific setting is unlikely to be translatable into the experience possible in a different setting. The relevant functional codes are therefore essentially incommensurable and incommunicable. From this point of view, any expectation that the moral experience of bearing witness to pacifism will necessarily be endowed with universal social transitivity is a premodern assumption directed – as it certainly appears to have been in Gandhi and, before him, in Thoreau and Tolstoy – towards a society that is informal, static and sub-differentiated. In short: an archaic society.

The Foundations of International Ethics

The ethics of international relations aspires – as does any ethical doctrine – to a statute of normative universality, but is not concerned with the formulation of precise deontological precepts or principles. Indeed, in respect of this aspect it differs notably from absolute pacifism, which appeals instead to the moral conscience of individuals, prescribing (or more often forbidding) certain specific types of behaviour, for instance with regard to the categorical prohibition on perpetrating violence and killing. The ethics of international relations refers to moral principles which are 'commonly accepted', or – as Michael Walzer expresses it – 'universally acknowledged'; yet, it avoids either enunciating them or giving a normative justification stating the reasons why they should be observed.[19]

An example of this may be seen in Charles Beitz, who, while setting his 'cosmopolitan' ethics against both Hobbesian scepticism and Hugo Grotius's theories of the 'morality of states', admits that he is not in a position to produce any argument against ethical scepticism in general. All that he claims to be able to argue is that once the validity of ethics and its applicability to politics is apodictically accepted, 'international scepticism' is unjustified.[20] In similar fashion, Michael Walzer not only eschews any inquiry into the general validity of the 'moral law' which he means to apply to international politics, but indeed he goes as far as to state that he is by no means sure of its foundations.[21] Joseph Nye, although he dedicates an entire chapter to 'moral reasoning', ignores the topic of the normative foundations of international ethics and immediately turns to the 'ethical point of view' of the United States.[22]

The truth is that in all these authors there is an implicit reference to the Judaeo-Christian tradition, interpreted mainly from the standpoint of Protestant Christianity. The 'practical' dimension of this tradition is taken for granted: namely it is regarded as identical to 'ordinary morality', i.e. that morality which in practice and by usage is considered 'normal' in western societies, especially in those of Anglo-American culture. It is held that, thanks to its nature as a background moral belief which is normally beyond dispute (even though not always scrupulously complied with), this ordinary morality is not in need of justification on a philosophical and epistemological level. Nor is it necessary to express it according to particular deontic enunciations. Alternatively – as in the case of Terry Nardin – a rationality and universality superior to that of any other possible moral tradition is by definition attributed to the western ethical tradition as traceable from the Bible to the Stoa, St Thomas Aquinas and Kant. Its normative cogency is claimed to come not from tradition, from habit or from a transcendent authority but directly from 'reason'.[23] In adherence of this view, Stanley Hoffman regards as superfluous even so much as the proposal put forward by a theorist of justice such as John Rawls, who has tried to found his own doctrine on moral intuition.[24] As is commonly recognized, in *A Theory of Justice* Rawls re-elaborates some Kantian formulations from *The Critique of Practical Reason*, stating that all human beings are endowed with a 'natural sense of justice' thanks to the 'moral nature' of humankind.[25]

In accordance with the Weberian distinction between an ethic of conviction and an ethic of responsibility, the theorists of international ethics freely acknowledge that in the international framework, in which nations for the most part and only marginally individuals are to be considered the subjects of moral issues, any moral principles adopted must give due consideration to circumstances and the calculation of results. Thus, at the conclusion of his lengthy volume on the 'normative theory' of international relations, Charles Beitz acknowledges that in politics it is inappropriate to make a decision in accordance with ethical principles without considering the complexity of empirical situations.[26] Joseph Nye, who is the most explicit on this topic, proposes a 'three-dimensional' scheme, within which he attempts a normative synthesis of criteria referring to intentions, means and consequences.[27] He declares himself to be a 'sophisticated consequentialist' who gives up the ideal of 'moral integrity' in favour of the efficacy of moral reasoning.

Proof of the efficacy of his 'three-dimensional ethics' appears, he claims, in the fact that his scheme allows him to develop arguments to show the moral superiority of the United States's armed interventions in Grenada and the Dominican Republic over the apparently analogous interventions by the Soviet Union in Czechoslovakia and Afghanistan, while at the same time maintaining that 'American idealism' led the United States to an involvement in Vietnam which was not totally correct from a moral point of view. On the level of intentions and consequences, he maintains, the United States's military actions have always been morally unexceptionable, given that their aim has been to restore democratic order and to safeguard the political independence of the countries attacked. Moreover, with the sole exception of Vietnam, their interventions have had some of the lowest body counts, with very contained loss of life.[28]

Stanley Hoffman, adopting, for his part, an even more eclectic stance, has the declared intention of combining the principles of international ethics with the traditionally opposed principles of political realism.[29] Any moral judgement applied to politics cannot be anything but a historical – and thus 'contextual and situational' – judgement. In international politics, moral choice has to be compatible with its costs; it has, in other words, to take foreseeable consequences into account and to aim at efficacy: it cannot be an ethic of principles or of intentions.[30] On the other hand, he says, it is a mistake to dramatize the opposition between interests and morality, between prudential behaviour and generosity. These two attitudes can be reconciled, provided that a morality requiring absolutely disinterested behaviour is not taken to be the one and only true morality.[31] International ethics is exactly the area in which it is necessary to prove that reconciliation between moral principles and calculations of interest is possible and even advantageous. Principles act as a guide, yet it is not possible to use them either to the full or under all circumstances. Even precepts of the form 'do not kill' and 'do not lie' can be objects only of conditional allegiance. It is morally correct to kill, to lie, to deceive if the murder, lie or deceit makes it possible to avoid 'a considerable disadvantage for the national interest'.[32]

Michael Walzer, as will be seen in detail in the next section, goes still further: renouncing any ethical legalistic scruple, he formulates a moral category of 'supreme emergency'. In a situation of supreme emergency, he claims, the violation of any moral rule or limit by a state is allowed; even the massacre of hundreds of thousands of innocent people may be therefore morally recommendable.[33]

The claim that these arguments offer a significant contribution to the solution of international problems, in terms both of moral philosophy and of political theory, must in my opinion be discussed and criticized in general terms. This is all the more true if we take seriously the practical target at which they profess to aim, i.e. the elaboration of effective standards of moral discipline in international politics and of the containment of war. I venture this statement even though it seems to me difficult to deny that from the standpoint of peacemaking these theories, as well as the traditional doctrines of the 'just war', have not so far achieved any great efficacy, or, if they have, the outcomes have been, to say the least, ambiguous. In the next section my critique will consist of three different points. For each of them – referring mainly to the authors mentioned above – I will try to focus on some of the general inconsistencies which in my own view are characteristic of the ethics of international relations. In the subsequent section I shall deal in a more analytical manner with the theory of the 'just war' and with Michael Walzer's recent reinterpretation of this concept.

General Inconsistencies

Social complexity and moral polytheism

In the absence of a normative foundation, supporters of international ethics base themselves, as has been seen above, on the moral criteria which in their opinion are 'commonly accepted' in western society, taking for granted their universal and rational character. Clearly, such assumptions cannot be confuted on a theoretical level: *quod gratis asseritur gratis negatur*. They can be opposed only by different means, including the weapon of political polemics. I shall produce no general argument, therefore, in order to assert that western 'ordinary morality' influenced by the Judaeo-Christian tradition has no foundations. Instead I shall restrict myself to the observation that this morality, like other ethical doctrines which aspire to a categorical and universal application, stands or falls with the fideistic presuppositions – the existence of God, immortality of the soul, objectiveness of creation, constancy of natural laws, etc. – to which it implicitly or explicitly refers. These presuppositions have no rational support; nevertheless, without them these doctrines are deprived of normative authority.

To assert the lack of foundation of universal ethical theories, especially those belonging to the Judaeo-Christian tradition, is obviously not equivalent to denying the anthropological importance of moral commitment, nor does it mean undervaluing the political function of a common heritage of moral expectations, claims and indignation. Indeed, the very critique of the formal and abstract character of universal ethical theories can act as the premise for a subjectivist, non-deontological, non-categorical moral alternative which is expressed in a proposal to orient one's life in accordance with particular values. By contrast, the ethical doctrines which draw inspiration from Kantian deontology seek to form a concept of justice from an impersonal, impartial and neutral point of view. They thus condemn themselves – as Bernard Williams and Charles Larmore have pointed out – to a *sub specie aeternitatis* standpoint which is deprived of psychological, sociological and historical determination.[34]

Yet, it seems to me that on the same pragmatic level on which international moralists take their stand, the very existence of an 'ordinary morality' universally accepted in western societies and applicable to relations among states has to be questioned. Western countries, assaulted by the revolution in technology and automation, show themselves to be societies of increasing complexity, characterized by growing functional differentiation. Traditional moral codes have ceased to apply to the whole of the social system, retaining a certain degree of normative cogency only within very specific social backgrounds or in personal interaction. The practical observance of these codes – e.g. the sexual ethics preached by the Catholic hierarchy, the pacifism of Jehovah's Witnesses or Mormons, or the deontological positions of the countless religious sects abounding in the West – is restricted to clearly defined social groups which strive to raise, as it were, insurmountable semantic barriers to ward off the contagious perils of secularization and 'moral polytheism'.

The sense of subjectivity and contingency of values seems to be an irreversible characteristic of the modern world, in which the privatization of moral beliefs turns any 'public morality' into a sort of 'larval' survival of old mechanisms of legitimation of social order. As opposed to the moralistic nature of the great positive religions, the fragmentation of ethical codes and the very instability of the criteria of rationality seem increasingly to reflect the incommensurability of language games and lifestyles that characterizes differentiated and complex societies. In a word: the 'ordinary morality' to which international moralists appeal would appear to be an academic hypothesis rather than a sociological datum to be assumed without further discussion.

State morality and cosmopolitan ethics

A second and equally serious difficulty presents itself. Even assuming that it is possible to formulate univocal and universally cogent moral judgements, there remains the problem of how to identify the subjects of an international moral order. Who has the legitimate right to demand respect of his or her own 'moral rights'? Who has the duty to fulfil and defend them? And which moral – not simply political or military – authorities can legitimately issue statements on topics of international ethics, or solve the dilemmas raised by conflicting moral claims? Can there be a modern avatar of the medieval European cosmopolis, in which Christian princes acknowledged the absolute spiritual power – and *therefore* also an international jurisdiction – of the Catholic Church?

Different, controversial, sometimes confusedly eclectic opinions exist on this subject. Joseph Nye, for instance, suggests a 'cosmopolitan-realist synthesis' of the divergent theses of political realism, the theory of state morality and the cosmopolitan standpoint. Such a synthesis would acknowledge the imperatives of transnational ethics, while at the same time taking into consideration that the present-day world is organized into sovereign states.[35]

In similar fashion, Stanley Hoffman maintains that both nations and individuals are agents of international ethics: states, despite the fact that they are artificial constructs, are today the main players on the international stage, and to ignore the ethical implications of their decisions would hardly be realistic. On the other hand, awareness of the cosmopolitan universality of the 'moral rights' of individuals is, though poorly developed to date, in all likelihood destined ultimately to be successful.[36]

Yet, apart from these theoretically uncertain propositions, there are two fundamental options. There is a 'statist' option, which to a large extent predominates, according to which states and states alone are the holders of moral rights and responsibilities in the field of international relations. Following Hugo Grotius's version of the doctrine of natural law, which has lately been taken up again by Michael Walzer as a 'legalist paradigm', it is assumed that in the international arena individuals are represented by states and that their 'moral rights' are included within the pool of 'moral rights' of states. Nations are themselves moral agents, ethical Leviathans or – to use the classical expression – *magni homines* drawing together within themselves the moral claims of citizens. Included within the rights to territorial integrity and to political independence which the international order awards to nations are the 'natural rights' to life and freedom which nations grant to their own citizens.[37]

In contrast to this, the cosmopolitan option grants the designation as original agents of the universal ethical order exclusively to individuals, in that they are both members of the human community and 'moral persons'. Ethical cosmopolitanism – in the different versions of Kantian federalism, religious ecumenism and anthropocentric ecology – thus denies that states may stake out claims different or even contrary to those of their own citizens. The unity and universality of 'world ethics' goes beyond the political and territorial particularism of states and their legal systems.[38] If it is strictly necessary, for contingent reasons, to include states in the sphere of cosmopolitan ethics, then states must be taken as performers of duties, not as holders of rights. Their main duty is not only to treat their own citizens democratically but to treat all people equally, regardless of diversity of race, sex, culture, social class, etc., and regardless even of a person's citizenship or membership in a state.[39] In order to permit the fulfilment of this duty, Charles Beitz argues, it is necessary to go beyond the principle, classically formulated by Christian Wolff and Emmerich de Vattel, of absolute observance of the sovereignty of states and of non-interference in their domestic affairs.[40]

There is also a non-'statist', non-individualistic variant of cosmopolitan ethics which may be termed 'speciesist ethical globalism'. According to this view, the subject of cosmopolitan 'moral rights' is humankind itself, whereas individuals and states fundamentally have the duty to refrain from behaviour that might jeopardize survival of the species. Dangerous behaviour, in this perspective, could be anything from the use of nuclear weapons to alteration of the 'biospheric conditions' which make existence of the animal *homo sapiens* possible on this planet.[41] A still further view, distinct from the last although its close theoretical affinities should not be overlooked, concerns non-anthropocentric ecological ethics held by the philosophers of 'deep ecology' and of animalism. They assign moral subjectivity and natural rights not only to humankind but also to the other living species, to the terrestrial biosphere and to the cosmos.[42]

Such disparity of opinion, however, amongst theorists of international ethics on such a crucial point as the assignation of moral (international or cosmopolitan) agency is, in my opinion, one sign of the theoretical frailty of the entire normative framework.

The cosmopolitan option fluctuates between a radical moral individualism (deriving directly from the Enlightenment and the doctrine of natural law), on the one hand, and, on the other hand, an ethical globalism which is in a sense its inverse, replete as it is with traces of mystical-religious, organicist and evolutionist ideas. In the first case, the well-known criticism levelled from the time of Hume against the doctrine of 'natural law' from an agnostic, realist and historicist viewpoint is all the more pertinent when brought to bear on the 'natural' character of subjective rights within the international field, that is to say in the field of so-called 'human rights'.

There are, as Norberto Bobbio has lucidly argued, no foundations in a universal ethical code to give 'natural' rights or 'human' rights an *a priori* justification on the basis of a metaphysical anthropology. They have gained currency as positive constitutional rights – which can be claimed and enforced – through a series of highly specific historical events which were mainly characterized by a high level of political conflict and which occurred exclusively in Europe.[43] It is widely known that many non-western authors now see the spread of the doctrine of 'human rights' and even the Universal Declaration of 1948 as phases of an ominous process of westernization of the world. This point I shall return to in detail in the following chapter.

As for ethical globalism, which tends to see humankind as the primary subject of moral cosmopolitan rights, objections on a philosophical level can be even more radical. Above all, it is not clear why the 'species' – a strictly biological, not cultural, notion – should enjoy ethical primacy over and above individual moral conscience. The whole development of human language, culture and civilization seems to be towards the liberation of individuals from the organic bonds which in archaic societies tied them to their own group and its biological-reproductive functions. The emergence of individual self-consciousness, in terms of cognitive and moral identity, appears inseparable from the evolutionary process of differentiation of individuals in comparison with their family, tribe, clans, *gens*, city, nation, species. In this sense, an ethics of the species which aims to impose limits and sacrifices on individuals in the name of 'moral rights' ascribed to the probable series of future generations can only be evolutionarily regressive. It ignores the incomparable singularity of individual lives, and their freedom and destiny, in the name of a 'speciesist' collectivism which negates, if nothing else, the dimension of individual pain and death. Moreover, it is utterly misleading to believe that adoption of a speciesist ethic – all the more so if, with Teilhard de Chardin, it is infused with a sort of millenarian cult of the human species – provides a master plan for averting the nuclear destruction of our planet or its pollution or the exhaustion of its resources. These objectives seem rather to require integrated – political, economic, technological, demographic – strategies aimed at containment of the enormous and constantly growing pressure which is exerted on the planetary ecosystem by the human species and which, even here and now, threatens the life and freedom of individuals.

Furthermore, an ethic granting a privilege to the species *homo sapiens*, by which the perpetuation of this particular animal species is held to be the first moral duty of its members, lays itself open to the keen criticism of non-anthropocentric types of ethics. The rational groundlessness of the two types being equal, the latter can at least vaunt its genuinely cosmic universality over the crude ethical particularism of anthropocentric cosmopolitanism. In any event, this speciesist battle appears to ignore the empirical data which, *rebus sic stantibus*, suggest with some reasonable reliability a forecast of the eventual extinction of humankind, as well as of any other living species on the earth.

The other basic option is, as we have seen, represented by the 'state morality' thesis. This boasts a long tradition, for it is commonly identified with the doctrine of Hugo Grotius and, more generally, with the ethical assumptions which have accompanied the birth of modern international law. In the view of many authors, and principally Michael Walzer, the 'moral standing of states' is closely linked to the 'legalistic paradigm', i.e. to the complex of the rights that the so-called international community recognizes and grants to states. From the viewpoint of normative foundation, the moral prerogatives of states do not appear to differ, according to these authors, from the political and legal prerogatives which the practice of international organizations, their legal systems and the whole network of international legal order accord to them.

What, then, is the specific meaning of the international ethics proposed by such authors? What duties do they allot to the individual states and, in particular, to 'rich countries' and the great powers? The topics generally addressed by the theorists of 'state morality' are mostly those of the moral use of force by states, of the advancement of human rights and of 'global distributive justice'.[44] For the present I shall dwell briefly on this last point only, for I will deal specifically with the others later on. I have two observations to make here.

The first concerns a difficulty which ought to be perceived by the theorists of international ethics as internal to their own argument. This is the difficulty of assigning 'moral qualities' to states – and thus to their territorial definition, regimes, governments, repressive machinery, armies, etc. – without due attention to any other moral evaluation. Thus Michael Walzer, among others, suggests adopting such simple criteria as the diplomatic recognition of states by international organizations or the absence of an ongoing civil war within their frontiers. Such questions as nationhood, status as a people, ethnic grouping, linguistic or religious community, or citizenship are totally overlooked.[45] All this is in accordance with the assumption – which may indeed be useful in the pragmatic field of law, but is unjustified on an ethical level – that states are the defenders of their citizens' life and freedom as well as of their common civil experience.[46] The problem is that a moral legalism and statism of this kind ultimately endows simple political configurations with some form of ethical value, and not infrequently attributes normative absoluteness to what is actually the result of military conflict or of hegemonic strategies pursued by the great powers. And indeed moralists such as Joseph Nye and Stanley Hoffman have even indulged in the formulation of a 'superpower ethic' for the exclusive use of the United States and the Soviet Union.[47]

In my second observation I wish to challenge the view that a modern political system, as seen in the international field in the form of the sovereign territorial state, can be conceived of as a moral agent subject to the imperatives of 'global distributive justice'. This view is one which is supported by a number of theorists of the 'just international order', in particular by Charles Beitz and Peter Singer. Beitz has no doubt whatsoever that it is both feasible and necessary to extend to global society the theory of justice elaborated for individuals by John Rawls within the sphere of the state.[48] Singer goes as far as to require rich countries to shoulder a 'moral burden of assistance' towards poor countries. In his opinion, rich countries have the moral duty to bring about a drastic decrease in the standard of welfare of their own citizens, in order to bring aid to the citizens of poorer countries. Nor should they help the least rich of their own citizens until they have assisted those of poorer countries, even though they may happen to be located in remote continents.[49]

The supporters of these theses are certainly moved by the best of intentions, yet they run the risk of failing to transcend a mere display of moral scruples. What appears to go unrecognized by these authors is that modern societies are characterized by a clear functional differentiation between the political code and the code of personal interactions. They fail to take into consideration that the modern state – the holder of the legitimate monopoly of force in order to ensure order at home and protection against outsiders – is in no position to act 'impartially' in accordance with a universalist ethic of a Kantian or neo-Kantian type.[50] A rigid functional constraint requires the state political system, like any other modern political system, to fulfil the task of assuring the protection of its own members and *these only*, as a precondition of its very existence and legitimacy. Unless they appeal to this original 'prejudicial condition', the structures of the political and territorial particularism of the state have no ground on which to constitute themselves and maintain themselves in existence. And the 'organization of prejudice' – to use the expression offered by Schattschneider[51] – requires differentiation between an internal area of affairs falling within the scope of the political group, in which 'safety' is jealously guarded, and an external sphere in which the sources of danger and fear, both physical and symbolic, are placed.[52] Furthermore, it is necessary to engender an asymmetrical organization of power relations within the group, giving the highest-ranking elements of the social body the power to use force against deviants and external enemies. Only by observing this twofold functional logic of exclusion and subordination can the state grant its citizens a selective regulation of social risks and a corresponding 'reduction of fear'.

In other words, the functional condition of the existence and legitimacy of a state – even of the most democratic – lies exactly in its capacity to make decisions in accordance with 'political' criteria, i.e. criteria lacking impartiality and universal ethical justification. Even the protection of rights to freedom, of market rules and of private property within liberal-democratic countries would be impossible without a power system able to guarantee political order by means of decisions which are to a large extent arbitrary if assessed from an ethical point of view. No amount of moralistic optimism can mask this 'severity of politics' without running the risk of falling into the irresponsibility of wishful thinking.[53]

Ethical eclecticism and normative inconclusiveness

The most serious consequence of eclecticism in the form in which it is methodically practised by the theorists of international ethics is the 'normative inconclusiveness' of their doctrines. By 'normative inconclusiveness' I mean a lack of deontic rigour in statements of international ethics, and it is certainly no coincidence that such statements, from Walzer on, call to mind the argumentative techniques of casuistry.[54] Once the non-pertinency of an ethic of principle has been declared and unlimited consequentialism embraced, the moral judgements which are passed in individual situations come to depend on the selective recon-struction of factual circumstances, on the prediction of future conse-quences and on the calculation of risks. It is hardly necessary to underline the epistemological frailty of the products of such operations, which are unavoidably compromised by the methodological decisions and value assumptions involved.[55] Added to this is the inherent uncer-tainty of any forecast concerning highly complex future events, such as the outcome of any international political decision, given that such decisions are bound to be made under pressure of time and in contexts of high interdependence and turbulence of the variables to be con-sidered. All of this renders the ethical evaluation of individual cases discretionary and entirely inscrutable: *stat pro ratione voluntas*.

When, therefore, the theorists of international ethics attempt to derive an evaluation of a specific case from the formulation of some general principle, the normative cogency of moral principles – which is never explicitly enunciated, however – is either heavily diluted amidst generic or compromise formulations, or subordinated to explicitly partisan pressures or else rendered void by the introduction of *ad hoc* exceptions.

A remarkable example of ambiguity and normative indeterminacy can be seen in the norms of nuclear ethics formulated by Joseph Nye through the application of his triadic synthesis of intentions, means and results. In the end, all that Nye feels he is able to propose to the US administration – the term 'prescribe' would be out of place here – is that, first, nuclear deterrence set up by the United States is morally justified by the right to self-defence and can be taken in the wider meaning of an 'extended deterrence'; second, nuclear weapons should never be considered as if they were conventional weapons; third, it is appropriate to endeavour to reduce to a minimum the killing of innocent people by nuclear means; fourth, it is advisable to lower the short-term risks of a nuclear war; fifth, it is recommendable that the United States should progressively cut down its military dependency on nuclear weapons.[56]

It is not for me to say whether such generic and pliable rules have any real meaning or even merit consideration by the authorities responsible for the nuclear strategy of the United States. But what I can definitely state is that the only remarkable aspect these standards have from the normative point of view is the implicit legitimation of the voluntary killing of 'innocent' people. And this seems to me to be a result that is not very encouraging on a moral level. Furthermore, I would argue that in the vocabulary of international moralists, influenced as they are by the medieval doctrine of the 'just war', the idea of innocence is gravely distorted.[57] It seems to me to be morally absurd to consider non-combatants innocent and, *therefore*, combatants non-innocent; all the more so today, in war situations which are light years away from the rudimentary models of the Middle Ages and even from those of the nineteenth century, in which the principle of the 'immunity of non-combatants' had a specific legal and military value. Today it is uncertain whether non-combatant civilians can be considered entirely uninvolved in a war which is fought in their country. At times, they become caught up in activities or responsibilities that are of considerable military importance. But above all it is senseless to think that the fact of belonging or not belonging to a military group, which may include even an army of conscripts under a despotic regime, can be considered to be so powerful a moral discriminant that it can affect people's right to life.

Similar observations may be made in respect of the moral imperatives stated by Seyom Brown at the conclusion of his recent book.[58] Brown includes these imperatives in his 'integrated strategy' for the prevention and control of war, while stating his full awareness that ethics alone cannot diminish the role that war plays in international relations. He therefore maintains that 'the moral imperatives must reinforce, and be reinforced by, calculations of self-interest by the holders of great material power.'[59]

In this radically consequentialist vein, Brown further enunciates, in two distinct expressions, one general maxim and one deontological precept which in his opinion should be observed by all states. The general maxim asserts that the level of immorality of an international political act must be measured by considering how many people have been killed or tortured as a consequence of the act itself.[60] The deontological precept, following a line of thought shared by many other international moralists, for example by Elizabeth Anscombe, Robert Phillips and Paul Ramsey, would place an absolute ban on the *intentional* killing of unarmed and innocent civilians.[61]

One can hardly fail to notice, however, that the general maxim which Brown puts forward touches on the extreme borders of ethical cynicism, for the reason that he attempts to resolve a moral question in purely quantitative terms. It does not forbid either the murder or the torture of innocent or less innocent people, but confines itself to recommending a parsimonious use of such actions in the international sphere. As for the precept which prohibits the *intentional* killing of innocent civilians, this, in a consequentialist context, is scarcely more restrictive than the general legitimation of the murder of innocents allowed by the nuclear ethics of Joseph Nye. There is no massacre of innocent people which is incapable of justification in a modern war, if it is interpreted as an indirect non-intentional effect of military operations necessary to attain certain strategic objectives (morally permissible, according to certain versions of military ethics). Thus, it can always be viewed as the lesser evil when compared with the relinquishing of such objectives.

In effect, those who – like Seyom Brown and the other moralists mentioned above – restrict themselves to condemning the *intentional* killing of unarmed innocent people are simply revamping a classic casuistic contrivance: the 'double effect' rule.[62] Such a rule is considered to be inapplicable today even by Stanley Hoffman, because it dangerously mingles, in the nuclear era, two absolutely contradictory Christian impulses: mildness and 'the crusading spirit'.[63] The killing of unarmed innocent people is permitted by the rule on the condition that the event is not the result of direct intention, even if it is foreseeable as an indirect consequence of an action of war, for instance the bombing of a military installation located in a densely inhabited area. In such a case, in order not to break the rule, it is necessary only to counterbalance the (non-intentional) killing of thousands of civilians with the (intentional) killing of thousands of soldiers, or with the destruction of military quarters or with the successful achievement of other essential strategic objectives.

Examples of the second type, namely of subordination of international ethics to partisan pressures, are extensively present in Michael Walzer's *Just and Unjust Wars*. Of these, the most remarkable, to my mind, is the one which concerns the ethical justification of preventive war. Walzer suggests a general norm which runs as follows: 'states may use military force in the face of the threats of war, whenever the failure to do so would seriously risk their territorial integrity or political independence.'[64]

As is well known, the rejection of preventive war is one of the basic principles which the international legal system has elaborated in order to restrict armed conflicts. This rule has been officially confirmed by the Covenant of the League of Nations, the Kellogg–Briand Pact, the Charter of the United Nations and more recently by two specific declarations of the United Nations General Assembly. These declarations have outlawed on the international level so-called 'preventive self-defence', and prohibit the use of force either for averting an impending military attack or for repelling 'indirect armed aggression'.[65]

In general, those who hold the principle of self-defence by a state under attack to be well founded not only from the legal but also from the ethical viewpoint are all the more careful to define the idea of 'aggression' in restrictive and verifiable terms, so that undue semantic extension of the concept can be prevented. As a rule, the actuality or real imminence of an armed attack or of a full-scale land invasion are required. Michael Walzer, who, as we shall find in the next section, advocates a total reinterpretation of the 'just war' doctrine in accordance with an ethical definition of 'aggression', nevertheless gives a moral justification for preventive war in highly generic terms, which thus admit of an extremely broad range of interpretations. In his view, preventive war is sufficiently legitimized by a 'threat of war' which seriously jeopardizes the territorial integrity or the political independence of a state.[66]

What is most surprising is not Walzer's ethical bellicosity. Far more startling is the kind of argument he chooses in order to propose what purports to be an ethical – and not merely legal, political or military – theory. He starts from the need, frankly stated and perceived as self-evident to those who, like him, are practising Jews and citizens of the United States, to provide a moral justification in terms of 'preventive self-defence' for the Israeli assault against Egypt (and Syria and Jordan) which opened the Six Day War in June 1967 and led to the occupation of large tracts of Palestinian territory.[67]

A sensational example of the third case – the suspension in exceptional circumstances of the normative efficacy of the entire moral code which is supposed to regulate all international relations – is to be found in yet another theory contrived by Michael Walzer, that of the 'supreme emergency'.[68] This theory is surprisingly reminiscent of Carl Schmitt's 'state of exception' theory, which is imbued with radical political realism. According to Walzer, no ethical limit need be respected by those who find themselves threatened by an 'unusual and dreadful' danger causing not only exceptionable fear but also moral repulsion.

Nazism, according to Walzer, was just such a threat: it presented 'a radical menace to human values', a genuine 'incarnation of evil in the world'.[69] In order to defeat this menace, it was necessary to resort to the very measures that the norms of 'just war' unconditionally forbid. The 'terrorist bombings' – the words are Walzer's own – which the British government authorized against the German civilian population, at the cost of more than three hundred thousand dead and eight hundred thousand injured in the wholesale destruction of German cities, were therefore legitimate. Only the final stage of those bombings – and also the atomic bombs on Hiroshima and Nagasaki – had no moral justification, because, in Walzer's opinion, the victory of the Allies was already certain and therefore the conditions for a 'supreme emergency' were not present.[70]

The *Justum Bellum* Doctrine According to Michael Walzer

'The restraint of war is the beginning of peace': it is with this twofold challenge to pacifism and to political realism that Walzer's *Just and Unjust Wars* concludes. In this book he sets out, with indisputable argumentational adroitness and an exceptional breadth of historical documentation, to restore theoretical dignity to the doctrine of the *justum bellum*. Nor can it be denied that he has to some extent succeeded in his attempt, since the extensive debate raised by his book has breathed new life into a tradition which, despite something of a revival in the Anglo-American cultural world, had long been languishing and had indeed very nearly fallen into oblivion.

Walzer has achieved this result almost in excess of his original intentions, because his goal was not so much that of restoring the authority of a theological tradition as that of reinterpreting it with all the freedom required to make of it an instrument of intervention in the current political situation. Not unnaturally the second edition of the book contains an introduction in which Walzer – in spite of voicing a few doubts about certain individual aspects of *jus in bello* – comes out firmly in favour of the 'morality' of the US intervention in the Gulf War and roundly condemns the 'immorality' of the enemy, Saddam Hussein's Iraq.[71]

The medieval Christian doctrine of the 'just war', as is well known, was intended to define the moral boundaries of war, so that it would be possible to distinguish 'just wars' from 'unjust wars'. War was thus accepted, though subject to certain conditions, within the ambit of Christian ethics. According to the intentions of its scholastic founders, from Thomas Aquinas to Francisco de Vitoria and Francisco Suárez, the distinction was intended to help to restrict war by obliging the Christian princes to wage only wars that could be justified on solid moral grounds and fought with legitimate means. In other words, the moral limitation extended not only to the 'causes' or reasons which could legitimate the beginning of war (the so-called *jus ad bellum*) but also to the actual handling of hostilities, including in particular the use of military instruments (*jus in bello*).[72]

The entire doctrine was to be seen in the political framework of the *respublica christiana* and presupposed the existence of a secure and stable *auctoritas spiritualis*, endowed with international legal power: the Roman Catholic Church. The *justum bellum* doctrine was supposed not only to restrict war but also to distinguish the wars waged between Christians (that is to say between opponents all of whom were subject to the authority of the Church) from 'feuds' (that is to say from the struggles between princes and peoples – such as the Turks, the Arabs and the Jews – who stubbornly declined to acknowledge the cosmopolitan authority of the Church).[73] The crusades and missionary wars authorized by the Church were *ipso jure* 'just wars', independently of the fact that they were wars of aggression or defence. Any war, however, waged upon Christendom was *ipso facto* an unjust war. Furthermore, during a just war, the enemy was not to be considered a *justus hostis*, in the formal meaning that would later be formulated by the founders of European public law: Alberico Gentili, Hugo Grotius and Samuel Pufendorf. The enemy was an infidel, an outlaw, a criminal.

Only with the abandonment of the moral-theological and cosmopolitan premises of the medieval *justum bellum* doctrine, from the seventeenth century onwards, was 'interstatal international law' to become influential throughout Europe.[74] As it was by then taken for granted that in the absence of a universal moral authority all contenders would consider their own war just – *bellum utrimque justum* – interstatal international law (no longer cosmopolitan) focused on the elaboration of exclusively formal and procedural norms. By ritualizing and regulating the use of weapons, an attempt was made to restrict the destructive effects of conflicts among states, although in fact only negligible results were actually achieved. In accordance with this intention, then, each European state was considered as a *persona moralis*, and thus as *justus hostis*, the holder of an original right to wage war. What survived, therefore, of the ancient *justum bellum* doctrine was solely a secular, legal and statalized version of *jus in bello*, the whole construct of *jus ad bellum* being in practice abandoned.

Since the First World War the very concept of 'aggression' has come to lose a moral sense, and to denote in legally neutral terms – as, for instance, in the Geneva Protocol of 1924 and the Kellogg–Briand Pact of 1928 – the adoption of military violence. The 'aggressor' has become simply the state which is the first to initiate war manoeuvres, regardless of whatever moral or other reasons are brought forward to justify the abandonment of diplomatic channels and the use of force. Finally, the United Nations Charter, drawn up on what was now the threshold of the nuclear era, not only places an absolute and comprehensive prohibition on the use of force by states, but even strongly reduces the right to armed defence by a state under attack. The Charter allows such states only the faculty of temporary resistance to aggression pending intervention by the UN Security Council. The Security Council, which is endowed with independent power ranking above that of either or any of the belligerents, has the authority to restore order by resorting for its own part to the use of force, without being compelled to take into account the military manoeuvres initiated either by the attacking or by the attacked state.[75]

It is interesting at this point to enquire into the nature of the interpretative exercise offered by Walzer. For, despite its great subtlety and complexity, it can also be said to display a certain lack of scruple. Walzer professes to start from an ethical-legal model of the interpretation of war, reflecting, he believes, western social conventions regarding law and order, on both the national and international level: this interpretation he terms the 'legalist paradigm'.[76] But on closer inspection it becomes clear that the 'legalist paradigm' in fact amounts to no more than the name by which Walzer has chosen to describe his own personal 'theory of aggression'.[77] In order to construct this theory, he exploits both the 'domestic analogy' and an explicitly discretionary use of elements of the western ethical and legal tradition (while subjecting his own theory to a series of notable exceptions or extensions as a somewhat paradoxical tribute to the casuistic method).[78] What becomes clear in the end is that Walzer's 'legalistic paradigm' turns out to be a restatement of the very *jus ad bellum* theory which modern international law – both secular and pragmatic – has succeeded in expunging from the medieval tradition of the just war. For Walzer maintains that

> aggression can be made out not only in the absence of a military attack or invasion but in the (probable) absence of any immediate intention to launch such an attack or invasion. The general formula must go something

like this: states may use force in the face of threats of war, whenever the failure to do so would seriously risk their territorial integrity or political independence.[79]

Thus, he believes that it is possible to reintroduce a *jus ad bellum* theory at the present time: first, by attributing moral (not merely legal, political or military) value to the idea of aggression against the territorial integrity and political sovereignty of a state; second, by considering the threat of aggression equivalent to actual aggression; third, by conferring moral legitimation both on armed resistance against an aggressor and on an attack made – in the guise of 'preventive self-defence' – against those who pose a serious threat of war; and fourth, by authorizing 'preventive self-defence' even in cases where an 'aggressor', although full of threatening talk of war, gives no tangible evidence of any immediately imminent offensive.

The net result of this suggestion is to take us, in my opinion, not a single step forward in comparison with the scholastic treatment of *jus ad bellum*. On the contrary, it even has the retrogressive consequence of nullifying some of the more forward-looking rules of the law of war that progress in modern legal thought had succeeded in establishing after the decline of the medieval Christian cosmopolis.

Walzer's military ethics in fact differs from the scholastic tradition of *jus ad bellum* only in the abandonment of obviously out-of-date and even, by modern standards, ridiculous concepts, such as the criteria of righteous intention, competent authority, the goal of peace, *extrema ratio* and so on. What he retains, however, is the presumption – typical of medieval theology – that in the case of an armed conflict there may be 'moral' reasons justifying *ab origine* the war waged by one or the other of two contenders. The existence of such reasons may be declared in absolute terms by a superior ethical authority or argued for on the basis of a universal moral code; in either case the war waged by one of the two belligerents would be turned into a 'just war', and the opponent's war into an 'unjust war', or 'war of aggression'. And, as we have seen, a situation of hostility can be defined as a war of aggression regardless of the fact that the 'aggressor' state may not have been the first to resort to violence, or indeed have shown any intention of using violence, confining itself instead to threats of war which lead to military retaliation from the state subjected to the alleged 'aggression'.

Consequently Walzer's military ethics may also be said to retain a second, equally typically medieval, idea. In defining the moral or immoral character of a war, he maintains, contrary to the whole thrust of modern international law, that it is immaterial to establish *who* has 'struck the first blow'. If, according to the theorists of the *justum bellum*, a war was thought to be just – as war against the infidel was typically held to be – then whether it was one of defence or of aggression was a minor consideration. So too, one might well say that for Walzer – as for the Catholic theologians who blessed the crusades or, more recently, justified the colonial exploits of Italian Fascism[80] – 'preventive self-defence' is morally justified, above all if it is applied to the detriment of *injusti hostes* and if those who wage the war are western armies.[81]

Quite apart from its unfortunate potential for justifying any kind of war,[82] the theory of aggression proposed by Walzer is in any event both hollow and circular, given that it stands or falls on the general assumption of 'state morality', that is to say of the universal moral nature of the territorial integrity and political sovereignty of any internationally recognized state. Such an assumption, as I have already maintained and as is cogently argued by Gerald Doppelt, belongs to a 'statism without foundations'.[83] It is of course precisely from contentions regarding the territorial legitimacy of a state or the right to existence of a political body that cases of armed conflict most often originate, as is amply, if tragically, exemplified by the former Soviet Union and the former Yugoslavia.

It may help to subject Walzer's position to the force of some contemporary examples. What sense would it have, for instance, to say that British territorial sovereignty over the Falkland Islands had – and still retains – universal ethical foundation? With what *moral*, and not merely legal or political, argument is it possible to assert that the Argentine attack against British sovereignty was 'unjust'? Is territorial sovereignty itself a moral absolute? If the war had been won by Argentina, could it be said that this South American country would then have had the *moral* duty to give the Falklands back to Great Britain? And were these islands not annexed by Great Britain in the last century by means of force or at least with the backing of force?

And what about Israeli territorial sovereignty over the areas from which Palestinian settlements were expelled at least in part by the use of terrorism, and which were later, in 1947, assigned to Israel by the United Nations after a decision of dubious international legitimacy? Or what about the lands subsequently conquered both through defensive and preventive wars? How, however, is one to assign universal ethical value to the political independence of despotic regimes which possess no internal legitimation – but are not thereby subjected to the ravages of civil wars – as was the case for decades in the Soviet Union or in Spain under Franco, or in Ceauşescu's Romania or in Tito's Yugoslavia? And what of the racist regime which ruled South Africa over a long period of years? Should all these cases be regarded as political situations governed by a universal ethics, which is however to be overturned on the basis of realistic considerations of the likely outcome of armed conflicts (which cannot be morally evaluated on the basis of a theory of aggression)? Any one of these questions represents, in my view, an irremediable flaw in the theory of aggression which Walzer proposes.

It may be just to acknowledge, however, that, where Walzer is unsuccessful, many others before him have previously failed. There exists no convincing definition of aggression between sovereign states in the strong sense of a 'morally or legally illegitimate military attack', rather than simply in the sense of a 'military attack by the state which is *the first* to resort to force' and is, on these grounds alone, forbidden by the international legal system. Not unnaturally, therefore, even the attempt of the General Assembly of the United Nations to define 'aggression' in terms which are not formalistically neutral has failed.[84] For such an endeavour entails seeking to revive in secular modern terms an incorrigibly theological doctrine – the medieval *jus as bellum* doctrine – application of which would, in addition, require the existence of an unchallenged spiritual authority endowed on the temporal level with a cosmopolitan power superior to that of all others.

Nor, finally, should it be overlooked that there is an analogy between 'criminalization' of the enemy, as so typically occurs in the just war doctrine (principally, though not exclusively, in its original medieval formulations), and Walzer's criminalization of the enemy as an 'incarnation of evil in the world', or as a 'radical menace to human values', or 'morally ignoble'. From these emotive considerations – humanly comprehensible though they may be – Walzer draws his astounding *non sequiturs*, such as the moral justification of terrorist bombings against German cities during the Second World War or the ethical extolling of the war waged by the western powers against Iraq, on the grounds that it was inspired by the highest of moral causes. (Here it may be recalled that during the Gulf War there was widespread discussion in western countries as to whether the figure of Saddam Hussein could be equated with that of Hitler.) Thus it is a revival of the theological moralism which underlies the doctrine of the just war which gives Walzer the authority to cast out the entire 'positive' legal construct of *jus in bello* laboriously created by theorists of modern international law. It is important to see that, in so doing, he scraps a system of law which, for all its limitations and decidedly restricted effect, has shown itself in modern times to be both separate from theology and distinct from ethics and morality.

The Relationship Between *Jus ad Bellum* and *Jus in Bello*

From the framework I have outlined a state of affairs emerges which leaves little scope for further doubt. The ethics of international relations represents neither a pragmatic rationalization of spiritualistic pacifism nor a theoretical alternative to so-called 'Machiavellian realism'. In all of the authors I have mentioned – and not only in Stanley Hoffman and Michael Walzer – recourse to consequentialist and casuistic eclecticism ultimately renders the normative dimension of moral arguments void of effect. Moral categories are freely shaped in order to bend to the whim of cognitive and evaluative prejudices. Ethics is reduced to a rhetorical-persuasive assemblage of a scholastic nature, if not perhaps even to mere academic jargon. Sometimes, as in the case of Michael Walzer's proposals, ethics appears to be shorn of all its moral characteristics – assuming, that is, that judging and acting morally must in some sense mean, as William Frankena states, living according to non-selfish principles and aiming to make them universal, in such a way that the good of each individual receives equal consideration.[85]

What, in particular, makes international ethics sterile from a normative point of view is that it allows itself to give way on one essential point: the acknowledgement of the moral character of the conscious killing of people, whether they be civilians or soldiers, regardless of any consideration of their individual responsibility, or of the personal reasons on account of which they have been drawn into a war, or of the means by which they pursue it.

This criticism is specifically directed to the relation between *jus ad bellum* and *jus in bello* as it is found in the 'just war' tradition. The scholastic distinction between the register of 'just causes' and the register of 'just means' introduces a heavily asymmetrical dualism, since it implicitly aims at awarding normative primacy to the *jus ad bellum* doctrine. Only after the just war has been undertaken do *jus in bello* criteria enter into play: a war which is just from the point of view of causes must also be just from the point of view of means. As Michael Walzer has written, it is necessary to be able to fight and to win 'well'.[86] The use of illegitimate means, however, has no retroactive effect on *jus ad bellum*: the basic reasons which have justified a war remain untouched. The war thus remains just in a crucial sense, in that it was in any case legitimate to undertake it and it remains legitimate to continue it.[87]

Yet if modern war, whatever its initial motives may be, can involve – or indeed is bound to involve – the killing, wounding or torture of (thousands or hundreds of thousands of) innocent people, one may ask in what sense moralists continue to speak of the 'justice' of war.[88] Evidently, they intend a sense which countenances the sacrifice of human life and limb in the cause of 'military necessity'. But once one admits the legitimacy of the hostile treatment of a person, including torture, mutilation or killing, *independently of the responsibility or otherwise of that person's behaviour*, then moral arguments seem to lose any capacity for theoretical direction or practical efficacy. They lose virtually all of their importance as an alternative to absolute pacifism and, above all, as a critique of political realism, of which they eventually represent no more than a sort of grotesque parody. One thus proceeds by leaps and bounds into what the non-consequentialist theorist Thomas Nagel has termed 'a moral blind alley'.[89]

A Realist Critique

Little resistance, as will now be evident, is presented to the central tenet of a realist critique that the whole consequentialist machinery of international ethics relies on a series of previously conducted intellectual operations and practical evaluations. Without these – in the admission of its own exponents – international ethics becomes ultimately futile, as it proves to be incommensurable with the functional requirements of international politics. The elements of previous evaluation, as has been seen, consist of such cognitive and evaluative operations as the definition of political objectives and their settings, the measuring of costs, the anticipation of (probable) consequences, careful consideration of risks, the calculation of interests and analysis of the strategies of the agents involved. In short, the whole store of knowledge and skills required for the efficacy of political decision-making.

For political ethics (and for international ethics in particular) all of this creates an over-arching and conditioning problematical dimension. At the same time it is precisely these circumstances which endow the Weberian profession of politics with a kind of dramatic fascination. For Weber it is a profession infused with the 'ethics of responsibility' (from which, not unexpectedly, Stanley Hoffman feels the need to keep his distance even in the very first pages of his book).[90] And these are the same circumstances which, forming the background to Machiavelli no less than to Pareto, Weber, Schumpeter and Luhmann, make politics into an art, a specific discipline and 'subsystem' governed by a differentiated functional code, i.e. that of the 'prudent' practice of power as a guarantee of security.

In reality, however, it should be recognized that what Weber – drawing on Machiavelli and Nietzsche – calls an 'ethic of responsibility' is in fact the viewpoint of political realism before it has been trivialized through simple reduction to Thucydides' 'Melian dialogue', or to Thrasymachus' argument or to the untroubled sleep of which Harry Truman boasted after the bombing of Hiroshima. It is a form of realism not reduced to a rudimentary conception of politics as being made up of deception, threats, violence and, above all, of the necessary and unavoidable oppression of the weak by the strong, even though such factors do obviously play a major role both in domestic and in international politics.

Rather than this, however, political realism needs to be seen as the Machiavellian and Hobbesian awareness that a dialectics of conflict, fear and protection determines the functional essence of politics. Such a character of political realism leads to a sharp divergence from the deontological code of universal ethics which was handed down from the classical-Christian tradition. Political conflict, and especially a conflict between states, is not a mere, even though violent, clash of interests which can be resolved according to a unified 'Table of Laws'. As Weber emphasizes, at the root of political violence and war there always lies an incompatibility of symbolic worlds, moral ideas, different value systems:[91] i.e., of the 'prejudices' around which expectations of safety and different systems of protection – all in some sense 'rational' and internally legitimated – revolve and cluster together.

Thus, one of the most serious flaws of international ethics is that it does not even attempt to trace the deeper roots of political violence, and it can therefore offer no appropriate answers to the question of how to contain the destructive effects of conflict and war. It may be true, as Michael Walzer suggests, that 'the restraint of war is the beginning of peace'. Yet, in order to have any effectiveness at all, this restraint must address the deep-seated reasons of international conflict. This, as I shall argue later on, requires far more serious arguments and intellectual commitment than the practice of a military neo-Jesuitism.

Certainly, not even international political realism, from Niebuhr to Morgenthau, Carr and the neo-realists such as Kenneth Waltz and Robert Gilpin, can boast that it is already in possession of a tested theory of peacemaking. International political realism, which is sometimes tainted by elementary positivistic epistemologies and by a strict 'statist' option, has at best succeeded in constructing (important) theories of international conflict and of war.[92] But one perception attributable to political realism is that modern war is beyond doubt a *morally intractable* phenomenon, because its destructive potential knows no limits and respects no proportions. (Of the truth of this point the Gulf War has, despite its international legitimation, again given proof.) For exactly as it would be pointless to work out a doctrine of

THE BLIND ALLEYS OF INTERNATIONAL ETHICS

legitimate reasons (*jus ad*) and of permitted means (*jus in*) to be adduced as moral justification of, say, slavery, torture, rape or genocide, so also it would be equally senseless to construct an ethics of modern war. Thus in its critique of the theoretical claim to be able to moralize war, the realist attitude is in effect much closer to absolute pacifism than to international ethics.

From the standpoint of a political realism inspired by Weber's teachings, war can be undertaken and judged only if one starts out from standards of political prudence and responsibility. Prudence requires that a cost-benefit analysis should include not only a consideration of the direct consequences – in terms of suffering and destruction – that war involves for a particular social group, but also an evaluation of the political, economic and ecological interdependences which can turn a modern war, even though not a nuclear one, as in the case of the Gulf War, into a 'scourge' for all people, including even the hypothetical victors. In addition, any analysis must also reckon with 'international terrorism'. Political responsibility towards one's own social group requires recognition of the fact that the use of violence is always a high-risk enterprise: it can lead to a tragically dangerous zero sum game. All the more so today, in a nuclear world in which the capacity to attack and destroy is infinitely greater than the capacity for defence. From the realist point of view, the burden of political responsibility cannot be lightened by the Jesuitic prosthesis of the justice of war.

In spite of all this, there may be occasions when opting for armed struggle and war is prudent and politically responsible, just as in politics it can sometimes be prudent and responsible to tell lies or to fail to keep promises. But although war may represent an inevitable choice for a given social group under conditions where it is imposed by an intolerable situation, those who profess to legitimize it as a 'just' war make themselves morally responsible for what is inevitable. And there is no intellectual practice more cynical than the action of those who summon the noblest of values to their cause – culture, morality, spiritual values or even the message of Christianity – in order to provide a moral justification for the world as it is.

The worst fault of international ethics is undoubtedly the call it feels to apologetics. Far beyond the intentions of its authors, this tends to act as a factor within the contrast of different symbolic worlds which lies at the root of violence and war. Indeed international ethics appears to be far more effective in this guise than in its ostensible function of restraining war. As it has been memorably expressed by E. H. Carr, it is not international politics that can be conceived of as a function of ethics, but rather it is international ethics that lends itself for use as a function of national politics.[93] This aspect, according to Carr, was especially evident in international ethics as elaborated in the Anglo-American setting in the first half of the twentieth century. Its unconscious but systematic tendency, he argued, was to mistake the particular interest of the British and North American world for the general interest of humankind. In Carr's words:

> Theories of international morality are the product of dominant nations or groups of nations. For the past hundred years, and more especially since 1918, the English-speaking peoples have formed the dominant group in the world; and current theories of international morality have been designed to perpetuate their supremacy and expressed in the idiom peculiar to them. [...] Both the view that the English-speaking peoples are monopolists of international morality and the view that they are consummate international hypocrites may be reduced to the plain fact that the current canons of international virtue have, by a natural and inevitable process, been mainly created by them.[94]

Over and beyond the quasi-Marxist schematism of such an analysis, there is perceivable in Carr's severe verdict a negative judgement of the tendency to apologetics apparent in 'Wilsonian ethics', a judgement which in my view receives confirmation from many of the references I have made so far to contemporary moralists.

Conclusion

A few lines will suffice to give a conclusive answer to the questions that were raised at the end of the first section. In the present circumstances, the tradition of 'ethical pacifism' is certainly able, as far as theories of non-violence are concerned, to make a noteworthy contribution to the construction of a political philosophy of peacemaking. For regardless of its normative baselessness and its practical limitations, the non-violent option remains a disturbing and stimulating challenge to political realism. In certain ways, as I have already pointed out and as will be seen in greater detail later on, the 'active non-violence' strategy is able to suggest concrete alternatives for the defence and foreign policy of democratic states.

As for the consequentialist ethics of international relations, however, and the *justum bellum* doctrine in particular, there is a very definite negative judgement implicit in the criticisms I have raised against its proponents: its contribution to a theory of peacemaking goes no further than casuistic arguments regarding moral prohibitions and obligations to be taken seriously by all states, including the greatest powers of the planet. However, one should not overlook the contribution made by the moral theory of *jus in bello* to the elaboration of a modern international law of war.

In spite of the limitations of both lines of development of ethical pacifism, the fact remains that this tradition implicitly reveals a serious gap in the institutional projects of 'perpetual peace' worked out in the framework of the cosmopolitan model of the Holy Alliance. These projects lack any attention to the possibility of capitalizing on the intellectual and moral energies of individuals as possible 'peacemakers', nor do these projects concern themselves with the social – and not merely institutional – roots of war or with the conditions of the democratic legitimation of the foreign policies of states.

Finally, it may be concluded that international ethics, notwithstanding its universalist aspirations and implicit reference to the idea of the moral unity of humankind, offers no arguments in favour of the globalistic and cosmopolitan perspective of 'world government'. Two opposing options lie within its scope, the 'statist' and the cosmopolitan options. Both seem to be unjustified and inconclusive. Furthermore, it remains possible to conceive of moral alternatives to universalist ethics, and, on the basis of these, reasons can then be adduced for a subjective rejection of the cosmopolitan, and in particular of the 'speciesist', perspective.

Notes

1 The term 'ethics' is used here to designate doctrines which, as is typically the case in Catholic sexual and matrimonial ethics, set out a universalist and deontological code binding on each person's conscience; by contrast, I use the term 'morality' to refer to any subjective scheme of personal behaviour which derives from principles, for instance those of mildness and friendship, which are not competitive or acquisitive. In reporting or discussing other authors' thought, however, I shall be unable to pursue this distinction with accuracy, since terms like 'ethics', 'ethical', 'morality' and 'moral' are often used as synonyms or even with a semantic polarization quite opposite to the sense which I myself propose.

2 N. Young, 'Peace Movements in Industrial Societies: Genesis, Evolution, Impact', in R. Väyrynen, D. Senghaas and C. Schmidt (eds), *The Quest for Peace*, London: Sage Publications, 1987, pp. 303–16.

3 For an example of nineteenth-century pacifism, see H. D. Thoreau, *On the Duty of Civil Disobedience*, Boston: Fellowship Press, 1853; on Tolstoy's pacifism, see Gallie, *Philosophers of Peace and War: Kant, Clausewitz, Marx, Engels and Tolstoy*, pp. 100–32; on the relation between Tolstoy and Gandhi, see B. Srinivasa Murthy (ed.), *Mahatma Gandhi and Tolstoy Letters*, Long Beach: Long Beach Publications, 1987; P. C. Bori and G. Sofri, *Gandhi e Tolstoj*, Bologna: Il Mulino, 1985; on Gandhism, see H. J. N. Horsburgh,

Non-violence and Aggression: A Study of Gandhi's Moral Equivalent of War, London: Oxford University Press, 1968; among recent works see B. Parekh, *Gandhi's Political Philosophy: A Critical Examination*, London: Macmillan, 1989; J. Hick and L. C. Hempel (eds), *Gandhi's Significance for Today*, London: Macmillan, 1989.

4 The ethics of war and international relations cannot be reduced in absolute terms to the just war tradition, although this does represent its most important development. Ethical reflections on war and international relations may be found, for instance, in the works of the English utilitarians of the eighteenth century.

5 Among recent works of this kind, see P. Ramsey, *War and the Christian Conscience: How Shall Modern War be Conducted Justly?*, Durham (NC): Duke University Press, 1961; W. V. O'Brien, *The Conduct of Just and Limited War*, New York: Praeger, 1981; J. T. Johnson, *Can Modern War be Just?*, New Haven: Yale University Press, 1984; see also the useful collection J. B. Elshtain (ed.), *Just War Theory*, Oxford: Basil Blackwell, 1992; and, for a non-consequentialist position, R. L. Holmes, *On War and Morality*, Princeton: Princeton University Press, 1989.

6 See Walzer, *Just and Unjust Wars*; C. R. Beitz, *Political Theory and International Relations*, Princeton: Princeton University Press, 1979; S. Hoffman, *Duties Beyond Borders: On the Limits and Possibilities of Ethical International Politics*, Syracuse: Syracuse University Press, 1981; J. S. Nye, Jr, *Nuclear Ethics*, New York: The Free Press, 1986. See also L. Bonanate, *Etica e politica internazionale*, Turin: Einaudi, 1992; Engl. trans., *Ethics and International Politics*, Cambridge: Polity, 1994; L. Bonanate, *I doveri degli Stati*, Rome–Bari: Laterza, 1994.

7 Walzer, *Just and Unjust Wars*, pp. 329–35.

8 H. L. Williams, *Kant's Political Philosophy*, Oxford: Basil Blackwell, 1983, pp. 260–8.

9 On Martin Luther King, see L. Bennet, Jr, *What Manner of Man*, Chicago: Johnson, 1968; J. J. Ansbro, *Martin Luther King, Jr.: The Making of a Mind*, Maryknoll (NY): Orbis Books, 1982; as for Gandhi's influence on King, see T. Kilgore, Jr, 'The Influence of Gandhi on Martin Luther King, Jr.', in Hick and Hempel (eds), *Gandhi's Significance for Today*, pp. 236–43. Unlike Gandhi, Martin Luther King was a member of a specific religious denomination and did not associate non-violence with any kind of personal asceticism.

10 On the notion of 'coercive diplomacy', cf. Brown *The Causes and Prevention of War*, pp. 79–88. On the game theory used in the field of international diplomacy, see among others: T. C. Schelling, *Arms and Influence*, New Haven (Ct): Yale University Press, 1966; G. H. Snyder and P. Diesing, *Conflict Among Nations: Bargaining, Decision Making, and System Structure in International Crises*, Princeton (NJ): Princeton University Press, 1977. To the best of my knowledge, no essay uses game theory to analyse the strategy of the 'Gandhian player'.

11 Compare Bobbio (*Il problema della guerra e le vie della pace*, p. 80): 'what makes the use of force unavoidable is the lack of a superior authority ranking higher than the individual states and able to decide which state is right and which is wrong, and then to enforce its own decision.'

12 See G. Sharp, *The Politics of Nonviolent Action*, Boston: Porter Sargent, 1973; G. Sharp, *Making Europe Unconquerable: The Potential of Civilian-based Deterrence and Defence*, Cambridge (Mass.): Ballinger, 1985; J.

Galtung, *The True Worlds: A Transnational Perspective*, New York: Free Press, 1980.

13 Parekh, *Gandhi's Political Philosophy*, p. 221.

14 Ibid., pp. 110–41.

15 M. K. Gandhi, *Non-Violent Resistance*, Ahmedabad (India): Navajivan Trust, no date, pp. 383–7.

16 M. K. Gandhi, *Non-violence in Peace and War*, Ahmedabad: Navajivan Publishing House, 1944, pp. 183–9, 190–3, 197–9, 204–7, 229–30, 234–8. Judah L. Magnes and Martin Buber's critical answers have been recently published in *Micromega*, 6 (1991), 2, pp. 137–84.

17 Parekh, *Gandhi's Political Philosophy*, pp. 221–2.

18 D. Zolo, *Reflexive Epistemology*, Dordrecht and Boston: Kluwer Academic Publishers, 1989, pp. 147–53; D. Zolo, *Democracy and Complexity*, Cambridge: Polity Press, 1992, pp. 9–10, 28–35.

19 Walzer, *Just and Unjust Wars*, pp. xxviii–xxix.

20 Beitz, *Political Theory and International Relations*, pp. 15–27; 'I assume without discussion that some such theory [of morality] can be provided. [. . .] I shall proceed on the assumption that we share some basic ideas about the nature and requirements of morality and see whether international skepticism is consistent with them,' ibid., pp. 16–17.

21 Walzer, *Just and Unjust Wars*, p. xxix ('I am not going to expound morality from the ground up. Were I to begin with the foundations, I would probably never get beyond them; in any case, I am by no means sure what the foundations are').

22 Nye, *Nuclear Ethics*, pp. 14–26.

23 T. Nardin, 'Ethical Tradition in International Affairs', in T. Nardin and D. R. Mapel (eds), *Traditions of International Ethics*, Cambridge: Cambridge University Press, 1992, pp. 9–14.

24 Hoffman, *Duties Beyond Borders*, pp. 2ff.

25 J. Rawls, *A Theory of Justice*, Cambridge (Mass.): Harvard University Press, 1971, pp. 40–5, 46–8, 580.

26 Beitz, *Political Theory and International Relations*, p. 183.

27 Nye, *Nuclear Ethics*, pp. 20–6.

28 Ibid., pp. 20–1, 25–6.

29 Hoffman, *Duties Beyond Borders*, p. xi.

30 Ibid., pp. 27–9, 33.

31 Ibid., p. 41.

32 Ibid., p. 43

33 Walzer, *Just and Unjust Wars*, pp. 251–68.

34 B. Williams, *Ethics and the Limits of Philosophy*, London: Fontana Press and Collins, 1985, pp. 54–70, 110ff; C. Larmore, *Patterns of Moral Complexity*, Cambridge: Cambridge University Press, 1987, passim. Both Williams and Larmore are critical of Aristotelian and Kantian deontologism. They state the impossibility of founding the universality of ethical principles, introduce the notion of 'moral judgement' as the free intervention of individual practice in the actual use of moral rules and recognize the possibility of conflict between different moral principles. Larmore, in particular, elaborates the category of 'moral complexity', i.e. of the differentiation of ethical principles with respect to different social spheres; see also S. Hampshire, *Morality and Conflict*, Oxford: Blackwell, 1983.

35 Nye, *Nuclear Ethics*, pp. 34–41.

36 Hoffman, *Duties Beyond Borders*, pp. 38–40; for an effort to reconcile individual moral rights with state sovereignty, cf. M. Frost, *Towards a Normative Theory of International Relations*, Cambridge: Cambridge University Press, 1986, pp. 161–86.
37 On this subject see the debate among C. R. Beitz, G. Doppelt, D. Luban and M. Walzer: C. R. Beitz, 'Bounded Morality: Justice and the State in World Politics', *International Organization*, 33 (1979), 3, pp. 405–24; G. Doppelt, 'Walzer's Theory of Morality on International Relations', *Philosophy and Public Affairs*, 8 (1978), 1, pp. 3–26; D. Luban, 'Just War and Human Rights', ibid., 9 (1979), 2, pp. 161–81; M. Walzer, 'The Moral Standing of States: A Response to Four Critics', ibid., 9 (1980), 3, pp. 209–29; G. Doppelt, 'Statism Without Foundations', ibid., 9 (1980), 4, pp. 398–403; compare also G. L. Scott and C. L. Carr, 'Are States Moral Agents?', *Social Theory and Practice*, 12 (1986), 1; Frost, *Towards a Normative Theory of International Relations*, pp. 150–6. It is worth noting that within the theoretical lexicon of the theorists of international ethics the term 'rights' is used with reference both to moral and legal positive rights.
38 Beitz, *Political Theory and International Relations*, pp. 71–83; C. R. Beitz, 'Sovereignty and Morality in International Affairs', in D. Held (ed.), *Political Theory Today*, Cambridge: Polity Press, 1991; H. Küng, *Projekt Weltethos*, Munich: Piper, 1990; Engl. trans., *Global Responsibility: In Search of a New World Ethic*, New York: Crossroad, 1991, pp. 25–35; K.-O. Apel, *Diskurs und Verantwortung: Das Problem des Überganges zur postkonventionellen Moral*, Frankfurt a.M.: Suhrkamp, 1988, passim; see also R. J. Vincent, *Human Rights and International Relations*, Cambridge: Cambridge University Press, 1986, pp. 44–57; R. J. Vincent, 'Western Conceptions of a Universal Moral Order', in R. Pettnam (ed.), *Moral Claims in World Affairs*, Canberra: Australian National University Press, 1979, pp. 52–78; H. J. McClosky, *Ecological Ethics and Politics*, Totowa (NJ): Rowman & Littlefield, 1983.
39 Bonanate, *Etica e politica internazionale*, especially pp. 18–23, 178–211; L. Ferrajoli, 'Dai diritti del cittadino ai diritti della persona', in D. Zolo (ed.), *La cittadinanza. Appartenenza, identità, diritti*, Rome–Bari: Laterza, 1994.
40 Beitz, *Political Theory and International Relations*, pp. 74ff. On the principle of non-intervention and on humanitarian intervention, see L. Brilmayer, *Justifying International Acts*, Ithaca–London: Cornell University Press, 1989, chapters 5–7, pp. 105–55.
41 Brown, *The Causes and Prevention of War*, pp. 217–19.
42 According to Hans Jonas: 'It is at least not senseless any more to ask whether the condition of extrahuman nature, the biosphere as a whole and in its parts, now subject to our power, has become a human trust and has something of a moral claim on us not only for our own sake but for its own right' (H. Jonas, *Das Prinzip Verantwortung: Versuch einer Ethik für die technologische Zivilization*, Frankfurt a.M.: Insel Verlag, 1979, p. 8; Engl. trans. *The Imperative of Responsibility*, Chicago: Chicago University Press, 1984, p. 8); compare also A. Naess, *Ecology, Community and Lifestyle*, Cambridge: Cambridge University Press, 1989; T. Regan and P. Singer, *Animal Rights and Human Obligations*, Englewood Cliffs (NJ): Prentice Hall, 1976; T. Regan, *The Case for Animal Rights*, Berkeley: University of California Press, 1983.
43 N. Bobbio, *L'età dei diritti*, Turin: Einaudi, 1990, pp. vii–xxi, 5–16.

44 S. Hoffman dedicates three specific chapters of his *Duties Beyond Borders* to these three topics; see also the third part of *Political Theory and International Relations*, in which Charles R. Beitz tries to use Rawls's theory of justice to solve the problem of 'international distributive justice' (pp. 125–76); see also B. Barry, 'Can States be Moral? International Morality and the Compliance Problem', in R. J. Myers (ed.), *International Ethics in the Nuclear Age*, Lanham (Md): University Press of America, 1987, pp. 85–112.

45 The papers on this subject, first delivered at the Workshop on 'Duties Beyond Borders' organized by the European Consortium for Political Research (Amsterdam, 10–15 April 1987), were published by *Ethics*. See in particular: D. Miller, 'The Ethical Significance of Nationality', *Ethics*, 98 (1988), 4, pp. 647–62; R. E. Goodin, 'What is so Special about Our Fellow Countrymen?', ibid., pp. 663–86; H. R. van Gusteren, 'Admission to Citizenship', ibid., pp. 731–41.

46 Walzer, *Just and Unjust Wars*, pp. 80–2.

47 Cf: J. S. Nye, Jr, 'Superpower Ethics: An Introduction', *Ethics and International Affairs*, 1 (1987), 1, pp. 1–7; S. Hoffman, 'The Rules of the Game', ibid., pp. 37–51.

48 Beitz, *Political Theory and International Relations*, pp. 129–43; C. R. Beitz, 'Justice and International Relations', in C. R. Beitz, M. Cohen, T. Scanlon and A. J. Simmons (eds), *International Ethics*, Princeton: Princeton University Press, 1985, pp. 282–311. For a criticism of Beitz's theses, compare S. Hoffman, *Duties Beyond Borders*, pp. 153ff; for a criticism of Rawls's hasty allusions to international ethics, cf. R. Admur, 'Rawls' Theory of Justice', *World Politics*, 29 (1977), 3, particularly pp. 452–60.

49 See P. Singer, 'Famine, Affluence and Morality', *Philosophy and Public Affairs*, 1 (1972), 3.

50 An analogous thesis may be maintained with respect to multinational corporations, which, to a greater extent than national states, are actors in the global economic system. The functional constraints of the (differentiated) economic code prevent them from taking into consideration the criteria of any possible 'international distributive justice', let alone the prescriptions of charity.

51 E. E. Schattschneider, *The Semi-sovereign People*, New York: Holt, Rinehart & Winston, 1960, pp. 30ff.

52 On the relationship between fear and politics, compare Zolo, *Democracy and Complexity*, pp. 35–45. The notions of fear and safety are at the centre of Barry Buzan's research on national and international politics; see B. Buzan, *People, State and Fear*, New York: Harvester Wheatsheaf, 1991.

53 The expression is derived from Nicola Matteucci's work on Machiavelli's demonstration, in *Il Principe*, of the 'severity of politics'; compare N. Matteucci, *Alla ricerca dell'ordine politico*, Bologna: Il Mulino, 1984, pp. 57–65.

54 Compare Walzer, *Just and Unjust Wars*, p. 9: 'the proper method of practical morality is casuistic'. For an epistemological criticism of the casuistic tradition, see A. Jonsen and S. Toulmin, *The Abuse of Casuistry: A History of Moral Reasoning*, Berkeley: University of California Press, 1988.

55 On methodological decisions and the relation between theoretical propositions and evaluations, compare Zolo, *Reflexive Epistemology*, pp. 27–50.

56 Nye, *Nuclear Ethics*, pp. 97–131.

57 On the basis of different theoretical premises G. I. Mavrodes maintains an analogous thesis: cf. 'Conventions and the Morality of War', in Beitz, Cohen, Scanlon and Simmons (eds), *International Ethics*, pp. 75–89.
58 Brown, *The Causes and Prevention of War*, pp. 215–22.
59 Ibid., p. 222.
60 Ibid., p. 221.
61 G. E. M. Anscombe, 'War and Murder', in R. Wasserstrom (ed.), *War and Morality*, Belmont (Ca.): Wadsworth Publishing Company, 1970, pp. 42–53; R. L. Phillips, *War and Justice*, Norman: University of Oklahoma Press, 1984, chapter 2; P. Ramsey, *The Just War: Force and the Political Responsibility*, New York: Charles Scribner's Sons, 1986, chapter 7, passim.
62 In its classical conception formulated according to the theological tradition of *justum bellum*, the double-effect rule states that killing non-combatants is morally tolerable under three conditions: first, it must be the indirect consequence of an action aiming at a morally permitted goal (for instance, killing soldiers or destroying enemy military bases); second, even though foreseen, it must not be desired as a consequence of the permitted effect (as in the case of the bombing of a nuclear power station deliberately conceived not only with the purpose of destroying the installation, but also that of causing death to the inhabitants of the surrounding area); third, according to the general principle of proportionality, the intended and morally permitted effect must be greater than the indirect unintended evil effect. It is clear that the crucial element here is a psychological condition, which is totally subjective and untestable. In other words, the certain and foreseeable death of innocent people may be caused if it is not 'desired'. As far as the principle of proportionality is concerned, in this case as in any other, it appears to be totally ineffective. According to what unity of measurement, one might ask, is it possible to make a moral comparison between the destruction of military plants and the murder of innocent people? For Michael Walzer's substantial support of the double-effect rule, see *Just and Unjust Wars*, pp. 151–9; see also J. Boyle, 'Towards Understanding the Principle of Double Effect', *Ethics*, 90 (1980), 3, pp. 527–38; G. E. M. Anscombe, 'Action, Intention and Double Effect', *The Proceedings of the American Catholic Philosophical Association*, (1982), 54, pp. 12–25; the first and the second part of J. P. Sterba (ed.), *The Ethics of War and Nuclear Deterrence*, Belmont (Ca.): Wadsworth Publishing Company, 1985, pp. 1–67.
63 Hoffman, *Duties Beyond Borders*, pp. 48–9.
64 Walzer, *Just and Unjust Wars*, p. 85.
65 See the Declaration of the General Assembly of the United Nations on Friendly Relationships (1970) and the Declaration concerning the definition of aggression (1974). The expression 'indirect armed aggression' denotes any form of economic or military assistance to armed groups fighting against a state; compare Cassese, *Il diritto internazionale nel mondo contemporaneo*, Engl. trans. pp. 137–42; on the notion of war from the point of view of the international legal system cf. H. Kelsen, *Principles of International Law*, ed. R. W. Tucker, New York: Holt, Rinehart & Winston, 1967, pp. 22–173.
66 Walzer, *Just and Unjust Wars*, p. 85.
67 Ibid., pp. 80–5. The book opens with a dedication to the martyrs of the Holocaust, to the rebels of ghettos, the partisans of the resistance, the Allied soldiers, and to eternity, which is contained in the Yad Vashem Memorial inscription in Jerusalem.

68 Walzer, *Just and Unjust Wars*, pp. 251–68.
69 Ibid., p. 253.
70 Ibid., pp. 263–8.
71 Ibid., pp. xi–xxiii. In a previous passage, already quoted above in chapter 2, note 27, Walzer contrasts the 'moral nobility' of military intervention by the United States with the 'infamous' nature of their adversary.
72 The scholastic formulation usually includes within *jus ad bellum* the following seven rules: just cause (defence against an attack, recovery of something wrongly taken, punishment of evil), right authority, right intention, the goal of peace, war as last resort, reasonable hope of success, proportionality of good over evil. *Jus in bello* includes the two criteria of proportionality of means and discrimination (non-combatant immunity according to the double effect rule). Compare for instance Johnson, *Can Modern War be Just?*, pp. 18–29; J. T. Johnson, 'The Just War and the American Military', in Johnson and Weigel, *Just War and the Gulf War*, pp. 3–42; 'The Challenge of Peace: God's Promise and Our Response', The Pastoral Letter on War and Peace by the United States Catholic Conference, Washington DC, 1983, in Elshtain (ed.), *Just War Theory*, pp. 98–104.
73 C. Schmitt, *Der Nomos der Erde im Völkerrecht des Jus Publicum Europaeum*, Berlin: Duncker & Humblot, 1974, pp. 89–96.
74 C. Schmitt, *Der Nomos der Erde*, pp. 112–21, 123–43.
75 Compare in particular articles 2 and 51 of the Charter of the United Nations.
76 Walzer, *Just and Unjust Wars*, pp. 61ff.
77 Walzer summarizes his theory of aggression in six propositions: (1) there exists an international society of independent states; (2) this international society has a law that establishes the rights of its members, above all the rights of territorial integrity and political sovereignty; (3) any use of force or imminent threat of force by one state against the political sovereignty or territorial integrity of another constitutes aggression and is a criminal act; (4) aggression justifies two kinds of violent response: a war of self-defence by the victim and a war of law-enforcement by the victim and any other member of international society; (5) nothing but aggression can justify war; (6) once the aggressor nation has been militarily repulsed, it can also be punished (cf. Walzer, *Just and Unjust Wars*, pp. 61–3).
78 After having defined the rules of his 'legalist paradigm' Walzer argues for the necessity of their violation. Particularly worthy of violation is the rule stating that 'nothing but aggression can justify war'. In fact Walzer considers it morally legitimate to launch a military attack against an independent state not only for 'pre-emptive self-defence' but also in order to (1) support secessionist movements which are fighting for 'national liberation'; (2) balance the intervention of other states in a civil war with a counter-intervention; (3) rescuing populations threatened with enslavement or massacre, as in the case of the Indian invasion of Bangladesh (compare Walzer, *Just and Unjust Wars*, pp. 86–108).
79 Walzer, *Just and Unjust Wars*, p. 85.
80 The influential journal of Italian Jesuits, *La civiltà cattolica*, used the moral categories of *jus ad bellum* to justify the Fascist colonial expeditions against Ethiopia. Italian Jesuits maintained that the aggression against Ethiopia was justified by the natural right of Italians – as they were numerous and their demographic density was expanding – to invade African territories which were sparsely populated and badly cultivated. The colonial expedition was

to be understood as legitimate pre-emptive self-defence against the real aggressor: the Ethiopian people who did not want to give up their country spontaneously to Italians; compare A. Messineo, 'Propagazione della civiltà ed espansione coloniale', *La civiltà cattolica* (1936), 2; A. Messineo, 'Necessità di vita e diritto di espansione', ibid. (1936), 3.

81 As is known, Israel is alone today in maintaining the international legitimacy of pre-emptive war as anticipatory self-defence (and has practised it, in particular in the Six Day War, against Palestinian camps in Lebanon in 1975, and, in 1981, by bombing the Iraqi nuclear reactor); cf. Cassese, *Il diritto internazionale nel mondo contemporaneo*, Engl. transl. pp. 230ff.

82 Holmes, *On War and Morality*, p. 162.

83 See G. Doppelt, 'Walzer's Theory of Morality in International Relations', pp. 3–26; G. Doppelt, 'Statism Without Foundations', pp. 398–403.

84 Holmes, *On War and Morality*, pp. 159–63; Bobbio, *Il terzo assente*, p. 173; Cassese, *Il diritto internazionale nel mondo contemporaneo*, Engl. transl. pp. 66–7, 137–42; A. Cassese, *Violenza e diritto nell'era nucleare*, Rome–Bari: Laterza, 1986; Eng. transl., Princeton: Princeton University Press, 1988, pp. 40ff.

85 W. Frankena, *Ethics*, Englewood Cliffs (NJ): Prentice-Hall, 1973, p. 96; Frankena takes this definition of morality from Kurt Baier's *The Moral Point of View*, New York: Random House, 1965, chapter 5.

86 Walzer, *Just and Unjust Wars*, pp. 127–37.

87 In this sense J. T. Johnson, in his intransigent defence of the image of the United States as a 'moral agent', stresses the autonomy and superiority of *jus ad bellum* as compared to *jus in bello* with regard to the case of the Gulf War; compare J. T. Johnson, 'The Just War Tradition and the American Military', in Johnson and Weigel, *Just War and the Gulf War*, pp. 10–12, 36; see also C. Greenwood, 'The Relationship between *Jus ad Bellum* and *Jus in Bello*', *Review of International Studies*, 9 (1986), 2, pp. 221–34.

88 An analogous thesis is maintained by a non-consequentialist moralist such as Robert Holmes: 'Unless one can justify the actions necessary to waging war, he cannot justify the conduct of war and the pursuits of its objectives; and if he cannot do this, he cannot justify going to war' (Holmes, *On War and Morality*, pp. 175–82). The theory of 'just war' is deemed to be 'not only obsolete but outright dangerous' by B. V. A. Röling, 'Are Grotius' Ideas Obsolete?', in Bull, Kingsbury and Roberts (eds), *Hugo Grotius and International Relations*, p. 285.

89 T. Nagel, 'War and Massacre', in Beitz, Cohen, Scanlon and Simmons (eds), *International Ethics*, p. 73. Thomas Nagel maintains that a hostile treatment of any person is morally justified only 'in terms of something *about that person* which makes the treatment appropriate' (ibid., p. 63); compare in the same vein Holmes, *On War and Morality*, particularly chapter 5 ('Can War be Morally Justified?'), pp. 146–82; for a documentation of the dispute between upholders of ethical deontologism and upholders of consequentialism, see S. Scheffler (ed.), *Consequentialism and its Critics*, Oxford: Oxford University Press, 1988.

90 Hoffman, *Duties Beyond Borders*, pp. 12–13.

91 On this aspect of Weber's thought see D. Beetham, *Max Weber and the Theory of Modern Politics*, Cambridge: Polity Press, 1985, pp. 102–12.

92 For instance, an elementary positivist causalism is common both to Morgenthau and Carr; compare the 'Six Principles of Political Realism' in Morgen-

thau, *Politics among Nations*, pp. 4–13; E. H. Carr, *The Twenty Years' Crisis 1919–1939*, London: Macmillan, 1940, pp. 82ff.
93 Carr, *The Twenty Years' Crisis*, pp. 82, 110–12.
94 Ibid., pp. 101–2.

4 *Civitas Maxima* and Cosmopolitan Law

Often the international jurist is left feeling like one of those intellectuals of whom Bertold Brecht said that they amused themselves painting still lives on the walls of a sinking ship.

A. Cassese, *International Law in a Divided World*

One cannot take a realistic approach to the question of the rights of man if this issue is considered in the abstract, without reference to the two great problems of our time, the problems of war and poverty, and of the absurd contrast between the excess of power which has created the conditions for a war of extermination, and the excess of powerlessness which condemns vast masses of human beings to hunger.

N. Bobbio, 'Presente e avvenire dei diritti dell'uomo'

Two Normative Models

The problem I wish to deal with in this chapter stems from a distinction which was formulated, following in the footsteps of Leo Gross, by Richard Falk and subsequently further developed by Antonio Cassese. This is the distinction between two normative models which, according to these authors, coexist within the international legal order: the 'Westphalian model' and the 'United Nations Charter model'.[1] By 'Westphalian model' Falk and Cassese mean the original framework of the international legal system established in Europe at the end of the Thirty Years War. This model, they argue, became consolidated in the course of over two centuries and underwent significant modification only with the Second World War. From a strictly legal point of view the Westphalian model seems to Falk and Cassese to present the following characteristics.

First, the subjects of international law are exclusively states, while individuals play a passive, secondary role. Collective entities other than states, such as peoples, nations, ethnic groups, economic organizations or voluntary associations are in no way recognized as international legal subjects.[2]

Second, there is no 'international legislator' with the power to decree norms that are automatically valid *erga omnes*. The source of international law is the sovereign authority of states in so far as the latter sign bilateral and multilateral treaties and recognize the force of customary norms.[3]

Third, the international legal system is made up almost exclusively of primary or material norms, while secondary or organizational norms are lacking. This lack differentiates the international legal system from that of states, within which there are normative bodies that regulate both the production and also the interpretation and implementation of laws. In other words, the Westphalian model does not envisage any binding jurisdiction that has the power to identify violations of international law, or a 'police' qualified to repress illegality preventively or consequent to its identification. The interpretation and implementation of international law is entrusted either to the domestic institutions of each state or to international procedures, such as arbitration, with respect to which the parties involved have already come to a provisional agreement.

Fourth, the sovereignty of states and their legal equality are absolute, unconditional principles. International law does not decree norms concerning the domestic legal structures of individual states or their behaviour towards citizens, nor does it envisage the power of a state or international organization to interfere in the domestic affairs of another state. The *de facto* inequality that distinguishes the great powers from the other states, or the industrialized countries from those that are less developed, is of no importance legally.[4]

Fifth, every state has the full right to resort to war or to analogous coercive measures to protect its own rights or interests. On an international level, illegal acts are a kind of private affair between the state which is the author of the illegality and its opponent. No other state or international organization has the right or the formal duty to intervene on behalf of one or other of the contenders.[5]

By contrast, the new model that has come into being on the basis of the normative framework of the United Nations Charter has essentially, according to the interpretation put forward by Falk and Cassese, the following aspects.

First, the subjects of international law are not only states but also international organizations, in particular the United Nations organization. A role, if extremely limited, is also granted to individuals, social groups and peoples having a representative organization. Simultaneously international norms that oblige states to respect the dignity and the fundamental rights of individuals have gradually come into force: a partial 'erosion of domestic jurisdiction' has in fact taken place.[6]

Second, actual 'general principles' of the international legal system have been established that are not only considered binding for all states but prevail, as a mandatory *jus cogens*, over treaties or customary norms.[7] Of these general principles Cassese indicates the following, while admitting that not all enjoy the same degree of effectiveness: the sovereign equality of states, the ban on the use of force for the resolution of controversies, non-interference in domestic affairs, respect for human rights.[8]

Third, the myth of the legal equality of states has been demolished and differences in power and wealth have assumed legal significance.[9]

Fourth, the right of states to resort to war has been restricted to self-defence. The punitive use of force has been entrusted to a centralized body, the United Nations Security Council. Non-compliance with international norms is no longer a private affair between individual states but becomes a public affair involving the whole international community, thereby introducing exceptions to the principle of the absolute sovereignty of states.[10]

According to Falk and Cassese, as I have already mentioned, these two models coexist within the international legal system. The old model clearly prevails from the point of view of actual effectiveness, since it corresponds to what Falk calls 'statist logic' and Cassese terms the 'individualism of states'. In practice the traditional legal system establishes a formal framework for the power claims of individual states and consecrates pure force (economic, political, military, etc.) without succeeding in ritualizing or restraining it through procedures of control or repression. According to Falk and Cassese, the new model, in contrast, represents a perspective that has remained essentially *in fieri*, since the communitarian, globalistic logic, which in their view characterizes the Charter and the normative practice of the United Nations, has been realized only to a very limited extent. This is attributable above all to the disputes that divided the great powers during the period of the Cold War, but is also partly due to the conflict of economic interests between the industrialized powers and the developing countries.[11]

Both for Falk and Cassese, progress in the international legal system can only be in the direction of a reinforcement of the 'new model' introduced by the United Nations Charter and of a complete replacement of the 'old model' dating back to Westphalia. For the latter reflects the 'primitive, individualistic' nature of relations between European states in the seventeenth and eighteenth centuries, while it is only with the United Nations Charter that a modern international legal order was founded.[12]

In the following sections I would like to question this perspective, which we might call 'legal cosmopolitanism', and show its inadequacies and difficulties. In legal cosmopolitanism four normative theses come together: first, that of the primacy of international law and the progressive reduction of the sovereignty of states, considered to be the major obstacle to the attainment of a legal order; second, that of jurisdictional centralism – in order for the primacy of international law to be truly established it needs to be completed by the development of norms and centralized bodies for the verification and coercive application of the law, which today are non-existent or ineffective; third, that of 'legal pacifism', which endeavours to place limitations on war and its destructive effects by relying upon the development and effective application of positive international law as a *jus contra bellum*, as a legal prohibition of war; and, finally, fourth, that of 'global constitutionalism', which is closely linked to the theory of human rights and emphasizes the ability of centralized supranational institutions to safeguard the fundamental liberties of individuals which states have shown themselves incapable of protecting.

I will deal in turn with each of these four themes in the next sections. In conclusion I will endeavour to answer the following questions. First, given the clear-cut division of the world into a limited number of rich and powerful countries and a large number of poor and weak countries, is it possible to create an international legal order that is not rigidly hierarchical and does not deny the principle of the formal equality of the subjects of law? Second, is it possible to attribute a mandatory character to a jurisdiction charged with interpreting and applying international law without entrusting its coercive execution to the military force of the great powers, hence removing the latter *de facto* and *de jure* from the remit of such a jurisdiction according to a typical absolutist scheme? Third, is the rejection of war as an international crime and the legal safeguarding of peace feasible in the context of the 'global centralism' that characterizes contemporary incarnations of the Holy Alliance? Fourth, can individuals become subjects of an international system capable of providing a real, impartial jurisdictional safeguard of their rights? Is it reasonable to entrust the defence of human rights to illiberal power structures?

The Primacy of International Law and the Legal Equality of States

While the Westphalian model, as Richard Falk and Antonio Cassese maintain, presents 'primitive, individualistic' characteristics, the United Nations Charter on the other hand sets up a genuine international legal order. It might be said that in their judgement the normative perspective of the Charter, going beyond both domestic or 'internal' public law and the so-called 'external public law', founds a veritable 'cosmopolitan law', the Kantian *Weltbürgerrecht*.[13] At a theoretical-legal level the positions of Falk and Cassese point back implicitly – but there are also explicit references[14] – to the Kelsenian theory of the primacy of international law, in the sense of an *original, exclusive and universal* legal system, and to the correlated denial of the sovereignty of the state.

In his classic work *Das Problem der Souveränität* and, thirty years later, in *Principles of International Law* Kelsen attempted to construct a monist legal theory in opposition to the dualism and pluralism of the sources of international law.[15] To this end he postulated the existence of international law as a unified legal system that includes all other systems, in particular the state legal systems, and is hierarchically ordered above such systems. On the basis of the strictly formal arguments of his 'pure theory of law' he contends that any notion of sovereignty, in the traditional sense of *civitas superiorem non recognoscens* – whether of the state itself or of the legal system of the state – cannot be entertained.[16] He therefore rejects the idea that the source of international law is the contractual self-obligation of states and that the compulsory nature of international norms derives from their implicit or explicit recognition by the governments or parliaments of the individual countries. Instead he argues that the internal law of states is a 'partial system' compared with the universality and 'objectivity' of the international legal order. Internal norms must therefore conform to international norms and, in the event of conflict between the two, it is the latter which should prevail. Thus at least in principle they can be assumed as *jus cogens* and applied by international courts without any need to be transformed into internal law.[17]

The unified character of the legal universe and, within it, the primacy of the international legal order are for Kelsen, above all for the mature Kelsen, 'epistemological postulates', the acceptance or rejection of which forms the object of a free evaluative choice.[18] Yet he asserts that the primacy of international law is dictated by ineluctable logical-conceptual necessity internal to the scientific interpretation of law: it is a hypothesis that 'cannot but be accepted if social relations are to be interpreted as legal relations'.[19] If this assumption is not made, he asserts, it is logically impossible to conceive what he considers to represent the very essence of the international system, that is, the idea of a community of states endowed with equal rights despite conspicuous differences in territorial extension, population and power. This conception, Kelsen asserts,

> is possible only with the aid of a legal hypothesis: namely, that above the legal bodies considered as States [...] there lies a legal system that delimits the scope of validity of the individual States, thereby preventing the interference of the one in the sphere of the other or linking such interference to certain conditions that are equal for all. Such a legal system should be conceived as regulating the reciprocal behaviour of these bodies by means of norms that are equal for all, and as therefore excluding at the very root, as far as the form of particular legal relationships among individual States is concerned, *any legal surplus-value of the one with respect to the other.* [...] It is only on account of the primacy of the international legal system that particular States are on the same legal level and, that, by virtue of being subject in equal measure to the higher-ranking international legal order, they *can count legally as entities of equal rank.*[20]

It is clear that the Kelsenian doctrine of the primacy of international law represents a rigorous formalistic development both of the legal doctrine of the Enlightenment and also of the cosmopolitan conception – derived from the tenets of natural law and having a distinctly anti-Hegelian slant – of international law.[21] Kelsen formalizes the categories elaborated within an extended tradition of thought, that which, from Francisco de Vitoria to Alberico Gentili and Grotius, replaced medieval universalism with the modern paradigm of an international society of sovereign states: states conceived as legal subjects that are independent of one other but at the same time under an obligation to respect the law of the *universalis societas gentium.*

It could be said that Kelsenian legal cosmopolitanism ends up by pushing to extremes and overturning this tradition when, as an ethical-political foundation of his approach, Kelsen takes up again the theological idea of the unity of humankind as *civitas maxima*:

> a multiplicity of legal bodies or communities must enjoy equal rights, that is, they must be of equal standing in a legal community [...] in which the liberty of the subjects (the States) is limited by their fundamental legal equality. This idea finds expression in the hypothesis, put forward by Christian Wolff, of the *civitas maxima*, which as a legal system is superior in equal measure to individual States.[22]

There can be no doubt that opting for the primacy of international law and against the idea of the sovereignty of states leads Kelsen, despite his claim to purity in matters concerning legal science, to a twofold epistemological and ethical-political exhortation, heavily overloaded with methodological decisions and value assumptions. On the one hand, the primacy of international law is equated with no less than a very generalized option in favour of the objectivity of knowledge: it presupposes an 'objective universal reason' and an 'objectivistic conception of the world'. In contrast, the subjectivism and gnoseological relativism from which the thesis of the primacy of the sovereignty of the state draws its inspiration, Kelsen argues, lead not only to the negation of law in general and of legal science but also to the assertion of a logic of 'pure power' in international relations.[23]

On the other hand, the primacy of international law is correlated with a pacifist, anti-imperialist ideology which necessarily culminates, Kelsen believes, in the idea of a 'world or universal State', in the sense of a 'universal community superior to the particular states, which are all entirely encompassed within it'.[24] When the one and only sovereign order of the world state has absorbed into itself all other orders, law will have become 'the organization of humanity and will therefore be one with the supreme ethical idea'.[25] Flinging all methodological caution to the winds, Kelsen even commits himself to a full-scale historical prophecy:

> only temporarily and certainly not for ever is mankind today divided into States, which have taken shape more or less arbitrarily. The legal unity of mankind, the *civitas maxima* as the form of organization of the world: such is the political core of the primacy of international law, which is however at the same time the fundamental idea of that brand of pacifism which in the sphere of international politics constitutes the reverse image of imperialism. Just as for an objectivistic conception of life the ethical concept of man is humanity, so for an objectivistic theory of law the concept of law is identified with that of international law, and for precisely this reason is at the same time also an ethical concept.[26]

It would be an academic exercise, after decades of criticism of Kelsenian normativism, to point out the logical fallacies of Kelsen's internationalism and legal pacifism, by borrowing arguments, say, from Carl Schmitt's blistering criticism. Kelsen's positivistic claim to scientific status for his doctrine, his humanistic rhetoric, and, last but not least, his cultural eurocentrism are all too easy to criticize. On one central point, however, Kelsen's position would appear to be difficult to refute, although it should be said that he himself made the mistake of never applying his doctrine to the real international legal order, despite the weighty volume that he dedicated to systematic comment on the United Nations Charter.[27]

The primacy of international law and the (progressive) removal of the sovereign prerogatives of states, Kelsen maintains, are inseparable from the idea of the legal equality of states as subjects of international law. This must hold at least until such time as, the Kelsenian prophecy having once come true, the states themselves have disappeared and have been completely absorbed into the global order of the *civitas maxima*. I would argue that here an extremely clear-cut theoretical-legal alternative takes shape. One can of course reject out of hand, for instance in the light of a warlike or economistic ideology, any legal consideration of international relations and with it the perspective of legal cosmopolitanism. Indeed Kelsen himself, as we have seen, admits as much. But if, in common with Falk and Cassese and many other cosmopolitan jurists as well, one subscribes unreservedly to this perspective, it seems difficult to avoid a violent collision with the normative logic upon which the legal system of the United Nations is based. For it is indeed a system which, apart from the idealizing and equivocal declaration of the 'sovereign equality of all its members' contained in article 2,[28] takes as its very foundation the criterion of the formal inequality of its members; that is, it confers a privilege in a technical sense on certain of its members, or, as Kelsen would have said, a 'legal surplus-value'. Article 23 also confers a privilege inasmuch as the formal inequality is not made to derive from a substantial rule that is in some way generalizable – on the basis, say, of a different extension of territory or size of population or economic potential – but depends, *tout court*, on the military outcome of the Second World War.

The attribution of this privilege, around which the whole normative and institutional mechanism of the United Nations revolves, cannot therefore refer to any customary tradition of the *jus gentium*. It can be justified only on the basis of a simple contractual bond: acceptance of the United Nations Charter as a *diktat* imposed by the great powers on the other states at the conclusion of the Conference of San Francisco – a *diktat* that is perpetuated in terms of a necessary acceptance of the international hierarchy by those newly independent states that aspire to recognition of their own sovereignty. The 'United Nations Charter model' – interpreted by Falk and Cassese as a highly developed normative model and as such contrasting with the legal primitiveness of the 'Westphalia model' – is in fact a normative *monstrum* within the entire tradition of the *jus publicum Europaeum*, since it violates the constitutive principle of any modern legal system: the uniqueness of the subject of law. From the point of view of the modern theory of law the whole normative and institutional system of the United Nations is therefore devoid of legal self-justification: what is lacking, in Kelsen's words, is a 'fundamental norm' that would establish the binding nature of its decisions. It is founded, in a Schmittian sense, on an act of pure political will. The refusal by a state to become a member of the United Nations, or its decision to leave the organization, would thus be backed not only by the formal arguments submitted by one of the most authoritative jurists of our time but also by the very logic of modern law.

Antonio Cassese recognizes that the United Nations Charter presents a characteristic that is without precedent in a modern normative text, whether national or international. For the first time the law of force is placed, *formally*, above the force of law:

> While in the past the lack of substantial restraints on the use of force simply confirmed that the powers were the overlords in the world community, now the law goes so far as to consecrate their might, providing, as it does, that while they must not use force contrary to the Charter, transgression will not invite sanctions under Chapter VII of the Charter owing to the veto power conferred on each of them.[29]

Cassese speaks of a 'huge shortcoming', yet on the one hand he seems to justify it on the grounds of the need to create 'realistic legal mechanisms', while on the other, though in a different context, he exults in observing that contemporary international law has 'torn to shreds the myth of legal equality of states' and that it has realistically taken into account the enormous 'economic and social inequalities' that characterize them[30] – for such developments, in the eyes of Cassese, mark a genuine step forward in international law.

But if this is the case, i.e. if it is recognized that within the international legal order the legal equality of states is nothing more than a myth, and if it is admitted that *de facto* situations and the logic of power cannot fail to influence the normative structure of international institutions by attributing a 'legal surplus-value' to certain particular states, then even cosmopolitanism risks appearing no better than wishful thinking, an escape into the pure world of what should be. If it is maintained that legal equality between the subjects of international law is not realistically feasible – and Cassese does maintain this – then it would be wise to attenuate 'communitarian' enthusiasm for the paradigm of the United Nations Charter and recognize that there are good grounds for more realistic positions. It would probably be more coherent to acknowledge that the Westphalian model – the model of equilibrium and co-ordination between sovereign, independent states – is, despite its serious flaws, legally less 'primitive' than the United Nations Charter model. And it would likewise be sensible to consider cautiously and selectively the cosmopolitan reasons that militate in favour of overcoming the 'individualism' of states in favour of a 'communitarian' solution. If nothing else, as Adolf Lasson contended – thereby incurring severe criticism from Kelsen – the pluralism of sovereign states may be an antidote to the tendency of the 'logic of power' to be translated into the legal forms of a sovereign international autocracy.[31]

Jurisdictional Centralism and 'International Regimes'

The international legal system, even after the advent of the United Nations Charter, consists almost exclusively of primary norms, which impose obligations, while secondary norms relating to the interpretation and coercive application of law are almost entirely lacking. This is particularly true from the point of view of the actual implementation of the system, given that, as we have seen, the provisions of the Charter that conferred on the Security Council broad powers of executive organization for the enforcement of its own decisions have fallen into disuse. Indeed the use of force – as we saw in exemplary fashion in the Gulf War and in the interventions by the United Nations in Somalia, Rwanda and Haiti – is *de facto* delegated to the military power of the individual powers, not unlike situations which used to occur in the League of Nations. Thus the implementing of sanctions decided by the Security Council is decentralized and to a large extent voluntary.

On the other hand the jurisdictional functions of the International Court of Justice hold very little sway: the Court – like any other international judge, it should be added – issues its statements only in order to resolve controversies between states that have already accepted its jurisdiction. Therefore the Court does not have in its employ an international police force endowed with the power to apply sanctions against violations of international law. Article 94 of the Charter entrusts the implementation of its decisions to the discretionary judgement of the Security Council. Moreover the Court has no power whatsoever to control or apply sanctions against the highest military-political organ of the United Nations.

These normative inadequacies and, above all, this lack of full legal effect – so the argument advanced by the advocates of legal cosmopolitanism runs – profoundly differentiate the international legal order from that of states, to the point of justifying the conceptual contraposition between 'international anarchy' and 'state order'. Along the lines established by John Austin and Herbert Hart, it can indeed be asked if a legal system which not only lacks specialized organs for the production and coercive implementation of the law, but lacks even a formal definition of its sources, is a legal system in a real sense or whether it is simply 'positive international morality'.[32] It can even be doubted whether its laws are legally binding. Or at least one may wonder, with Kelsen, whether such a system may not be so rudimentary as to require urgent completion and development in the direction of a centralized, compulsory and universal jurisdiction.[33] Only after this has been achieved, it is claimed, will international law cease to be a law that concerns only inter-state relations: it will at last become a cosmopolitan law in the full sense, concerning relations between all the citizens of the world, be they organized in the form of a state or not. Only then will it be possible to say with Kant that the violation of a law occurring at one point on the earth is felt at all its points.

Until then – according to a widely shared thesis of Bobbio's – the situation whereby international law is essentially shorn of its full legal effectiveness will be matched by what amounts to international anarchy. And in a regime of anarchy there may even be doubts over the criteria to be adopted for the legal characterization of the behaviour of the international actors, as well as for sanctions against such behaviour. In the presence of 'primitive' international law – 'primitive' because devoid of a higher jurisdictional authority – one or more subjects can sovereignly interpret international laws according to their own self-interest. Subjects can pursue their own interests by resorting to the use of force in a manner which is discretionary, but in the last analysis legitimate. In the absence of universally respected and enforced rules of the game, Bobbio continues, it is hardly surprising that all types of means, including even those of a terrorist nature, should be adopted by a democratic state engaged in the repression of international terrorism.[34]

This position is not without a rigid internal coherence, but is not in my opinion convincing, since, once again, it is dominated by the paradigm of the 'domestic analogy'. For, as Hedley Bull has cogently argued,[35] reference to the analogy of the state legal system prevents a proper understanding of the specific aspects that the twofold alternative law/anomie and order/anarchy presents in the framework of international relations. This is true in at least the following senses.

First, in the international sphere the absence of a centralized jurisdiction is not equivalent to a situation of anomie and anarchy in the radical Hobbesian sense of the *bellum omnium contra omnes*. Hobbes himself, after all, distinguished between the 'pure natural state' of individuals and the 'state of nature' of states and implicitly attenuated, in the latter case, the panconflictualistic hypothesis.[36] Despite the possibility of war – always imminent and frequently occurring – it cannot be said, even from a rigorously realist point of view, that a situation of *status statui lupus*, so to speak, represents normality in relations between states. The state actors, hampered though they are by the absence of a general harmony of interests and therefore in bitter competition with each other, do not live in a permanent, unilateral situation of a zero sum conflict. On the contrary, they display the tendency, albeit extremely selectively and in a context of striking asymmetries of power and resources, to interact, to 'adapt' and to co-operate with other actors in the search for mutual advantages. What one finds, then, is a condition that could be defined as 'co-operative anarchy' or, to use the insightful oxymoron suggested by Kenneth Waltz, 'anarchic order'.[37] Or else, to emphasize the relations of sociality which, when all is told, do character-ize the 'anarchic' system of sovereign states, one could speak of an 'anarchic society', according to the realist interpretation of the Grotian tradition proposed by Hedley Bull in his classic work.[38]

Only an archaic, dogmatic realism can still continue to represent states, in particular democratic states, as 'rational' actors in a Paretian sense, committed to maximizing their power and wealth in a context of perfect anarchy and therefore at the expense of all other subjects. The great powers themselves, it has been shown, tend much more towards stability than towards the continuous expansion of their power. On this point the 'neo-realist' critique, from Kenneth Waltz to Robert Gilpin and Robert Keohane,[39] has intervened effectively, and, without intro-ducing the slightest trace of a harmonistic hypothesis, has succeeded in going beyond the idea of an inevitable alternative between hegemony and conflict or, in slightly different terms, between hierarchical central-ization and anarchy. To Keohane in particular is owed an important self-critical revision of the theory of 'hegemonic stability', which in its original version subordinated the whole range of behaviour and prefer-ences of international subjects to a deterministically realist notion of power and of the 'selfish interest' of states.[40]

Second, the absence of a universal, binding jurisdiction does not exclude the possibility that, under certain conditions, particular sets of issues may be considered and negotiated jointly by the majority of international actors. Nor does it preclude the eventuality that, within such 'issue-areas', sanctions in various forms may be applied to behav-iour that departs from rules that have been agreed to: such a situation obtains, for example, in sectors such as diplomatic and consular rela-tions, the mutual protection of citizens abroad, international trade, the exchange system, ocean fishing, space research, meteorology, the disci-plining of human activities in the Antarctic. One need only cite in particular – notwithstanding value judgements regarding the political objectives actually achieved – the undoubted effectiveness of normative organisms such as GATT (currently World Trade Organization), the non-nuclear proliferation treaty or the regional seas programme and, more generally, the multilateral conventions framed under the auspices of the International Labour Organization or under the aegis of the United Nations. It cannot therefore be maintained in general, as by Bobbio, that the absence of a *super partes* power inhibits even the legal characterization of international behaviour, though this may well be true in particular instances.

Third, the growing complexity of the international environment and the growing interdependence among its variables – in the spheres of science, high technology, mass media, demography, trade, finance, oil production, etc. – tend to produce a systemic situation which James Rosenau has defined as 'governance without government',[41] i.e. a situation in which the absence of a government possessing formal authority (government) co-occurs with a context of extensive phenomena of self-regulative aggregation (governance) of international agents. It is therefore a situation that contradicts the logic of centralized, binding and universal jurisdiction advocated by jurists who derive their inspiration from Kelsenian cosmopolitanism.

In conditions of high complexity systemic dynamics tend to give rise to a polycentric normative matrix, which arises from widespread processes of strategic interaction and multilateral negotiation. This matrix has more the structure of a web, or rather a series of webs in a fractal pattern, than the pyramidal structure of the celebrated Kelsenian *Stufenbau*. The decentralized and mainly spontaneous character of the phenomenon shows how the possibility of disciplining international relations does not depend rigidly on the elimination of the sovereignty of states, even though it clearly involves a reduction of their powers and prerogatives. However, despite the necessary self-limitations, nation states remain – and seem destined to remain so in the near future – the most important sources of the complex self-organization of international law. Naturally this does not mean that they form the exclusive source of international and transgovernmental relations or that the emergence of international agents other than states should be ignored. On the contrary, such new relations and new agents, whose presence contributes greatly to an increase in the complexity of the international arena, belong to phenomena of segmentation and dispersal of international power which are, no less than the traditional sovereignty of states, opposed to the perspective of centralist, hierarchical cosmopolitanism.

It is evident that the arguments presented here form a theoretical-legal development of the doctrine of 'international regimes'. More specifically, they are based on the neo-realist version of this doctrine, elaborated in particular by Robert Keohane and Stephen Krasner.[42] It is indeed to Krasner, as is widely known, that we owe the canonical definition of the concept of an international regime, as

> sets of implicit or explicit principles, norms, rules and decision-making procedures around which actors' expectations converge in a given area of international relations. Principles are belief of fact, causation, and rectitude. Norms are standards of behaviour defined in terms of rights and obligations. Rules are specific prescriptions or proscriptions for action. Decision-making procedures are prevailing practices for making and implementing collective choice.[43]

From a strictly normative point of view, 'international regimes' establish frames of legal responsibility by formulating sets of general norms, of specific rules and procedures which have the aim of disciplining interaction between actors, defining their rights and guiding their behaviour in various ways. At the same time, in contexts of normative uncertainty and political and economic risk, 'regimes' establish stable frameworks of negotiation, reinforcing the actors' expectations, reducing transaction costs and improving the quality and quantity of information available.[44]

Setting aside the details and the many variants put forward in the vast literature on these issues,[45] what is important in this doctrine from the point of view of the legal anti-cosmopolitanism proposed here is its central theory: in conditions of elevated interdependence among international factors, multilateral negotiation is a decentralized source of the production and application of international law that operates effectively despite the absence – or rather thanks to the absence – of centralized functions of government. In Keohane's view, there are two aspects of the international context that are decisive for the genesis of 'regimes':

> Two features of the international context are particularly important: world politics lacks authoritative governmental institutions, and is characterised by pervasive uncertainty. Within this setting, a major function of international regimes is to facilitate the making of mutually beneficial agreements among governments so that the structural condition of anarchy does not lead to a complete 'war of all against all'.[46]

Analogously, he states that

> regimes may have significant impact in a highly complex world in which ad hoc, individualistic calculations of interest could not possibly provide the necessary level of coordination. If there is a general movement toward a world of complex interdependence, then the number of areas in which regimes can matter is growing.[47]

Although predominantly a conscious product of interaction between state actors, 'international regimes' enjoy relative autonomy with respect to the sources of power that initially constituted them, and presuppose a fluid, dynamic normative context. Moreover – *pace* the Kelsenian assumption of the unity, completeness and coherence of the legal system – this now holds broadly within states as well, if it is true that in postindustrial societies there is a crisis of the regulatory capacity of the state system, and therefore of the certainty of the law, so that there is a multiplication of areas allowing some degree of independence in enacting regulations *ultra legem* and, frequently, *contra legem*.[48]

According to the classical systemic proposition, in environmental conditions of increasing complexity, interdependence and turbulence, one may find order emerging spontaneously from disorder, albeit in imperfect, precarious forms. It is however a flexible, polycentric, essentially non-hierarchical order.[49] On the other hand, despite appearances to the contrary, a monocentric, hierarchical normative structure can over the long term have the effect of inhibiting the development of factors of systemic equilibrium and thereby bring about more serious conflicts. Hence there is considerable reason to wonder whether, in the presence of a high level of complexity and turbulence in the international environment, a similarly large dose of indeterminacy and normative disorder might not be preferable to the quest for a complete, universal legal system.

Peace through Law?

'If international law is in some ways at the vanishing point of law,' Hersch Lauterpacht has authoritatively written, 'the law of war is, perhaps even more conspicuously, at the vanishing point of international law.'[50] Is it possible to overcome this pessimism concerning the ability of law to counter war or at least limit its destructive effects? Is it possible to maintain that law is an effective instrument for guaranteeing peace, or even, as Hans Kelsen has maintained, and as has been maintained by cosmopolitan jurists following in his wake, that the law is the only instrument capable of achieving stable and universal peace? *Peace through Law* is in fact the title of the celebrated 1944 essay in which Hans Kelsen designed a legal strategy for achieving peace.[51] Kelsen believed that the post-war period, characterized by the presence of no more than three or four great powers not intent on making excessive territorial claims, would be conducive to agreements among these powers: it would therefore become possible to achieve in practice 'the idea of international peace through international law'.[52] His legal pacifism (and optimism) were however tied, as will be seen, to the perspective of an abandonment of the state-centred paradigm and a profound reform of international institutions in a globalistic, centralistic direction. The expectation was that this would provide a remedy not only for the incompleteness of the international order but also for the widely proclaimed ineffectiveness of war law.

It is undeniable – in fact it is generally recognized – that the law of war, understood in a Grotian sense as *temperamentum belli*, has so far been the sector of international law that has least come into effect. Yet it cannot be denied that on the subject of the legal disciplining of war there have been significant developments in Europe from the seventeenth century onwards, both theoretically and in the sphere of normative production.

On the level of theoretical elaboration the most significant progress, as we have earlier seen, occurred with the gradual supplanting of the medieval doctrine of *justum bellum* – and in particular of the theological conception of *jus ad bellum* – by *jus in bello*, on which normative efforts began to focus. It was a phenomenon of secularization, positivization and statalization of the law of war which, as is well recognized, went hand-in-hand with the birth and development of modern international law, from Baltasar Ayala to Alberico Gentili, Grotius and Emmerich de Vattel.[53] In these authors the search for the 'just causes' of war is abandoned, giving way to recognition of the 'public' character of conflict between states and to definition of the formal, procedural and jurisdictional conditions that make it possible to award the contenders the legal qualification of *hostes equaliter justi*. Through this qualification, legally recognized enemies can be and are treated quite differently from the way in which a bandit, a criminal or a brute is treated. Indeed it is the legal equality of sovereign states within the Westphalian system that allows the legal formalization of war, without any further discrimination between *justi* and *injusti hostes* from the ethical-theological point of view.

This centuries-long process of emergence of a European law of war from its original theological and cosmological shell has over time, and in more modern times, brought about an extensive production of a positive law of war. The goals this form of law seeks to achieve include both dissuasion from recourse to military violence, regardless of its 'causes' – hence, as we have seen, the metamorphosis of the notion of aggression – and, above all, that of reducing the more destructive or 'unnecessarily' destructive aspects of war. In the meantime the destructive aspects of war have notoriously become apocalyptic as a result of progress in military technology and the power of both conventional and nuclear weapons. The very distinction between these two kinds of weapons, as was shown by the Gulf War, is now deprived of a precise meaning because non-nuclear weapons can, on account of their selective destructiveness, prove to be far more devastatingly effective than nuclear armaments.

It is on the basis of these premises that from the second half of the nineteenth century onwards the law of war as *jus in bello* has been endowed with formal status through a long series of conferences, conventions and multilateral treaties: in particular the Geneva protocol of 1924, the Kellogg–Briand Pact of 1928 and the conventions, above all the Geneva Conventions, which from 1949 up to the present time have gradually revised and updated previous legal statements in the (vain) attempt to keep up with the continuous development of military technology. This same trend is reflected in the recent Convention on 'inhuman' weapons.[54]

One characteristic of the Covenant of the League of Nations and the Kellogg–Briand Pact was the attempt to establish procedural rules for preventing, ritualizing and controlling war internationally, yet without prohibiting it in absolute terms and without inflated claims of its capacity to be abolished. Thus under certain conditions – above all in response to an armed attack and as an extreme collective sanction imposed by international law – war remained a legitimate option available to every member of the international community.[55] On the other hand, and here too the Covenant and the Kellogg–Briand Pact are paradigmatic, the road to bilateral and multilateral agreements for arms reduction was opened up and an attempt was made to discipline the production and trade of weaponry, discouraging (but never prohibiting) arms production, in particular production by private industry.[56] Since then, numerous multilateral treaties have been signed over the years with the aim of 'humanizing' war, by banning or limiting the use of particular types of weapons, such as poisonous, chemical and bacteriological weapons, asphyxiating gases, anti-personnel mines etc., and by updating the rules concerning 'discrimination' of non-combatants and the treatment of prisoners and the wounded. Some of the more recent rulings have moreover prohibited the use or placement of weapons of mass destruction, particularly nuclear weapons, in outer space or on the sea-bed.[57] Finally, courts have been constituted to judge war crimes and crimes against humanity and peace, from the international military tribunals of Nuremberg and Tokyo to the International Criminal Tribunal for the former Yugoslavia, with its seat in The Hague, and the recent International Criminal Tribunal for Rwanda.

What should be said about this enormous normative production is precisely that it is, as Hersch Lauterpacht has written, 'evanescent law', a thin web that places no more than very limited restrictions on the military activities of states. There needs to be realistic recognition that within the *issue-area* of international violence no 'legal regime' has managed to establish itself and create a coherent normative framework and an effective system of sanctions. The more important military powers have never accepted general restrictions, so that, as far as the legal limitation of the conduct of war activities is concerned, the international normative system is characterized by 'deficiencies, loopholes and ambiguity'.[58] Very often conventions ban only the relatively ineffective or unreliable means of destruction, i.e. those that are capable of jeopardizing the lives even of those who use them for offensive purposes. Consequently, not only has the dropping of bombs from aeroplanes never been banned, but neither has a formal ban on the use of atomic and nuclear weapons ever been ratified. As is well known, not even the nuclear non-proliferation treaty provides for any kind of limitation in this sense.[59] Furthermore, the industrialized countries are always able to produce new and more sophisticated weapons that do not fall under the specific bans of existing legislation:[60] here it is sufficient to mention only the 'conventional' weapons used by the Allies in the Gulf War. As for the international criminal courts, it has been observed by, among others, Hedley Bull[61] that their symbolic function – for in this case one cannot speak of jurisdictional functions in any real sense, even if their judgements are implemented with the use of force – has so far been tarnished by the selective character of their pronouncements. It is the 'victors' and in any case the great powers that organize these tribunals and without exception perform the role of judges, while a handful of 'scapegoats' representing the defeated normally appear in the dock. Never has there been a case – *pace* the fond hopes cherished by Hans Kelsen after the Second World War – of the victorious states accepting the idea that their own citizens should be put on trial. That they could be tried by the defeated is treated as an unutterable anathema, but the concept of being tried by the same courts as those instituted to judge the defeated fares no better.[62]

In comparison with this tradition of 'evanescent' *jus in bello*, a drastic change – and from this point of view we cannot but agree with Falk and Cassese – has been introduced with the United Nations Charter. With regard to the international regulation of war the 'Charter model' on the one hand introduces a drastic limitation, if not an absolute denial, of the *jus ad bellum* which in the Westphalian model was conceded to the sovereign states, while on the other hand it totally neglects the traditional side of *jus in bello*. The Charter is committed exclusively to elaborating a mechanism of concentration of military power in the hands of the Security Council, so that this organ can operate as the supreme guarantor of a stable, universal peace. In short, the legislators of Dumbarton Oaks, turning away from a tradition of over a thousand years, took a decisive step in the direction of *jus contra bellum*. As Hans Kelsen has observed, even the word 'war' has disappeared from the vocabulary of the Charter and has been systematically replaced by the term 'use of armed force'.[63]

Indeed, as we have seen, the United Nations Charter not only imposes a general prohibition on the use of force by states but also drastically limits the right to self-defence of a state that has been attacked militarily, since it concedes to a state only the faculty of resisting attack provisionally, pending the intervention of the Security Council. It is the Security Council that possesses the supreme power – unlimited, discretionary and uncontrollable – to re-establish order by resorting in turn to the use of force if it deems this necessary. Should the Security Council make a decision in favour of military intervention, in doing so it is not even obliged to take into account any military operations initiated by the state that is the victim of aggression.

Hans Kelsen has strongly emphasized the fact that the United Nations Charter finally introduces 'an international security system marked by a high degree of centralisation',[64] but complains that the excessive discretionary power conferred on the Security Council prevents it from operating as a legal organ, that is, as a source of centralized, universal and 'equal' jurisdiction, able to create an effective system of alternative sanctions to war, in particular to 'defensive war'.[65] For these reasons, in his essay *Peace through Law* he recommended a series of institutional and normative innovations – such as the organization of a permanent league for the maintenance of peace, the constitution of an international criminal jurisdiction, personal responsibility for acts of war – that converge in the direction of a complete centralization of the monopoly of force as a contribution to security and world peace and a spur to the superseding of the sovereignty of states by a federal world state.[66]

Taking as their inspiration the teachings of Kelsen, a number of political scientists and cosmopolitan jurists have recently proposed a further series of normative interventions under the banner of the radical antinomy between war and law. Such proposals include the formal qualification of any war initiative as a crime against international law, the banning of all instruments of war and therefore the general prohibition of the production of weapons of war, the creation of an international police force, operating under the aegis of the United Nations and holding a world monopoly of the use of force, the subsequent disarming of states, the creation of an international criminal code and an international criminal court.[67]

What can be noted – and this should also constitute, in general, a theoretical criticism of legal pacifism – is that the sum of these proposals is characterized by the rationalist assumption that it is possible to 'disarm states' and 'abolish war' by relying essentially on normative instruments, that is, by creating a power which is by definition 'legal' in the sense that it is rational, regulated and enlightened.[68] On the other hand, these proposals unconsciously espouse the military ideology that inspired the legislators of Dumbarton Oaks, who thought that a stable, universal peace could be achieved by concentrating into the hands of an international organization – that is into their own hands – a military force so powerful as to be capable of quashing any local or regional conflict simply by smothering it with overwhelming military force. It was for this reason that they not only opposed any project for a general control of weapons but were also committed to elaborating the rules of *jus in bello*.

In the third place – and from the point of view of a theory of peacekeeping this is the most delicate point – the concentration of military power in the hands of an (extremely powerful) international organism amounts to nothing less than concentrating in this organism the *jus ad bellum* taken away from states. Any 'policing operation' carried out by a supranational organ that possesses the world monopoly of force – let us say, an organ such as the Security Council of the United Nations, however democratized this organ may be, or held up as the expression of world public opinion or even elected by a planetary electorate – is destined to take on all the connotations of war. The Gulf War showed the theoretical and practical impossibility of distinguishing between an operation of international policing and a full-blown war in a true sense. When an armed conflict of vast proportions flares up, the logic of the 'destruction of the enemy' and of saving the lives of one's own combatants inevitably prevails, all the more so if the holder of military power is so strong as not to be susceptible to any form of control from the point of view of *jus in bello*.

Finally – and here too the Gulf War should have given a severe warning – a war conducted in the name of or on behalf of a supreme international organism inevitably tends to assume the characteristics not only of a lawful and legitimate war but also of a 'just war', of a crusade in the name of the world order. Thanks to the sensationalist contributions of the media, the image of the *injustus hostis* is inexorably attributed to the enemy, who tends to be criminalized as morally ignoble, as an enemy of humanity and the incarnation of evil. And indeed just such a development actually took place in the course of the Gulf War. It is obvious – compare the theory of Michael Walzer concerning the 'supreme emergency' – that in a just war against an 'unjust enemy' no account can be taken of any criterion of *jus in bello*: it is a war that is not only militarily but also morally and legally without proportion and without limits.

To conclude: replacement of the old 'Westphalian model' by the 'United Nations Charter model', as proposed by legal pacifism, paradoxically risks reintroducing precisely the very same archaic notion of *jus ad bellum* that the modern international law, formed after the peace of Westphalia, had succeeded in removing from the horizon of civilization. Moreover, the Enlightenment assumption that it is possible to abolish war 'through law' ends up leaving aside that protective net, the *jus in bello*, which, fragile though it may be, for the moment represents the only practical result of the centuries-old attempt to deploy law against war.

A Planetary Rule of Law for the Protection of Human Rights?

Only a supranational institution based on the 'United Nations Charter model' – so Richard Falk and Antonio Cassese maintain, and with them a multitude of advocates of legal cosmopolitanism – is able to ensure effective protection of human rights.

A thesis of this kind cannot but be based implicitly on a broad series of assumptions, some of which are very general indeed. It is necessary to assume, above all, that the doctrine of human rights can be argued rationally and is therefore, in a non-trivial sense, 'universal'. In the second place, the hypothesis presupposes that human rights are 'rights' in the full sense: namely, that they can be defined and delimited with precision and that they are 'positive rights', legally binding and not pertaining only to the moral level. In the third place, it must be assumed that the protection of human rights cannot be adequately guaranteed by nation states, even the most liberal and democratic. In actual fact it cannot be denied that individual states lack the resources, power and to a large extent even the jurisdictional competence to guarantee the rights of subjects who do not come under their jurisdiction, who are not, that is, their 'citizens'. The most that states are able to do is to guarantee foreigners present on their territory the 'rights of citizenship', as well as naturally guaranteeing the same rights to their own resident citizens.[69] It is equally true, on the other hand, that the protection of human rights would very often appear to require legal action against the very state of which the subjects concerned are citizens. Bobbio has written with his usual clarity that:

We shall be able to speak of international protection of human rights only when an international jurisdiction succeeds in imposing itself over national jurisdictions, and the passage from a guarantee *within* the state, which still predominantly distinguishes the present phase, to a guarantee *against* the state has occurred.[70]

And again:

The international protection of human rights is made difficult, if not almost impossible, by the same condition that makes war possible. This condition is the *de facto* unlimited sovereignty of *sovereign states*. Human rights can be truly guaranteed only when the individual subject's right to appeal to higher tribunals than those of the state, in the final instance to international bodies, is recognized and when these bodies are provided with sufficient power to obtain [. . .] respect for their own decisions.[71]

It could be said, in other words, that the doctrine of human rights presents a cosmopolitan bias, since by breaking with the centuries-old tradition of the *jus publicum Europaeum*, it imparts the nature of subjects of the international legal order not only to states (or in any case to collective subjects) but also to individuals. Or better, it tends to impart the status of international subjects predominantly to individuals.[72] Against the notions of 'citizenship' and of 'rights of citizenship' outlined in the classic treatment by Thomas Marshall – notions that are strictly linked to a subject's belonging to a particular national legal system – the doctrine of human rights tends to construct the perspective of a 'cosmopolitan citizenship': a citizenship and a legal system without frontiers, where the fundamental rights (civil, political, social and cultural) of all people, as rational beings and 'persons', are recognized and protected.[73] As Cassese writes:

Human rights are based on an expansive desire to *unify the world* by drawing up a list of *guidelines* for all governments. They are an attempt to highlight the *values* [. . .] that all states should take as parameters for assessing their actions. In a nutshell, human rights are an attempt by the contemporary world to introduce a measure of reason into its history.[74]

The doctrine of human rights therefore accords, in Kantian and Kelsenian mode, with the 'ethical idea' of a universal community, of a *civitas maxima* of which all people are members. Not unconnected with this is the fact that the first article of the Universal Declaration goes so far as to state that all human beings, having been born free and equal in dignity and rights, and all possessing reason and conscience, should treat each other in a mutual spirit of brotherhood. Clearly this philosophy of international relations is a long way from the Grotian (and

Hobbesian) paradigm of 'international society' as a society of states – not of 'persons', let alone of 'brothers' – tied by legal relations of coexistence and co-operation, but also of competition and conflict.[75] The universal protection of human rights demands therefore not only an 'erosion of domestic jurisdiction' but, as Richard Falk has explicitly declared, nothing less than a gradual abandonment of the Westphalian principle of the non-interference of a state or international entity in the 'domestic affairs' of a sovereign state. Thus the protection of *human* rights lies at the foundation of the right and duty to *humanitarian* interference.[76]

Finally, from the point of view of jurisdictional guarantees, the international protection of human rights necessarily implies, as Richard Falk consistently maintains, the idea of a 'global constitutionalism'. It requires the European model of the state in which the rule of law obtains – typified by its institutions embodying the principle of legality, the political independence of judges, the separation between law and morality, the limitation of the political sphere, and, last but not least, the protection of private property – to be taken as the paradigm of the supranational institution which is destined to replace states. Despite the wish that even states which abide by the rule of law should dissolve and give way to the destiny of the future Cosmopolis, the European model of the state in which the rule of law obtains has a universal value and must be universally applied. Protection of the fundamental rights of individuals can be entrusted, in the last analysis, only to the jurisdictional guarantees enshrined in a planetary rule of law, of a 'legal Cosmopolis' based on western political values.[77]

It is hard not to appreciate the gravity and urgency of the problems to which the doctrine of human rights attempts to give an answer. The lure of its moral inspiration and its intentions is indeed powerful. Suffice it to remember that more than two billion people – about half of the world population – are at present suffering on account of the lack or systematic violation of the fundamental rights normally recognized by any western state in which the rule of law holds (although 'recognized' does not necessarily mean they are protected). These violations include a long series of atrocities and acts of violence: genocide, torture, summary execution, disappearance, political murder, violence against children, rape, sexual mutilation of adolescents, the violent removal of organs destined for clandestine trade, slavery, illegal arrest, ill-treatment of political refugees and immigrants, capital execution of minors and disabled persons, corporal punishment, degrading treatment of prisoners, exploitation of prostitution, racial discrimination, but also, and above all, grinding poverty and starvation. Particularly alarming is the situation that emerges from an analysis of the documents of the two

United Nations conferences on human rights (Tehran 1968, Vienna 1993) and which is denounced annually by the reports of Amnesty International: the violation of fundamental rights is a phenomenon of growing proportions, concerning a very large number of states – over 150, including all the western states[78] – and does not seem even to have been touched by the intense activity of non-governmental organizations or by the increasing awareness generally widespread in world culture, let alone by official initiatives.

Despite all this, it is only natural that, from the realist, anti-cosmopolitan point of view put forward here, the doctrine of human rights, with its dual corollary of 'humanitarian interventionism' and 'global constitutionalism', should be evaluated with great theoretical caution and with a certain dose of practical scepticism.

Indeed Kelsen was among the first to assert that the doctrine of human rights, as it was formulated in the Universal Declaration of 1948, was far from possessing the requisites of a legally binding discipline, not only because of the well-known lack of normative powers invested in the body which passed it – the General Assembly of the United Nations – but also because of the non-imperative formulation of the text and the total absence of secondary norms which would enable an international court to punish violations of proclaimed rights.[79] Again it was Kelsen who observed that the doctrine of human rights is linked to a highly controversial European philosophy, the theological-metaphysical conception of natural law which claims to define the moral qualities of human beings by inferring them from the natural order or by deducing them from their very rationality.[80]

Norberto Bobbio has added that this philosophy is characterized by a twofold form of ethical rationalism: on the one hand it assumes that 'absolute foundations' of normative propositions are possible – and here we have a classic case of the naturalistic fallacy criticized by Hume – and on the other it makes the obligatory nature of rights depend on their supposed foundation. In actual fact human rights, above all in the very broad sense they have come to assume in the international vocabulary, cannot lay claim to any absolute, unitary foundation: if for no other reason than on account of the antinomies that create oppositions between the various categories of rights included in the heterogeneous and imprecise catalogues contained in international documents.[81] Acquisitive rights are in conflict with consumption rights, civil rights and rights to freedom are largely incompatible with economic-social rights, and there is a tension between individual rights and collective rights, including the right of self-determination of peoples. Put generally, a power to act will at the same time limit, and conflict with, the faculty (of others) to choose.[82]

The truth is that 'human rights', like all other rights, have no foundation other than in the historical events from which they have emerged and in the aspirations of those political and social forces which have fought for recognition of those rights, usually in the course of bitter conflicts. Such events have been exclusively European or, at most, western. It should therefore come as no surprise that the conception of human rights which eventually prevailed in the formulation of the Universal Declaration should be an essentially western conception, one therefore that is imbued with the political philosophy of individualism, despite certain compromises imposed by socialist and Latin American countries. This is to a large extent also true of such subsequent documents – the only ones possessing normative cogency – as the 'Pact on civil and political rights' and the 'Pact on economic, social and cultural rights', both approved in 1966, despite the fact that these reflected to a greater degree the presence of newly emancipated Third World countries within the United Nations, after liberation from colonial domination.[83]

The universal character of 'human rights' is therefore a rationalistic postulate not only without substantiation in the theoretical sphere but also historically contested by cultures different from western culture. Such objections have mainly taken the form of resistance to the western ideology of 'humanitarian intervention', a resistance to which Hedley Bull has given the name 'revolt against the West'. The disputed ideology is a perfect continuation of the missionary, colonizing tradition of the western powers and goes back at least to the start of the nineteenth century, at the time of the armed interventions by Europeans against the Ottoman empire and in Syria – from which the United States's intervention in Cuba was no different – which supported minorities in conflict with their governments.[84]

In addition, the 'revolt against the West' has set against the cultural imperialism of the western powers – in particular of the United States, Britain and France – the differing conceptions of human rights which are present in cultures other than those of the West. It cannot, of course, be denied that certain elementary rules of social life – for example, respect for the physical integrity of individuals or the keeping of promises – are widespread in the vast majority of cultures and are implicitly present within widely divergent value systems.[85] It remains the case, however, that the complex of civil, political and social values that constitute the premise of the doctrine of human rights is to a large extent incompatible with the dominant ethos in countries like, for example, China, Pakistan, Saudi Arabia, the Sudan or Nigeria. Hence it is no coincidence that in these countries such rights are for the most part inoperative.

In the individualistic, liberal vision of the West human rights are normative prostheses designed to protect personal liberty, individual property and privacy against interference by other individuals, social institutions and above all political authorities. This concept of liberty is quite foreign to Islamic culture, even non-'integralist' Islamic culture, profoundly marked as it is by a religious sense of belonging to the community. The individual identifies with such a community not by claiming rights but by fulfilling duties, that is, scrupulously following collective rules of political-religious behaviour.[86] The same can be said of the Chinese Confucian tradition, which has survived intact despite the violent importation of the Marxist creed. According to Confucian ethics, social life is constituted by hierarchical and strongly asymmetrical relationships based on reciprocal ties of mutual collaboration and obligation rather than on equal and opposed rights and duties. So foreign is the very notion of 'law' to the semantics of the Chinese language that, as Chung-Shu Lo recalled, the early translators of western political classics, working at the end of the nineteenth century, were obliged to coin a new word, *chuan-li*, literally 'power and interest', to render the idea of individual rights.[87] One need only glance at the Banjul Charter on Human and Peoples' Rights, passed in 1981 by the Organization for African Unity, to see that economic-social rights conceived as collective rights of peoples clearly prevail over the civil and political rights of individuals.[88]

Rebus sic stantibus, the risk is thus very great that the cosmopolitan project implicit in the western doctrine and policy of human rights is in actual fact operating as – and is perceived as – an aspect of that process of the 'westernization of the world' which is currently overrunning the technologically and economically weaker cultures, depriving them of their identity and dignity.[89] Such a suspicion also falls on the international policies of 'humanitarian intervention': there is no more eloquent testimony to the risks of such policies than the recent failures of the United Nations – that is, of the Security Council under the hegemony of the United States – in Somalia, Bosnia and Rwanda. The suspicion applies also to the attempt to create new international organisms, endowed with a jurisdictional power in relation to violations of human rights.

From this point of view the polemic which raged in the course of the second Conference of the United Nations on Human Rights, held in Vienna in June 1993, is significant. On that occasion, for the first time after the ending of the East–West blocs, two largely incompatible conceptions of human rights confronted each other. On the one hand there was the thesis, backed by western countries, of the universality and indivisibility of fundamental rights, deriving implicitly from the idea of the cultural and moral homogeneity of the 'planetary civil society'. On the other hand, there was the position of the majority of the Latin American and Asian countries, with Cuba and China in the front rank: these countries contended that the necessary condition for any jurisdictional initiative on human rights was a firm commitment to address the global, 'collective' question of economic and social development, that is to say, the struggle against poverty and debt in the Third World. They denounced the ideology of 'humanitarian interventionism' as a new form of 'hegemonism' by the western countries, accusing them of planning to take advantage of the end of bipolar equilibrium in order to impose their values, their political system and their economic supremacy on the rest of the world. The clash became particularly violent over the proposal of the United States, supported by the European countries, to create a high commission for human rights, operating within the sphere of the United Nations and possessing broad powers of control and intervention. The majority of non-western countries opposed the project of assigning jurisdiction over human rights to an international bureaucracy dominated by the western powers.

This opposition was doubtless also inspired by not totally transparent 'reasons of state' – in particular so far as China was concerned – yet it is undeniably difficult to counter the objection of the non-western countries, also espoused by Amnesty International, that the protection of human rights could not be assigned to the hierarchical, bureaucratic power structure of the United Nations. For what this kind of structure lacks, they claimed, is precisely the major legal institutions that characterize the rule of law, whereas in the logic of global constitutionalism it is in fact these very institutions – such as the division of powers, the independence of the judiciary and constitutional control over the acts of the executive – that are supposed to represent the guarantee of fundamental rights. Instead, it was argued, the international protection of rights could perhaps be better entrusted to a body which would act as the expression of the General Assembly of the United Nations.

At least two other arguments, which integrate and give a more realistic slant to the thesis of Amnesty International, must in my opinion be added to this one. First, those who, like Norberto Bobbio and David Held, propose the establishment of international criminal tribunals and maintain that human rights can be guaranteed only when the power of each individual to appeal to jurisdictional entities higher than the state is recognized, unhesitatingly side with the 'rule of law'. By so doing, however, they entirely neglect the value of the 'rule of men', forgetting that the most delicate problem of any jurisdiction is the 'justice of the individual case' and, consequently, fair judgement. Apart from the extremely serious practical problems which would need to be resolved in order to organize the various levels of a world jurisdiction and to make it really workable for all people, there is no doubt that impersonality and functional abstractness would be the dominating features of the administration of cosmopolitan justice.

In the second place it must be realized that even the most liberal and democratic form of 'world constitutionalism' will remain a pure institutional fiction so long as the organs of coercive application of the international order coincide with the military set-up of a small number of powers formally exempted, thanks to their overwhelming economic and military power, from any jurisdictional control. Indeed it is obvious that the great powers, although hypothetically no longer possessing a 'legal surplus-value', are nevertheless, in practice, *legibus soluti*, and would be all the more so in the event of a single planetary superpower.

Conclusion

It appears inevitable that an international institution possessing extremely extensive powers of political and military intervention should have a hierarchical structure and a function shaped according to the archaic legal model of the formal inequality of the subjects of law. It appears equally inevitable that within such an institution the great powers should be, both *de facto* and *de jure*, beyond jurisdictional control. On the other hand it must be recognized that the gap which separates the elite of the powerful and rich countries from the mass of weak and poor countries cannot be closed solely through the instruments of institutional engineering and still less through those of 'global constitutionalism'. An international jurisdiction and police force, even in the context of a liberal and democratic world state, would have to possess a power above that of the major (nuclear) powers, unless, of course, the hypothesis is introduced of unilateral disarmament and voluntary renunciation by the superpowers of the advantages of 'hegemonic stability'. Excluding this consoling but improbable scenario, the plan for a further concentration of international power following the paradigm of the United Nations Charter would end in the creation of an absolutely 'sovereign' and uncontrollable institution and would consequently make both the international protection of rights and the search for peace even more precarious. It is therefore necessary to identify a strategy – and the quest for a political and economic strategy must take precedence over a legal strategy – capable of overcoming the anarchical aspects of the Westphalian model but capable at the same time of rejecting the centralistic model of legal cosmopolitanism.

Is it possible to conceive of diverse and polycentric political and legal forms which will set themselves the task of performing a small number of functions as compared with the present international institutions, and will therefore possess fewer powers than the latter, yet will precisely for this reason be more effective in the long term in preserving peace and protecting rights? Does the growing complexity and interdependence of international relations demand – and at the same time allow – this new strategic orientation of the theory and practice of international relations? Is it possible to achieve a 'conversion', to use a term of Thomas Kuhn's, from the paradigm of the planetary Leviathan to the paradigm of Lilliput? These are the difficult questions which I shall attempt to answer in the course of the next, concluding chapter.

Notes

1 Gross, 'The Peace of Westphalia 1648–1948', pp. 20–41; Falk, 'The Interplay of Westphalia and Charter Conceptions of International Legal Order', pp. 43–64; Cassese, *Il diritto internazionale nel mondo contemporaneo*, Engl. trans., pp. 4, 13–14, 163–5, 246–50, 396–403. For references to the 'Westphalian system' see also: L. H. Miller, *Global Order: Values and Power in International Politics*, Boulder: Westview Press, 1990; F. H. Hinsley, *Power and the Pursuit of Peace*, Cambridge: Cambridge University Press, 1978; M. Wright, *Systems of States*, Leicester: Leicester University Press, 1977; J. Mayall, *Nationalism and International Society*, Cambridge: Cambridge University Press, 1990; M. W. Zacher, 'The Decaying Pillars of the Westphalian Temple: Implications for International Order and Governance', in J. N. Rosenau and E.-O Czempiel (eds), *Governance without Government: Order and Change in World Politics*, Cambridge: Cambridge University Press, 1992.
2 Falk, 'The Interplay of Westphalia', pp. 43–4; Cassese, *Il diritto internazionale nel mondo contemporaneo*, Engl. trans., pp. 11–13, 99–103.
3 Falk, 'The Interplay of Westphalia', pp. 43, 48; Cassese, *Il diritto internazionale nel mondo contemporaneo*, Engl. trans., pp. 14–17.
4 Cassese, *Il diritto internazionale nel mondo contemporaneo*, Engl. trans., pp. 13–14, 396–9.
5 Falk, 'The Interplay of Westphalia', pp. 14ff; Cassese, *Il diritto internazionale nel mondo contemporaneo*, Engl. trans., pp. 246, 396–7.
6 Falk, 'The Interplay of Westphalia', pp. 59–62.
7 Ibid., pp. 55–8.
8 Cassese. *Il diritto internazionale nel mondo contemporaneo*, Engl. trans., pp. 126–65.
9 Ibid., pp. 397ff.
10 Falk, 'The Interplay of Westphalia', pp. 49–55; Cassese, *Il diritto internazionale nel mondo contemporaneo*, Engl. trans., pp. 246–7, 398.
11 Cassese, *Il diritto internazionale nel mondo contemporaneo*, Engl. trans., pp.

4–5, 163–5, 399–407; R. A. Falk, *Positive Prescriptions for the Near Future*, passim.

12 Cassese, *Il diritto internazionale nel mondo contemporaneo*, Engl. trans., p. 396.

13 Bobbio, *L'età dei diritti*, p. 139. According to Kant, the realization of perpetual peace needs, in addition to the federation of republican states ruled by international law, also the realization of 'cosmopolitan law', in order to govern the relationships between each state and the citizens of every other state, as 'citizens of the globe' (cf. *Zum ewigen Frieden*).

14 R. A. Falk, *The Status of Law in International Society*, Princeton: Princeton University Press, 1970, pp. x–xi, 41–59 ('My own outlook has been very much shaped by the intellectual dialectic that exists between the work of Hans Kelsen and Myres S. McDougal, two great international lawyers of our era who have each developed and sustained a coherent interpretation of the international order', ibid, p. x); Cassese, *Il diritto internazionale nel mondo contemporaneo*, Engl. trans., pp. 20–2. According to Cassese, Kelsen's doctrine of the primacy of international law 'has been instrumental in consolidating the notion that state agencies should abide by international legal standards and ought therefore to put international imperatives before national postulates' (ibid., p. 22).

15 See H. Kelsen, *Das Problem der Souveränität und die Theorie des Völkerrechts: Beitrag zu einer reinen Rechstlehre*, Tübingen: Mohr, 1920; H. Kelsen, *Principles of International Law*, New York: Holt, Rinehart & Winston, Inc., 1952; H. Kelsen, *General Theory of Law and State*, Cambridge (Mass.): Harvard University Press, 1945.

16 Kelsen, *Das Problem der Souveränität*, pp. 9–101.

17 Ibid., pp. 206ff.

18 Ibid., pp. 314–17; Kelsen, *Principles of International Law*, pp. 569–88.

19 Kelsen, *Principles of International Law*, p. 587.

20 Kelsen, *Das Problem der Souveränität*, pp. 204–5. Italics are mine. Cf. also Kelsen, *Principles of International Law*, p. 586: 'the idea of the equality of all States can be maintained only if we base our interpretation of legal phenomena on the primacy of the international law. The States as legal orders can be considered as equal only if they are not presupposed to be sovereign, because they are equal only insofar as they are equally subjected to one and the same international legal order.'

21 Kelsen, *Das Problem des Souveränität*, pp. 196ff.

22 Ibid., pp. 251–2.

23 Ibid., pp. 314–17.

24 Ibid., pp. 249–50.

25 Ibid., p. 205.

26 Ibid., p. 319.

27 See H. Kelsen, *The Law of the United Nations*, New York: Frederick A. Praeger, 1950.

28 On the notion of 'sovereign equality' and its ambiguity, compare Cassese, *Il diritto internazionale nel mondo contemporaneo*, Engl. trans., pp. 129–31; cf. also W. Levi, *Law and Politics in International Society*, Beverly Hills: Sage Publications, 1976, pp. 121–33.

29 Cassese, *Il diritto internazionale nel mondo contemporaneo*, Engl. transl. p. 247.

30 'Contemporary international law has torn to shreds the myth of legal

equality of states and set itself the task of concerning itself with economic and social inequalities' (Cassese, *Il diritto internazionale nel mondo contemporaneo*, Engl. trans., p. 399). For a qualification of the principle of legal equality of states as a myth and for a parallel exaltation of the 'philosophy of the veto' as based on realistic and democratic motivations, compare I. L. Claude, Jr, *Swords into Plowshares: The Problems and Progress of International Organization*, New York: Random House, 1971, pp. 152–62.

31 A. Lasson, *Prinzip und Zukunft des Völkerrechts*, Berlin, 1871, p. 9.

32 See J. Austin, *The Province of Jurisprudence Determined* (1832), ed. H. L. A. Hart, Oxford: Oxford University Press, 1954, lecture VI; H. L. A. Hart, *The Concept of Law*, Oxford: Clarendon Press, 1981. Compare also N. Bobbio, *Teoria generale del diritto*, Turin: Giappichelli, 1993, pp. 138–40; Bull, *The Anarchical Society*, pp. 130ff.

33 Kelsen, *Principles of International Law*, p. 20.

34 N. Bobbio, 'Cercate di attenuare i vostri peccati', *Liberazione*, 7 March 1992, p. 9.

35 Bull, *The Anarchical Society*, pp. 46–51 ('The domestic analogy is no more than an analogy; the fact that states form a society without government reflects features of their situation that are unique', ibid., p. 51).

36 T. Hobbes, *Opera Philosophica*, ed. W. Molesworth, London, 1839–1845, vol. 2, pp. 164, 210. Hedley Bull maintains that according to Hobbes states are less vulnerable than individuals. Therefore they have less fear of dying, they are unequal in power and resources and are less aggressive and more inclined to cooperation; compare H. Bull, 'Hobbes and the International Anarchy', *Social Research*, 48 (1981), 4, pp. 717–38; Bull, *The Anarchical Society*, pp. 46–51; for a different interpretation, cf. D. P. Gauthier, 'Hobbes on International Relations', appendix to *The Logic of Leviathan*, Oxford: Clarendon Press, 1969, pp. 207–12.

37 See K. Waltz, *Theory of International Politics*, New York: Newbery Award Records, 1979.

38 See Bull, *The Anarchical Society*, passim. According to Bull, the two pillars of international order are the (Hobbesian) balance of power and the (Grotian) rules and norms agreed on. On Bull and the relevance of his thought, see A. Hurrell, 'In Defence of International Society', in B. A. Roberson (ed.), *International Society Reconsidered*, London: Pinter, forthcoming.

39 Waltz, *Theory of International Politics*; R. Gilpin, *War and Change in World Politics*, Cambridge: Cambridge University Press, 1981; R. O. Keohane, *Neorealism and Its Critics*, New York: Columbia University Press, 1986.

40 R. O. Keohane, *After Hegemony: Cooperation and Discord in the World Political Economy*, Princeton: Princeton University Press, 1984, pp. 31ff, 49–64, 83–4. The revision of realism has led Keohane to elaborate a theory of 'international regimes' freed from the idea that they have to be conceived as a deterministic consequence of hegemonic stability (namely, as if the hegemony of a great power were the condition of their genesis and maintenance).

41 J. N. Rosenau, 'Governance, Order, and Change in World Politics', in Rosenau and Czempiel (eds), *Governance without Government*, pp. 1–11. At pp. 8–9 Rosenau analyses the relationship between the notion of 'governance without government' and that of 'international regimes'.

42 The notion of 'international regimes' was introduced in 1975 by John G. Ruggie ('International Responses to Technology: Concepts and Trends',

International Organization, 29 (1975), 3, pp. 557–84). For its neo-realist revision, see R. O. Keohane, 'The Demand for International Regimes', now in S. D. Krasner (ed.), *International Regimes*, Ithaca (NY): Cornell University Press, 1983, pp. 141–71; Keohane, *After Hegemony*; S. D. Krasner, 'Regimes and the Limits of Realism: Regimes as Autonomous Variables', now in Krasner (ed.), *International Regimes*.

43 S. D. Krasner, 'Structural Causes and Regime Consequences: Regimes as Intervening Variables', now in Krasner (ed.), *International Regimes*, p. 2. Keohane has elaborated the following neo-realist definition: 'institutions with explicit rules, agreed upon by governments, which pertain to particular sets of issues in international relations' (*International Institutions and State Power*, Boulder: Westview Press, 1989).

44 Keohane, 'The Demand for International Regimes', pp. 148ff, 161–71.

45 For a critique of the theory of international regimes, see S. Strange, 'Cave! Hic dragones: a Critique of Regime Analysis', now in Krasner (ed.), *International Regimes*, pp. 337–54; see also A. Hurrell, 'International Society and the Study of International Regimes', in V. Rittberger (ed.), *Beyond Anarchy: International Cooperation and Regimes*, Oxford: Oxford University Press, 1994.

46 Keohane, 'The Demand for International Regimes', p. 148.

47 Krasner, 'Structural Causes and Regime Consequences', pp. 7–8.

48 For an interesting, even if highly controversial, attempt to apply the systemic categories of complexity to legal phenomena, see the proponents of the theory of 'reflexive law': Gunther Teubner, 'Social Order from Legislative Noise?', in G. Teubner and A. Febbrajo (eds), *State, Law and Economy as Autopoietic Systems*, Milan: Giuffré, 1992 (*European Yearbook in the Sociology of Law*, 1991–2); G. Teubner and H. Willke, 'Kontext und Autonomie: Gesellschaftliche Selbststeuerung durch reflexives Recht', *Zeitschrift für Rechtssoziologie*, 6 (1984), 1, pp. 4–35; P. Hejl, 'Die Theorie autopoietischer Systeme: Perspektiven für die soziologische Systemtheorie', *Rechtstheorie*, 12 (1982), pp. 45–88.

49 See H. Atlan, *Entre le cristal et la fumée. Essai sur l'organisation du vivant*, Paris: Seuil, 1979; I. Prigogine and I. Stengers, *La Nouvelle Alliance: Métamorphose de la science*, Paris: Gallimard, 1979; E. Jantsch, *The Self-Organizing Universe*, Oxford: Pergamon Press, 1980; F. A. von Hayek, *Kinds of Order in Society*, Studies in Social Theory no. 5, Menlo Park: Institute for Humane Studies, 1975; F. A. Hayek, 'The Theory of Complex Phenomena', in M. Bunge (ed.), *The Critical Approach to Science and Philosophy*, New York: Free Press, 1964.

50 H. Lauterpacht, 'The Revision of the Law of War', *British Yearbook of International Law*, 29 (1952), p. 138.

51 See H. Kelsen, *Peace through Law*, Chapel Hill: University of North Carolina Press, 1944 (see also the new edition, with the Introduction by I. Silver, New York: Garland, 1973).

52 Kelsen, *Peace through Law*, p. 9.

53 Schmitt, *Der Nomos der Erde im Völkerrecht des Jus Publicum Europaeum*, pp. 123–40; Kelsen, *Principles of International Law*, pp. 29–39.

54 Cassese, *Il diritto internazionale nel mondo contemporaneo*, Engl. trans., pp. 253–86. The Convention on Inhuman Weapons, signed by thirty-one states and effective as from December 1983, prohibits the use of bullets whose fragments cannot be detected through X rays, prohibits or restricts the use

of anti-personnel mines and explosive devices which are apparently harm-
less, prohibits or restricts the use of incendiary weapons. The last important
convention concerns the use of chemical weapons.

55 Kelsen, *Principles of International Law*, pp. 34–9.
56 See articles 8 and 23 of the Covenant.
57 See the Outer Space Treaty, signed by ninety-two states and effective as
from October 1967, and the Sea-bed Treaty, signed by eighty-three states
and effective as from May 1972; cf. more generally Cassese, *Il diritto
internazionale nel mondo contemporaneo*, Engl. trans., pp. 257–66, 269–74.
58 Cassese, *Il diritto internazionale nel mondo contemporaneo*, Engl. trans., p.
285.
59 Brown, *The Causes and Prevention of War*, pp. 204–7; A. W. Marks (ed.),
NPT: Paradoxes and Problems, Washington (DC): Arms Control Association, 1975.
60 Cassese, *Il diritto internazionale nel mondo contemporaneo*, Engl. trans., pp.
255, 259, 269ff.
61 Bull, *The Anarchical Society*, p. 89.
62 Kelsen, *Peace through Law*, p. 114 ('The victorious States, too, should be
willing to transfer jurisdiction over their own subjects who have offended the
laws of warfare to the same independent and impartial international tribunal').
63 Kelsen, *Principles of International Law*, p. 26.
64 Ibid., p. 40.
65 Ibid., pp. 47–51.
66 Kelsen, *Peace through Law*, pp. 5, 13ff, 110–24. For a criticism of Kelsen's
excessive normative ambitions, see H. Bull, 'Hans Kelsen and International
Law', in R. Tur and W. Twining (eds), *Essays on Kelsen*, Oxford: Oxford
University Press, 1986.
67 D. Held, 'Democrazia e nuovo ordine internazionale', *Europa Europe*, 3
(1994), 1, pp. 48–50; Ferrajoli and Senese, 'Quattro proposte per la pace',
pp. 247–9, 253–6; N. Bobbio, 'La pace attraverso il diritto', in Bobbio, *Il
terzo assente*, pp. 126–35; Bobbio, 'Diritto e guerra', now in Bobbio, *Il
problema della guerra e le vie della pace*, pp. 97–118.
68 H. Bull notes that the advocates of world government make the tacit
assumption that it is their own moral and political preferences which will be
embodied in it (*The Anarchical Society*, p. 291).
69 States may try foreign citizens and stateless persons only if they have
committed a crime within national territory.
70 N. Bobbio, 'Presente e avvenire dei diritti dell'uomo', in N. Bobbio, *L'età
dei diritti*, p. 37.
71 Bobbio, *Il terzo assente*, p. 95.
72 See, for instance, Beitz, *Political Theory and International Relations*; Bonanate, *Etica e politica internazionale*; Bonanate, *I doveri degli Stati*.
73 See T. H. Marshall, 'Citizenship and Social Class', in T. H. Marshall, *Class,
Citizenship, and Social Development*, Chicago: The University of Chicago
Press, 1964; R. J. Vincent, *Human Rights and International Relations*,
Cambridge: Cambridge University Press, 1986, pp. 2–3, 92–108; R. J.
Vincent, 'Grotius, Human Rights, and Intervention', in Bull, Kingsbury and
Roberts (eds), *Hugo Grotius and International Relations*, pp. 241–56.
74 A. Cassese, *I diritti umani nel mondo contemporaneo*, Rome–Bari: Laterza,
1988, Engl. trans., Cambridge: Polity Press, 1990, p. 159.
75 H. Bull, 'The Grotian Conception of International Society', in H. Butterfield

and M. Wight (eds), *Diplomatic Investigations*, London: Allen & Unwin, 1966, pp. 51–73; Bull, *The Anarchical Society*, pp. 26–7.

76 See R. A. Falk, *Human Rights and State Sovereignty*, New York: Holmes & Meier, 1981, particularly chapter 1. However, in recent works, such as *Explorations at the Edge of Time* and *On Humane Governance*, Falk appears more ambivalent about 'legal cosmopolitanism' and also more prudent about the positive effects of globalization.

77 D. Held, 'Democrazia e nuovo ordine internazionale', pp. 48–50.

78 See A. Cassese, *Umano-Disumano. Commissariati e prigioni nell'Europa di oggi*, Rome–Bari: Laterza, 1994.

79 Kelsen, *The Law of the United Nations*, p. 41; Cassese, *I diritti umani nel mondo contemporaneo*, Engl. trans., p. 44.

80 Kelsen, *The Law of the United Nations*, pp. 40–1. Kelsen points out that the Brazilian delegation 'saw no reason why a Declaration on Human Rights should be introduced by philosophical postulates taken from outdated theories of natural law' (ibid., p. 40, note 4). This opinion was also expressed by Benedetto Croce: compare B. Croce, 'I diritti dell'uomo e il momento storico presente', in M. Gandhi, E. H. Carr, et al., *Dei diritti dell'uomo*, ed. UNESCO, Milan: Comunità, 1952, pp. 133–5.

81 For a tentative catalogue, cf. Vincent, *Human Rights and International Relations*, pp. 11–12.

82 N. Bobbio, 'Sul fondamento dei diritti dell'uomo', in Bobbio, *L'età dei diritti*, pp. 12–14. See also my essay 'La strategia della cittadinanza', in D. Zolo (ed.), *La cittadinanza. Appartenenza, identità, diritti*, pp. 3–46; E. Santoro, 'Le antinomie della cittadinanza: libertà negativa, diritti sociali, autonomia individuale' (ibid., pp. 93–128); F. P. Vertova, 'Cittadinanza liberale, identità collettive, diritti sociali' (ibid., pp. 167–202).

83 Cassese, *I diritti umani nel mondo contemporaneo*, Engl. trans., pp. 35ff; A. D. Renteln, *International Human Rights: Universalism versus Relativism*, Newbury Park (Cal.): Sage Publications, 1990, pp. 30ff; H. Bull, 'Human Rights and World Politics', in R. Pettman (ed.), *Moral Claims in World Affairs*, London: Croom Helm, 1978, p. 81; J. Galtung, *Human Rights in Another Key*, Cambridge: Polity Press, 1994, pp. 1–25.

84 Bull, 'Human Rights and World Politics', pp. 83–4.

85 Vincent, *Human Rights and International Relations*, pp. 13–16, 48ff; Renteln, *International Human Rights*, pp. 61ff; J Donnelly, *Universal Human Rights in Theory and Practice*, Ithaca (NY): Cornell University Press, 1989, pp. 109–24.

86 See B. Tibi, *The Crisis of Modern Islam: A Preindustrial Culture in the Scientific-Technological Age*, Salt Lake City: University of Utah Press, 1988.

87 Chung-Shu Lo, 'Les droits de l'homme dans la tradition chinoise', in M. Gandhi, E. H. Carr et al., *Autour de la nouvelle déclaration universelle des droits de l'homme*, ed. UNESCO, 1951.

88 Vincent, *Human Rights and International Relations*, pp. 39–44; H. Bull, 'The Revolt Against the West', in H. Bull and A. Watson (eds), *The Expansion of International Society*, Oxford: Clarendon Press, 1984, pp. 217–28; H. Bull, *The Concept of Justice in International Relations*, The Hagey Lectures, Waterloo (Ont.): University of Waterloo, 1984.

89 See S. Latouche, *L'occidentalisation du monde. Essai sur la signification, la portée et les limites de l'uniformisation planétaire*, Paris: Editions La Découverte, 1989.

5 Towards a 'Weak Pacifism'

You can starve to death beside a computer.

S. Latouche, *L'occidentalisation du monde*

If the political image of Modernity was Leviathan, the standing of national powers and superpowers will, for the future, be captured in the picture of Lemuel Gulliver, waking from an unthinking sleep, to find himself tethered by innumerable tiny bonds.

S. Toulmin, *Cosmopolis*

Three Final Theses

I can now take up more directly the thread of the argument that I began in the first chapter, and attempt to sketch an answer to the questions raised at the end of both the first and the second chapters. I posed the question of whether in general there might not be something profoundly wrong in the projects for 'stable and universal' peace which the highest international institutions have attempted to realize over the last two centuries. I advanced the hypothesis that the main reason for the repeated failures of institutional pacifism could lie in the latter's universalist and centralist option: in the claim, shared by cosmopolitan pacifism, that stable peace can be guaranteed by a universal government constituted according to the model of the Holy Alliance and applying the framework of the domestic analogy. I likewise drew attention to the poverty of this theory of peacemaking, which, apart from an elementary analogical reference to the formation of the modern European state, did not seem to be supported by an analysis of the dynamics of international conflict, nor by a broader philosophical-political analysis. Finally, I expressed a radical doubt, wondering whether the search for a stable and universal peace is not an unjustifiable aspiration, since

aggression and war are so deeply rooted in the biological nature of
homo sapiens – and are in any case so ever-present in human evolutionary history – as to be necessarily considered thoroughly natural and
even functional.

The answers which I believe I am now in a position to give to these
questions are the following.

First, contemporary cosmopolitan pacifism emphasizes and interprets
in a distorted manner, on the lines of the domestic analogy, the
processes of globalization taking place in the various sectors of international life, presenting them in a 'Lockian' sense as a tendency towards
a superseding of the 'states system' and the formation of an increasingly
homogeneous 'global civil society'.

Second, cosmopolitan pacifism underestimates the influence of econ-
omic-financial factors in the dynamics of international conflict and is
unaware that the increasing differentiation of the rhythms of 'human
development' is paradoxically favoured by the processes of globalization
of the international economy to which the highest international economic institutions contribute.

Third, from the point of view of a realist theory of peacemaking –
that is, a non-moralistic theory which is not, in Kelsenian fashion,
idealistically normative – aggression and reconciliation (together with
conflict and pacification) are evolutionary constants of the human
species that rule out the cosmopolitan project for a stable and universal
peace.

In the following paragraphs I shall present arguments in support of
these three theses and conclude with the proposal of a 'weak pacifism'.

A Global 'Civil Society'?

For some cosmopolitan theorists of law and politics – in particular
Richard Falk and David Held – the application of the 'domestic analogy'
has gone as far as proposing the use at international level of a classical
category of the European theoretical-political syntax: that of 'civil
society'. Ralf Dahrendorf has recently also made use of the term 'global
civil society' as part of actual proposals, and indeed this expression now
also appears in official documents of the United Nations.[1] This notion
is meant to refer to the complex of activities, movements and associations of a voluntary character which especially during the 1980s has
developed on an international scale, often as an explicit alternative to
official institutions. More generally, reference is made to the awareness,
claimed to be widespread in world opinion, of the global character and
the interdependence of the problems that today crowd the international

agenda. The most common reference is to the so-called 'non-govern-mental organizations' (NGOs), such as Amnesty International, Méde-cins sans Frontières or Greenpeace, whose lively activism is inspired by globalist ideologies of a humanitarian or ecological kind.[2] It is the growth of these ideologies, together with the objective processes of the globalization of politics, economics, finance and communications, that in the judgement of Falk and Held will gradually point the way towards planetary social integration and thereby constitute the premise for the construction of a world constitutional state and a transnational democ-racy capable of promoting peace, guaranteeing rights and protecting the environment.

The notion of 'civil society' commonly – from Ferguson to Locke and Marx – denotes the sphere within which, in some countries of northern Europe, family and professional life, bourgeois culture and the market economy developed 'autonomously' in the course of the industrial revolution.[3] 'Civil society' acted as the focal point from which the demand for individual liberties and economic liberties (entrepreneurial and commercial) emerged against the formalized power of the 'political state' – in particular of the modern absolute state. To use the vocabulary of Thomas Marshall, one can state that civil society is the social and economic sphere from which arose the social energies that set the values and institutions of modern citizenship against the 'old regime'. Thus on the one hand, in this historical framework, the 'rights of citizenship' were defined as prerogatives of the status of member *pleno jure* of the political community: a status which included, first, civil rights and then, gradually, political rights. On the other hand, definitions were also given of the pre-legal conditions of membership of the political community, that is, of the unified, nation state. In such conditions, citizens in the full sense were required to be native, adult, property-owning males and therefore members of the national bourgeoisie of the given state.

It was precisely the cultural and economic hegemony of the national bourgeoisie in these countries that guaranteed conditions of social homogeneity and political loyalty within the northern European geo-political sphere. This in turn set the stage for the realization of the project of unification and political centralization, which was eventually to give birth to the liberal state in which the rule of law obtains.[4] It was a momentous project indeed, which succeeded in gaining credence despite the functional tensions among different citizens belonging to the same national group: for there was inevitably friction between the consumerist logic of the market economy, incorporated in civil rights, and the largely egalitarian logic of political rights and, somewhat later, of social rights.[5] For more than a hundred years this tension was to express itself in the conflict between bourgeoisie and proletariat, but at no time was the substantial cultural and economic homogeneity of European political systems seriously undermined. Nor, except for the ephemeral adventure of the Commune of Paris, were the bonds of political loyalty of all the social forces towards the nation state broken. Social integration was guaranteed on the one hand by the trade union movement and the social democratic parties, and on the other hand by the acceptance, even by the most intransigent of political oppositions, of the framework of 'progressive' values championed by the bourgeois Enlightenment and industrialism. From this point of view even the 'Marxist heresy', at least in its western versions, also falls within the frame of this substantial geopolitical orthodoxy.

Is it possible, following this historical-theoretical account, to take up the notion of 'civil society' as an interpretative category of the dynamics of social integration on a planetary level and, on this basis, to propose a Lockian version – in place of the elementarily Hobbesian version that capitalizes on 'international anarchy' – of the 'domestic analogy'? Can it be said that we are facing a worldwide process of cultural homogenization and economic integration, one that is opening up the prospect of a new 'project' of unification and political centralization – this time, however, not contained within the confines of a handful of European territorial states, but extended to all cultures and all the economies of the planet? If this is so, then let us be clear that it would have to be a 'Lockian' project of 'contractualist' unification of the global political system, and not an attempt at imperial or in some sense hegemonic unification.

In my opinion this version of the 'domestic analogy' proves, no less than the previous ones, to be fallacious and misguided. Even granting the legitimacy of its analogical reference to the process of formation of European states, contractualist cosmopolitanism can be refuted by demonstrating that the political unification of the planet under the aegis of a 'constitutional Leviathan' would require at least the following three general conditions.

First, pronounced delegitimation of existing political entities – that is, essentially, of nation states, with the sole important regional variant of the European Union – and a corresponding legitimation of the present international institutions, to be acknowledged throughout all continents as a genuine expression of 'global civil society'.

Second, a strongly felt tendency to cultural homogenization of the planet thanks to widespread processes of 'ecumenical' integration between lifestyles, cultural traditions, political ideologies and religious beliefs. In other words, a true 'world society' would have to be realized, compactly united by interests and common values.

Third, a significant attenuation of distributive conflicts by virtue of the further development of the global processes which are helping to reduce the gap that today separates the industrially advanced countries, western and Asian, from the countries whose backwardness is expressed not only in terms of 'gross domestic product' but also, above all, of 'human development'.[6]

I do not intend to analyse the first point further, since it has already been dealt with at several points in previous chapters. I would simply point out that the delegitimation of nation states by subnational social and political entities – a phenomenon certainly occurring on a world level – cannot be interpreted as a thrust towards a 'global civil society'. Admittedly, it is often a question of a demand for autonomy in opposition to the official power structures, in a manner not altogether dissimilar to the demand for individual liberties against the structures of the 'old regime' that lay at the origin of the development of the rule of law in European states. Nevertheless, as we have seen, individual liberties are one thing, collective liberties quite another, and indeed in many cases there exists an antagonistic relationship between the two types of liberty. In addition, ethnic-national claims multiply the complexity and turbulence of the international arena, making the global political system less governable and less easily unifiable into a pattern that can avoid merely reproducing, so to speak, the model of the Holy Roman Empire. Finally, a tendency can be observed for some states to integrate themselves into wider regional units, of which far the most significant case is that of the European Union, followed, at a distance for the moment, by NAFTA, while the Organization for African Unity and the Organization of American States possess little importance. Yet such developments offer little confirmation of the cosmopolitan hypothesis. As Hedley Bull has observed, even if the present European states were to give up their sovereignty in order to create a single European state of subcontinental dimensions, the final result would be a considerable reinforcement of European particularism, a far cry indeed from an impetus towards a cosmopolitan transcending of the international interests and ambitions of Europe.[7]

As for the general thesis of the 'extinction of states' – almost a new avatar of the unfortunate Marxist doctrine of the withering of the state and law – I believe that this must be decisively opposed. As Bull has vigorously asserted, the future of the international order does not depend on the replacement of the system of states. It depends, rather, on their capacity for 'governance', or, in other words, on their propensity to strengthen the 'co-operative' dimension of 'anarchy' in the direction, it may be said, of a virtuous self-replacement of sovereignty. But in any case the extinction of states and the (hypothetical) creation of a sovereign state and a legal order of planetary dimensions cannot be expected to lead, *tout court*, to an epiphany of law, democracy and peace. It is therefore in my opinion misguided to assume that the division of the world into sovereign states – that is, the pluralistic fragmentation of sovereignty – is the main source of disorder or even, as has actually been stated, the 'cause' of international conflict.'[8] If the 'domestic analogy' has any validity at all, then there are good reasons for advancing quite the opposite hypothesis, namely, that in certain conditions of co-operation and general equilibrium, the spreading and localization of power could perform a 'guaranteeing' function at an international level just as 'polyarchy' does within states.

As for the radical federalist thesis, I believe that it has been overemphasized. Even within the framework of a broad morphological pluralism of international agents, national states will retain important functions for a long time to come. Regional aggregations will not succeed in absorbing all such functions, contrary to inflated claims made by federalist advocates of integral European unification, or to the intriguing proposals for world federalism drafted thirty years ago by the Indian Rajini Kothari.'[9] In all cases where the political form of the modern state achieves an optimal relationship between geopolitical extension and civil loyalty, it is by this very accomplishment already performing a valuable function, and may even keep in check some of the worst excesses of ethnocentric nationalism. This is likely to be all the more true when the state in question is one in which the rule of law obtains, and is therefore committed to the protection of the fundamental rights of citizens and foreigners. Furthermore, the state also performs an important protective function inasmuch as it safeguards the collective identity of weak countries, those most exposed to the pressures of an alienating globalization.[10] And if it is true that states may very often be identified as bearing prime responsibility for violations of the fundamental rights of citizens, then this should probably in itself be the starting point for the 'struggle for law', without setting off into ideological blind alleys or wildly unrealistic ventures.[11]

This by no means, however, entails an underestimation of the democratic potentialities of federalism. Disregarding the empty rhetoric of globalization and 'cosmopolitan citizenship', the theory of democratic federalism deserves to be profoundly rethought as a scheme for relocating political responsibilities and functions from the periphery to the centre and from the centre to the periphery. But it should be a scheme that does not take for granted the superseding of the nation state and does not underestimate the cohesive force of the ethnic and national roots of social groups, seeking instead, patiently and painstakingly, to distinguish the system of liberties and safeguards of fundamental rights from the prepolitical particularisms of group membership and collective identity.[12] Such an approach would be in harmony with the highest liberal tradition.

The Westernization of the Planet

Two themes that are closely linked to the theoretical hypothesis of the 'global civil society' require more detailed discussion. First and foremost, there is a need to analyse the very notion of 'globalization' – together with the closely associated notion of 'global interdependence' – and to free it, as much as possible, from its semantic ambiguities and from the rhetorical emphasis which, taken to extremes, goes as far as equating it with expectations of an imminent moral and spiritual unification of the entire human race.[13] In the second place – and I will deal with this next – it is a matter of understanding whether the 'human development' that can reasonably be predicted to occur over the next few decades will confirm or contradict the hypothesis of Lockian cosmopolitanism.

There can be no doubt that today, in all continents, perception of the interdependence that links the destinies of individuals and peoples has grown considerably. It is equally certain that this awareness is closely correlated with a genuinely ongoing phenomenon of globalization such as can be observed in important sectors of politics, economy, finance and mass communications.[14] The impressive development of transnational corporations, now present and well established in many countries once belonging to the Third World, is the most striking indicator of this impelling force of international economic integration.[15] It is a phenomenon which goes hand in hand with the relentless development of technological research and its industrial applications, above all in the areas of new materials, electronics, telecommunications and artificial intelligence. It is also closely connected with the process of modernization and secularization which, despite greatly differing intensities – Iran is not Singapore, Nepal is not Taiwan – has affected practically all cultures of the globe. Both of these tendencies have their foundation in the West and are components of a cultural drift of vast dimensions: the westernization of the world. With this relentless drift coincides what in the West is normally called globalization and global interdependence.

Can this process of the homologation of existential models, styles of thought and production practices be interpreted as a trend towards a cultural integration of world society that is truly a prelude to the formation of a 'global civil society'? Will it usher in an era of 'world constitutionalism' and of 'transnational democracy'? This is a crucial question. The answer furnished by the advocates of cosmopolitanism obviously cannot be other than affirmative: this cultural trend exists and should be supported by measures to encourage institutional centralization on a political and economic level. Other western authors, including globalization sociologists, are more cautious: Featherstone and Turner, for instance, see the compression of the world as producing frames of cultural reference which can hardly be called 'global culture'.[16] What is happening on a world scale is rather a process of 'creolization', that is, the adoption by a large number of 'indigenous populations' of a foreign, i.e. technical-scientific-industrial, culture which does not result in order and communitarian integration but on the contrary produces contamination, resistance and disorder. Or alternatively, another manifestation of the same underlying phenomenon is the emergence of 'third cultures', deterritorialized and linked to the accelerated pace of international exchange, tourism and consumerism, developed by those who, in the west, are cosmopolitan for professional reasons. This, however, reflects a phenomenon that is sociologically very limited and devoid of universality. In short, globalization does not, despite the overconfident claims advanced by the theorists of modernization and convergence, produce a cultural homogenization of the world: quite the opposite, for it arouses particularistic reactions that assert the identity of cultural codes rooted in nations and ethnic groups.[17]

Finally, other authors, who include Hedley Bull, Serge Latouche and Pier Paolo Portinaro, are even more critical. Bull has contended that 'global interdependence' is somewhat ambiguous jargon used to rationalize relationships of international dependence:

> some transnational relationships are of global importance, but their effect is to promote not the integration of world society as a whole, but rather the integration of a dominant culture. It is familiar that the effect of the multinational corporations, the great foundations and the scientific and professional associations, whose centers lie in the advanced capitalist countries, and especially in the United States, is to promote a kind of integration that links together the societies of those advanced countries and elite groups within the poor countries, but whose effect is also to widen the social and cultural distance between advanced societies and poor societies, and between modernised elite groups and the ordinary people within the latter.[18]

Latouche, for his part, has stated in his essay on the significance, range and limits of the *uniformisation planétaire*[19] that the cultural globalization induced by the communicative and economic hegemony of the West produces no integration of world society. On the contrary, it brings about a deculturation and uprooting of peoples and social groups who are unable to withstand its onslaughts. Countries like Singapore, Taiwan, Hong Kong, South Korea – the four Asian 'tigers' of accelerated industrial growth – are exemplary from this point of view, despite their sensational economic and financial success. Throughout the world, in the wake of market penetration into every corner of the inhabited earth, the West operates like a 'technical-scientific megamachine', which, although originally starting out as the product of a specific historical civilization, can now no longer be seen as the product of one geopolitical area. It is an impersonal machine which at all latitudes, and not only in the Third World, is wrenching populations from their homelands, disrupting their social bonds and hurling them – emigrants all of them, whether within the confines of their own country or in foreign lands – into the wasteland of metropolitan urbanization.[20]

The elites that live under the protective umbrella of the world market are matched by the growing army of dispossessed masses, men and women now deprived of a social context and cultural identity who migrate in search of asylum, besieging the wealthier countries. The inexorably advancing western machine crushes and disperses their roots, but does not integrate them, except in an utterly marginal fashion, into the process of industrialization, technicization and bureaucratization which it promotes universally.[21] This machine achieves an increase in functional differentiation in terms of the growing international division of labour and increase of technical-scientific specialization, but it does so without constructing an authentic cultural universalism, a core of shared values to generate a new form of popular imagination in place of the social particularisms which it dissolves. Given these effects of 'deculturation', 'deterritorialization' and 'planetary uprooting', Latouche argues for no less a verdict than a full-scale failure of the project of western 'modernization', the demise of its Promethean universalism.[22] Once the failure of this project is conceded – and it should be noted that the collapse of Eastern bloc socialism also belongs to this scenario – then the world appears as the *planète des naufragés*. No longer do there exist First, Second and Third Worlds but only 'Fourth Worlds' which include in their number the marginalized underclass of the rich countries, the native minorities and the poor countries.[23] The only remaining hope of these lies in an ability to escape from the mortal embrace of western globalization, in resistance to unification of the planet, including the unification appearing under the artful guise of the 'world civil society' and 'transnational democracy'.

Finally, in the opinion of Portinaro, the phenomena of globalization and interdependence induced by the hegemony of western culture and economy fail, through the evident asynchrony of development and heterogeneous interests and values, to put an end to friend–enemy juxtapositions or to the national and international tensions produced by the inequality of power. In the face of the explosion of ethnic-national particularisms which make non-negotiable demands in so far as they are anchored to the code of collective membership and identities, the liberal utopia more than ever lays bare its limitations and normative emphasis. For not only does the global market not operate as a vehicle for the neutralization of conflicts and the procedural reduction of politics, but the process of globalization of the economy and westernization of the world risks driving the world to ecological collapse. Yet again, modernization is revealed as something quite other than the progressive and universalist project it claims to be.[24]

One may not share, or one may share only in part, the pessimism of this analysis. For the complex, multifaceted reality of non-governmental international associationism may be credited with a degree of political potential – though certainly not a current political relevance – which will justify some moderate expectation of the spread of an internationalist, pacifist culture resistant to western hegemony. Furthermore, one can point to the fact that today a feature long seen as among the most elementary and biologically anchored reasons for conflict between states – territorial controversies – seems to have become largely obsolete. However, in my opinion, the profoundly ambiguous character of the processes of globalization remains unquestionable and, *rebus sic stantibus*, so does their total unsuitability to stand as the foundation of cosmopolitan pacifism and transnational democracy. What western cosmopolitans call 'global civil society' in fact goes no further than a network of connections and functional interdependencies which has developed within certain important sectors of the 'global market', above all finance, technology, automation, manufacturing industry and the service sector. Nor, moreover, does it go much beyond the optimistic expectation of affluent westerners to be able to feel and be universally recognized as citizens of the world – citizens of a welcoming, peaceful, ordered and democratic 'global village' – without for a moment or in any way ceasing to be 'themselves', i.e. western citizens.

The rhetoric of civil globalization and of a rising 'cosmopolitan citizenship' underestimates one of the most characteristic and most serious consequences of the way in which westernization is cultural homogenization without integration: namely, the antagonism between the esteemed citizenships of the West and the countless masses belonging to regional and subcontinental areas without development and with a high rate of demographic growth. This antagonism assumes the form of a mass migration of individuals often possessing a good level of knowledge and practical skills, but economically and politically very weak. Indeed they are tantamount to agents without citizenship and without birthrights, who, thanks to their capillary infiltration into the interstices of western societies, exercise an irresistible pressure for equality. Far from expressing the maturing of a sense of cosmopolitan belonging, the response of countries threatened by this 'universalist' pressure – in terms both of the rejection or violent expulsion of immigrants, and of the effective negation of their status as civil subjects – is fast becoming one of the most grievous chapters of the civil and political history of western countries. And all signs point to a worsening of the situation over the coming decades.

It is the Marshallian notion of citizenship itself that is being challenged at its very roots, in that growing numbers of subjects not belonging to the western indigenous majorities are clamouring to become citizens *pleno jure* of the countries where they live and work. This represents a radical challenge in that the very relationship between 'citizen' and 'foreigner' is distorted by the scale of migrations and their uncontrollability and irreversibility. It is also an explosive challenge because it tends to disrupt not only the elements of the 'prepolitical' constitution of citizenship, but also the sociological processes of the formation of collective identities and, in addition, the structures which provide the foundation for the rule of law. It is to these structures that the pressing demand is addressed for 'multi-ethnic' recognition, not only of the individual rights of immigrant citizens, but even of the ethnic identities of minorities characterized by a considerable cultural distance from their host societies.[25]

We should therefore distinguish very clearly between the holistic character of some of the dramatic problems that currently assail the political agenda of international institutions – the containment of armed conflict, preservation of the fundamental rights of citizens and foreigners, protection of the environment, demographic equilibrium – and the thesis which argues that such problems are solvable only 'globally', that is, by resorting to a supranational authority or at least by gradually laying the groundwork for its advent. For the first point refers to issues which it would be unrealistic to contest, but the second is by contrast an erroneous inference. To say that 'global' problems require an intense activity of co-ordination and co-operation between the many national, transnational and international agents involved – in other words, that they require the formation of 'international regimes' – is quite different from belief in the thaumaturgic effects of a cosmopolitan implosion of international power such as would lead to a drastic reduction in the complexity of the world 'political environment'.

Globalization, Economic Development and 'Human Development'

One assumption implicit in cosmopolitan pacifism and 'global constitutionalism' is that the processes of globalization of the international economy tend to reduce the gap between the economies of the rich countries – that is, of a restricted number of great and medium industrial powers, to which have recently been added the so-called NICs (Newly Industrializing Countries) – and the economies of the poor countries, which form the vast majority. This assumption is necessary because there is, as we shall see, a close correlation, if not a deterministic relationship, between economic development and 'human development', and it is unthinkable that a 'global civil society' will be formed as long as a billion individuals remain below a minimum level of literacy.[26] It is likewise a necessary assumption because neither peace nor the advent of a 'transnational democracy' is conceivable without a reduction in the conflictuality which originates from an overall asymmetry in development. A political power strongly concentrated in supranational institutions, and acting against a background of growing economic and social disparities and of a corresponding increase in conflictuality, could not but assume the distinguishing characteristics of a violently repressive and antidemocratic planetary Leviathan.

A very summary overview of data produced by official institutions shows that the dynamics of unequal growth over the last thirty years and present economic disparities may be described on a world level in the following terms.

At the beginning of the 1960s the richest 20 per cent of the world population had a disposable income thirty times greater than the poorest 20 per cent. Today, after some three decades, the richest 20 per cent enjoys an income sixty times greater than the poorest section of the world population. This proportion however is calculated on the basis of a comparison between states. If distributive inequalities within each country are also taken into account – in Brazil, for example, the richest 20 per cent of the population receives about 70 per cent of the national income while less than 2 per cent goes to the poorest 20 per cent – then the global disparity increases still further: the richest 20 per cent of the total world population receives a share of wealth 150 times that of the poorest 20 per cent. In thirty years the distance between the poorer and the richer countries, calculated in terms of GNP – although analogous results are also obtained by measuring world trade shares, the quantity of savings and internal investments – has more than doubled.[27] Moreover, it is predicted that, if present rates of global development and present distributive relationships do not drastically change, by the year 2020 the gap between the richest quarter of the world population and the poorest quarter will be 300 per cent higher than at present.[28]

Data from 1991 show that more than a billion people – i.e., about a quarter of the world population – were living in conditions of 'absolute poverty' in the economically backward countries: about half in southern Asia, a third concentrated in sub-Saharan Africa (where in the period 1981–91 individual income decreased by 25 per cent) and a considerable part in Latin America.[29] Absolute poverty is widespread in agricultural areas, but is concentrated in particularly degrading forms in shanty towns fringing the great metropolitan agglomerations. Women and children are worse affected than adult males. The World Health Organization estimates that more than ten million children die every year of malnutrition or of illnesses derived from maternal undernourishment, and that another ten million children under the age of five are at risk of death from starvation. It is also calculated that seven hundred million adults are seriously undernourished. Yet this by no means arises from global scarcity of food resources, since food production, despite the widespread Malthusian predictions that are sometimes applied instrumentally, has increased considerably over the few last decades and at a significantly higher rate than demographic growth.[30]

The connection, as has already been mentioned, between economic development and 'human development' is very close, even though it is still true that for a given GNP levels of 'human development' can vary considerably from country to country, measured according to indices such as average life expectancy, levels of primary education, availability of material resources for an acceptable quality of life and the enjoyment of fundamental rights, in particular of political liberties. Thus a comparison between a country like Sri Lanka on the one hand, and Brazil and Saudi Arabia on the other, seems to offer a convincing confirmation of the non-mechanical character of the link between economic development and quality of life: the former country, though notably poorer, enjoys much higher levels of life expectancy and literacy than the other two.[31] Obviously, much depends on the distributive policies within each country and on the way in which available resources are used. These in turn are conditioned by the structures of internal power: the more the political constitution of a country is, in a broad sense, democratic, the more it will be found that 'human development' follows close on the heels of economic development. This holds true in general despite the apparent counter-examples of certain rich and democratic countries – notoriously the United States itself – in which there exists a large underclass of citizens living in conditions of absolute poverty and the gap between affluence and destitution is very wide. It can however be stated with certainty that medium to low levels of GNP are correlated without exception to medium to low levels of 'human development' and, with the sole paradoxical exception of India, to non-democratic political systems.[32]

These data and these general observations are largely beyond dispute and already represent a form of objective confutation of the idea of an emerging 'global civil society' and of the appearance of as yet unknown opportunities for a cosmopolitan democratization of the planet. More controversial, but all the more significant for our purposes, are the theoretical interpretations of 'unbalanced development' and the ensuing attempts to propose suitable economic policies and to identify the national and international agents who, it is hoped, will prove capable of reversing the ever-widening gap between strong and weak economies.

Orthodox Marxist interpretations, based on a class concept of history and on a 'materialist' critique of the capitalist economy and its imperialist developments, now enjoy only very limited credit.[33] But heavy criticism has also been levelled at other neo-imperialist and neocolonialist – generically neo-Marxist – versions, such as the 'dependency theory' elaborated by, among others, André Gunder Frank, and the 'world system' theory of Immanuel Wallerstein.[34] What is disputed in particular in these theories is the thesis of a causal connection between the wealth of the industrialized countries and the poverty of the industrially backward countries, as if the former had grown rich 'at the expense of the latter' and not thanks to any independent productive superiority of their own. Against what they consider a generic Third World ideology, many authors are proclaiming the 'end of the Third World': the gap between the rich countries and the poor countries, it is suggested, does not depend on international exploitation or on the structural iniquity of the 'terms of trade'. Rather, these arguments claim, it depends on the differing degree of productivity of the national economic systems, and therefore on the levels of culture, technical qualification, administrative competence and spirit of initiative characterizing different countries.[35]

With this established, it is then maintained that the only significant theoretical prospect of any significance remains the classical liberal approach of opening up the markets, and hence a globalization of all the factors of economic development. In the long term a solution to the gap between the rich and poor countries can be found, it is claimed, within the global framework of a competitive economy: an economy freed from the residues of traditional mercantilism and protectionism and from the new practices of economic nationalism.[36] As Robert Gilpin typically maintains, the less developed countries have a high degree of dependence and continue to be vulnerable precisely because they are underdeveloped rather than vice versa. They are weak in a world of the strong. The lack of an effective and appropriate development strategy to overcome this situation is most important in holding them back. Their foremost problem is not external dependence but internal efficiency. Those less developed countries that have created efficient domestic economies on their own initiative are the ones that have succeeded in achieving rapid rates of economic growth. [...] The Third World no longer exists as a meaningful single entity.[37]

There is obviously some truth in these criticisms. The Third World no longer exists – just as the vertical geopolitical contraposition between North and South no longer exists – at least in the sense that within the vast area of underdevelopment significant phenomena of differentiation have occurred. Proof of this is seen in the economic successes achieved by the NICs, that is, by countries, mostly relatively small and situated in the East, that have achieved miniature reproductions first of the Japanese and then of the Hong Kong and Singapore paradigms. More generally, it is undeniable that the whole panorama which for some decades now has gone under the blanket term of the Third World is undergoing rapid transformation, and it is hardly rash to predict that in the next few decades profound upheavals in the gradation and classification of economic powers will be witnessed. This is likely to be brought about primarily by the importation of manufacturing activities from the West, whose exclusive preserve they were until just a few decades ago, into once uniformly underdeveloped areas.[38] In the span of another few decades countries like China and India could exploit their 'comparative advantages' so intensely as to catch up with or even overtake the present major economic powers and recover the position of absolute pre-eminence in world manufacturing markets that they held two and a half centuries ago.

Yet cosmopolitan optimism not only draws no comfort from the 'end of the Third World', but in many respects the differentiation of the rate of economic development among the poor countries seems destined to multiply the disparities, increase competition and, potentially, to unleash new conflicts. It does not, in any case, appear to be the harbinger of unification and progressive homogenization of world society: in short, globalization of production factors can in no way be equated with the socio-economic integration of the planet. It is no coincidence that the newly industrialized countries have already been accused of adopting predatory economic policies towards countries they have rapidly overtaken on the road to development: policies that are alleged to be no less detrimental than the ones classically adopted by western countries.[39] The highest price of even more differentiated and fragmented development falls, and will for a long time continue to fall, on the poorest of the poor countries, representing a sizeable majority of the population of the world living in southern Asia, most of Africa, the more backward countries of Latin America and probably also countries like Brazil and Mexico, which more optimistic observers today consider the potential American NICs.

More generally – and decisively – the economic policies of the industrial nations to a large extent coincide with the strategies of the most powerful transnational corporations, and are only apparently inspired by the great liberal principles of the opening-up and global extension of markets. Thus, despite their profession of faith in liberal principles, the major industrial powers practise complex strategies which, as Robert Gilpin has written, combine mercantilistic competition between states, economic regionalism (EU, NAFTA, APEC and other regional conglomerations currently forming in the Pacific basin, etc.) and sectorial protectionism.[40] Globalistic economic policies, sometimes verging on 'forced internationalization' of the weaker economies, coexist with practices that are characteristic of economic nationalism. The opening-up of markets is greatest in sectors where global competition is all to the advantage of the strongest: typical examples of this are the financial market and 'high tech' manufacturing. For if globality is the condition for development of the financial market, and if 'global manufacturing' can establish itself in the North, in the South or the East with the techniques of the 'global goods chain' illustrated by Gary Gareffi, then, it is maintained, nation states have exhausted all possible functions and nothing short of an economic war must be waged against them.[41]

By contrast, in the labour-intensive manufacturing sector or in that of exported unskilled labour the 'new protectionism' reigns supreme and discriminates against weaker countries, in particular the more backward areas of sub-Saharan Africa and southern Asia. Discrimination assumes the traditional form of customs tariffs, in particular on goods from countries which export partially processed raw materials; but to a much wider and constantly increasing extent it also takes on the form of 'non-tariff' barriers that make it possible to circumvent the principles of non-discrimination and multilaterality which are the foundation of the international trade regime set up by GATT (now in the form of the World Trade Organization).[42] Of the twenty-four OECD countries – the most industrialized ones in the world – at least twenty are today clearly more protectionist than they were a decade ago and about 30 per cent of their imports from the non-industrialized countries are affected by non-tariff barriers. At the beginning of the 1990s only 7 per cent of world trade respected the liberal rules of GATT: sectors such as agriculture, tropical products, textiles, services, intellectual property and investments evaded the rules of the 'global market', thereby causing an annual loss of about one hundred billion dollars to be borne by the economically weaker countries. Altogether commercial restrictions and contractual disparity annually cost the non-industrialized countries about 20 per cent of their GNP and more than six times the amount they invest in the 'human development' of their populations.[43]

Total subordination to these general tendencies of the world economy has been the hallmark of the way in which the highest-ranking international economic institutions – in particular the World Bank and the International Monetary Fund – have operated over recent decades. At best, the most charitable verdict is that their centralist and globalist interference in the dynamics of development of the international economy has been either irrelevant or totally favourable to the major industrial powers, which, after all, control them from every point of view, since the majority shares of capital lie in their hands. Indeed, so estranged have both the World Bank and the International Monetary Fund become from the functions formally attributed to them at Bretton Woods in 1944 that over the last decade they have actually despoiled the poorer countries – who imprudently ran up large debts before the collapse during the 1980s of the international prices of their 'cash crops' – of massive quantities of financial resources, which ended up in the coffers of the rich countries. In evidence of this, it need only be noted that the international level of the prices of raw materials obviously does not depend on natural events or on an impartial 'hidden hand': rather, it is to a large extent conditioned by the economic and monetary policies (and military policies as well) adopted by the industrial countries, together with the market choices of the most powerful corporations. It is therefore no exaggeration to speak of a full-scale 'extortion racket on an international scale'. As is known, the real interest rate paid by poor countries to service their foreign debts is equivalent to the nominal rate of interest in relation to the dollar exchange rate of the price of their exports. Following the collapse of these prices, the more backward countries paid during the 1980s an average rate of real interest amounting to 17 per cent on loans granted through the international monetary institutions of the rich countries, while the latter were normally paying a 4 per cent interest rate.[44]

Nor is this the full extent of the matter: the International Monetary Fund, in particular, exerted – and is still exerting – control and pressure over the domestic economies of the seventy most severely indebted countries, through the so-called 'structural adjustment programs'.[45] By setting up what amounts to a sort of parallel government influencing the economies of these countries, the Fund effectively obliges them to adopt economic policies whereby they indiscriminately open up their economies to the world market. Such a phenomenon is undeniably disadvantageous for their weak economies, and at the same time it also forces them into a drastic reduction of investment in the 'human development' of their populations, and induces them to adopt specious projects of demographic containment.

Added to this is the notorious failure in international aid, for which the ruling classes of the aid-receiving countries are themselves partly responsible, aggravated by the perverse effects of inadequately co-ordinated agricultural and infrastructural projects and food relief.[46] Against this background, it is hard to resist the conclusion proposed by Paul Ekins and seconded by, amongst others, Anthony Giddens: any assumption of positive and lasting effects on the 'human development' of the poorer countries springing from the aid measures enacted by the international bureaucracies must be scrapped. Apart from cases of extreme urgency where food aid and medical relief must be delivered immediately, it would be more appropriate to favour 'bottom-up' development, i.e. development based on small-scale projects using unsophisticated technology and making the most of local resources including, first and foremost, human resources.[47]

On these premises, there is certainly good reason for adopting a stance firmly opposed to any attempt to reinforce presently existing international financial institutions, or to set up a 'Global Central Bank' under the auspices of the United Nations, still less to supplement what is at present the Security Council of the United Nations with a 'Development Security Council' endowed with wide-ranging powers of intervention in the world economy. Equally unacceptable is the suggestion of drawing up a new 'world social charter' entrusting the United Nations with the role of 'principal custodian of global human security'.[48] The prospect of broadening and reinforcing the protective umbrella of the United Nations so that it comes to embrace the entire world economy, to the point of creating a sort of planetary welfare state – a welfare state with much more of a Bismarckian flavour to it than a genuinely social-democratic slant – would amount to the most short-sighted and misleading application of the 'domestic analogy'.

The conclusions to be drawn from this rapid overview of the dynamics of the international political economy are, I think, self-evident: the process of globalization of the international economy does not go hand-in-hand with any discernible process of planetary social integration, nor does it automatically bring with it any reduction in the immense distance separating the poor countries from the rich countries in the contemporary world. On the contrary, this distance is probably destined to increase over the next few decades rather than to melt away, despite the 'end of the Third World', and in fact partly as a consequence of that ending.

There may be some truth in the suggestion of the economist Jan Timbergen that it will take at least five centuries before the yawning gap separating the poor countries from the rich ones can be bridged, although it is not clear exactly how reliable econometric projections of this magnitude are likely to be.[49] Possibly – and so it may be hoped, for the sake of future generations – change will proceed much faster. But in any case, reduction of the currently existing gap will not depend on the globalization of the international economy, given that, as already seen, this process does not in itself favour either economic development or 'human development' in the poor countries. Likewise, it will certainly not depend on the social security benefits and hand-outs of a planetary welfare state: development, no differently from democracy and peace, cannot be 'exported'. Rather, development is much more likely to rest on structural changes deriving from technical-scientific innovation and from long-term processes of evolutionary adaptation, which cannot yet be foreseen. Moreover, it will also depend on the degree of aggressiveness of the poorer countries, on their capacity to resist the steam-roller effect of the westernization of the world, their perseverance in seeking their own economic solutions without letting themselves be deluged by the technocratic paradigm, and their ability to produce new types of international equilibrium through competition and conflict. Even such features as their pride, their sense of independence or their dignity may well play a significant role. Last but not least, much will also depend on the wars, and civil wars, which will undoubtedly break out over the next few decades.

Aggression and Peacemaking Rituals

Criticism has already been expressed in chapter 3 of the idea that stable and universal peace is an objective that can be exclusively or primarily pursued by legal and institutional means. Such a concept, as I mentioned earlier, fails to consider the influence of economic factors on conditions of war and peace. Nor is this all; for it also overlooks the deeper reasons that make war a form of 'sociological universal' within the experience of *homo sapiens*. By concentrating on the normative aspects of social engineering, legal-institutional pacifism ignores not only all questions of ethics and of individual morality but also the anthropological, sociological and psychological attributes of violence. Consequently, it offers a perspective which disregards the relation obtaining between three essential concepts of a non-trivial theory of peacemaking: 'war' as destructive and strategically planned group violence, 'conflict' as antagonistic interaction among social groups, and 'aggression' as an individual and collective predisposition to the use of violence.

In opposition to the normative idealism which tends to 'negate' war in institutional and legal terms, a realist theory of peacemaking should not restrict itself to maintaining that war cannot be eradicated by repressive supranational tools. A realist theory should instead take the argument much further: a suitable starting point would be the assumption that there exists a close-knit relationship between war and aggression (conceptually mediated through 'group conflict'), and that aggression has inbuilt biological roots not only in *homo sapiens* but in higher animals in general and in anthropomorphic primates in particular. Such a view would be in harmony with research on human ethology and the ethology of war, from Irenäus Eibl-Eibesfeldt to Frans de Waal.[50] But if this viewpoint is adopted, then even absolute ethical pacifism seems inevitably to lose ground, in that it is seen to set itself impossible goals and to commit itself to activities that are as generous and symbolically seductive as they are almost invariably ineffectual.

There can no longer be any doubt today that war is a phenomenon of 'intraspecies' group aggression, and consequently that it is the result of a strictly human evolutionary trend, which does not in itself rest on any overarching biological basis. In higher animals other than humans, destructive intraspecies conflict – i.e., war between groups belonging to the same species – is an extremely rare event.[51] It is for this reason that a relation has been suggested between war as destructive group aggression and 'cultural pseudospeciation', an exclusively human phenomenon. Human cultures differ from one another in language, mythology, religion, folklore, sexual and marriage customs, food traditions etc., and come into conflict with one another as if they were genuinely different species.[52] Once pseudospeciation has taken place, cultural groups find themselves occupying different 'niches', and thus begin to defend their collective identity against everything external to their group. They repel outsiders as if the latter were not members of the human species, and subsequently, having once 'dehumanized' the offending outsiders, they set about using out-and-out destructive weapons against their adversaries. In defending its own identity against external threat, a 'pseudospeciated' group can count on an individual predisposition to obedience and on extraordinarily heightened emotional resources, as has clearly been shown by research into collective psychology and human ethology.[53]

Konrad Lorenz has shown that aggression has become stabilized in this way over the course of evolution without any parallel development of behavioural mechanisms providing for the automatic inhibition of aggression, whereas such mechanisms are widespread in the animal world.[54] The biological imperatives, which ought to impose collaborative interaction between subjects belonging to the same species, have thereby been overlain by the filter of cultural norms authorizing the use of violence and killing.[55] Consequently, the concept that war is 'genetically programmed' in human nature is totally untenable. The hypothesis that it may be exclusively the outcome of phylogenetic adaptation – rather than being the result of learning and of cultural transmission – and consequently that war is associated with a destructive impulse humans are supposed to have inherited from higher animals has so far not been confirmed by any empirical theory. Nor is it to be maintained that during the course of the evolution of humankind a selection process has favoured aggressive behaviour as compared with other types of behaviour. Indeed this idea, which obtained considerable advancement from Konrad Lorenz's well-known thesis of the utility of aggressive behaviour for the purposes of the preservation of the species, has been severely criticized as an over-hasty extrapolation of empirical observations which, at best, may be valid for animals other than humans. It has been further and authoritatively confuted by the celebrated Seville Statement on Violence.[56]

The importance of the Seville Statement transcends the significance of its specific theses through the contribution it makes to discrediting the belief that the empirical research of biology and ethology offers support to a deterministic notion of 'human nature' as a basis of a metaphysical anthropology and a political philosophy, whether pessimistically or optimistically oriented. More specifically, a modern realist standpoint is not condemned to start from the biological-anthropological assumption of the irremediably egoistic, aggressive and violent nature of humankind – an assumption which, from Machiavelli to Morgenthau, has characterized classical political realism.

For the purposes of refuting the spiritualistic or rationalistic optimism which envisages the possibility of humankind's conversion from egoism to generosity and from violence to mildness, a far weaker anthropological hypothesis is amply sufficient. For this one need look no further than a notion of the evolutionary plasticity of *homo sapiens*: i.e., that interaction over many thousands of years with the environment has gradually moulded the fundamental impulses of this higher primate and transformed it into an essentially cultural animal, ever less constrained by biological determinism. The biological and anthropological characteristics present in humans at their current – and probably very primitive – stage of evolution are therefore destined, as a result of increasingly cultural types of interaction with the environment, to undergo further change over time. By the same token, war, which is an exclusively human cultural phenomenon, has changed profoundly over the course of history, and there is no reason to think that it may not change further in the future, or indeed eventually disappear completely. But such a development, if it ever comes to pass, will arise as the result of very slow and complex evolutionary processes in which the crucial factor will be not so much individual morals as the overall impact of cultural evolution on the deep-set impulses that characterize the members of the species today. And it appears hard to deny that at the present time these impulses include adaptive dispositions of an aggressive type to which it would be irrational not to relate the inclination of *homo sapiens* towards conflict and, under certain cultural conditions, war.

The fact that war is essentially a cultural phenomenon does not mean – as Eibl-Eibesfeldt has authoritatively maintained – that it does not correspond to biologically deep-rooted and widespread adaptive predispositions: to aggressive emotion, above all, followed by group solidarity, territorial instincts, the tendency to respond to signals of competition from outsiders and an antagonistic urge to predominate.[57]

The ultimate root of war, then – although not, it should be immediately stressed, its 'biological cause' – lies in human aggression. This, combined with group spirit, territorial instincts and in-group power dependency relations, is essentially a response to exposure to the 'environment' and thus to the need for security that *homo sapiens* shares with the higher animals.[58] In an environment perceived as dangerous, in the sense that it appears as a real or potential source of frustrations that can thwart vital expectations such as individual and group survival, protection of the group's territory, maintaining food supplies or creating the conditions for sexual reproduction, aggression becomes an attempt at 'reduction of fear'.[59] The use of aggressive violence as an alternative to flight from danger or simple defence represents a means of engaging in active opposition against the 'risks' contained in the environment, and of re-establishing a situation of homeostatic equilibrium, order and peacefulness.

In the light of these arguments, not only should aggression, conflict and war not be 'negated' but it becomes on the contrary necessary to attempt to integrate these factors into the lives of individuals and of groups. But 'integrating war' is a far cry from simply accepting war without further qualification. What it really means is on the one hand the need to recognize that war is the outcome of such an extended evolutionary process that it would be naive or hypocritical to imagine it could be stamped out by force within a short space of time; on the other hand, however, it also entails the need to activate aggression-controlling mechanisms in order to reduce the frequency with which conflict between human groups produces destructive effects. And this is all the more important today, given the extremely high destructive potential of modern armaments, both nuclear and conventional. Modern warfare is particularly destructive because of the irreversible damage which, in addition to the loss of human life, it causes to the environment. It could fairly be said that modern war is the extreme negation of complexity, variety and beauty. Further: it is the triumph of fear, the destruction of communication and the dissolution of all positive competitive spirit between civilizations and cultures.

Such may be the nature of war. But, in order for containment and control of war to become genuinely possible, it is also necessary to seek to understand exactly why its presence is so pervasive throughout the whole of humankind. There is little use in passing moral judgements or considering war as a pathological condition deriving from irrational instincts or from evil lying deep within the human heart, as is the tendency – albeit with very different motivations – among the proponents of institutional pacifism and absolute pacifism. In the words of Eibl-Eibesfeldt, 'peace requires that one recognizes the functions fulfilled by warfare and that one does not simply dispense with war as a pathological degenerate phenomenon.'[60]

For despite the immense burden of suffering, atrocities and destruction that have always been the complement of war, there can be no doubt that, from an evolutionary point of view, wars have always performed integrative and associative functions not only within groups engaged in conflict on the same side but, paradoxically, even between the opposite warring parties. (The European Union might well be considered as a classic example of this paradoxical effect.) In the absence of such functions, one would be at a loss to explain its evolutionary persistence. Moreover, numerous authors maintain that, by exacerbating conditions of selectivity, war has actually accelerated cultural evolution and has stimulated the division of labour and the rise of social complexity.[61]

If this is the case, then the objective of a realist theory of peacemaking cannot be the ambitious – indeed overambitious – one of exterminating war. Rather, efforts should be directed towards defining corrective measures and possible functional equivalents of war which will succeed in rendering aggression and conflict non-destructive, or at least less fiercely destructive, without actually aiming at the suppression of these phenomena. In other words, what is required is the establishment of 'social structures' (in the sense suggested by Arnold Gehlen and further elaborated by Niklas Luhmann) capable of operating as 'aggression-lightening' structures, as *Entlastungen* that will provide a cultural remedy for the 'instinctual poverty' characterizing *homo sapiens* as compared with all other higher animals.[62]

Where may such corrective measures and functional equivalents be found? The research on the ethology of war on which I have drawn extensively in the above considerations offers a number of valuable, if general, indications. Essentially, there is a need to enhance those mechanisms of automatic inhibition of intraspecies aggression which are an innate component of the nature of *homo sapiens* just as they are of all the other primates: for every human being experiences a strong aversion towards the killing of another similar being, an aversion which however is not so keenly felt as regards the killing of animals, and is increasingly less perceived the more the creatures appear morphologically different from humans.[63] It follows that steps should be taken to foster a cultural and institutional approach whereby the inhibition of intraspecies aggression can become effective in resolving human conflict as well, thus neutralizing the effects of cultural pseudospeciation.[64] It would be necessary to refine and apply to the collective area of conflict amongst human groups the 'peacemaking rituals' that form a widespread pattern of behaviour among anthropomorphic primates but which are either inoperative or seriously inadequate for coping with the nature and dimensions of modern war as it is waged among humans.[65]

In higher animals the mechanisms automatically inhibiting intraspecies aggression are represented by various procedures enabling the contenders to be brought into direct communication with one another. These procedures oblige them to establish face-to-face contact, with the result that clashes are ritualized and peacemaking signals are sent out that automatically induce the emotive inhibition of aggression.[66] The details of these peacemaking rituals have been studied by Frans de Waal, who showed that in anthropomorphic primates aggression and pacification are two deep-rooted and inextricably linked impulses. Non-human primates manifest a high level of aggression, but at the same time they are willing to settle their differences immediately after a clash. In order to achieve this end, they engage in highly elaborate strategies. Conflict triggers negative feedback that erases all psychological traces of the attack launched or endured, thus preventing an escalation of violence.'[67]

De Waal points out that even within human groups there exist traces of these elementary violence-inhibiting mechanisms. Some villages on the island of Bali, for instance, have a special hut to which people are sent to settle disagreements. The hut, located in a field outside the village, is composed simply of two poles with a roof atop. The absence of walls allows villagers to keep an eye on the two troublemakers. They sit with their backs against the poles, which are only a few metres apart, and may not return until their differences are healed.[68]

The interesting feature, to my mind, of this archaic and elementary model of peacemaking is that the social group does not forcibly impose sanctions on the aggressive and conflict-oriented behaviour of its members, but rather prescribes pacification rituals that are in some sense private and secret. Ritual institutionalization of the peacemaking process coexists with the contenders' autonomy in the management of their conflict. Institutional control and pressure from the community remain external to the reconciliation mechanism, to the point that any form of third-party mediation or arbitration is avoided.

In a highly differentiated and complex human world – one that is riddled with countless divisions and 'pseudospeciation' processes – any attempt to devise a cultural reactivation of these aggression-inhibiting mechanisms and peacemaking rituals would, as need hardly be pointed out, require infinitely more sophisticated and complex institutions, which would be far more costly from every point of view than the elementary hut on the island of Bali. Skyscrapers, rather than huts, would now appear to be more in order. Moreover, the attempt could not be anything other than the outcome of conscious processes of decision and international political negotiation: a far cry from the spontaneous product of 'global civil society'.

Nevertheless it seems to me that sight should not be lost of the valuable suggestion that, in order to prevent destructive conflict among human groups, an attempt should be made first and foremost to neutralize the ancestral mechanisms of pseudospeciation. And to this end it would probably be necessary to set up international institutions entrusted with the exclusive task of intensifying the symbolic contacts between cultures and civilizations. Ideally, these contacts should draw the greatest advantage possible from the exchange relations currently fostered by the globalization of markets, and indeed seek to go greatly beyond such relations. Furthermore, in order to contain and resolve conflicts that have effectively broken out, the first aim should be to make use of peacemaking mechanisms which are internal to the conflict or which emerge from the conflict itself. The underlying concept would thus be to work with the conflict rather than to impose violent solutions from without.

Weak Pacifism

A brief restatement of the general thesis of this chapter will serve to introduce a concluding proposal, that of 'weak pacifism'.

The suggestion of the rise of a 'global civil society' lacks all foundation, as does the hypothesis of a transnational democracy founded on such a society. A world government interpretable as the projection of current international political and economic institutions could not emerge as anything other than a despotic and totalitarian Leviathan, which would have no other option open to it than to counter the predictable spread of anti-cosmopolitan terrorism with methods of an equally terrorist nature. The processes of cultural and economic globalization which are the driving forces today behind relations of functional interdependence within the 'world system' are manifestly failing to produce cultural and economic integration within the unitary framework of a 'world society'. On the contrary, on both the cultural and the economic level, phenomena of globalization appear to be destined to produce further differentiation and fragmentation of the international arena over the next few decades. Thus terms such as global civil society, universal citizenship, world constitutionalism and transnational democracy may be said to belong to a normative vocabulary which draws strongly on wishful thinking. Furthermore, not only are the objectives they refer to almost certainly unrealizable in the foreseeable future, they are also of limited desirability.

For it is hard to see wherein lies the attraction of a world authority whose scope of action is not limited to guaranteeing a 'minimal political order' – to use the apt expression owed to Hedley Bull – but aims instead, in accordance with the ideology of the 'western globalists', to establish an 'optimal political order': i.e. a guarantee of stable and universal peace, distributive justice, the definition and protection of rights, the ecological integrity of the planet, determination of the proper weighting between available resources and demographic growth.[69] A cosmopolitan authority of this type, however much it might strive to set up a liberal democracy, could not fail to be pervasive and intensely interventionist, thereby giving rise to a political system describable as 'evolutionarily regressive', inasmuch as it would work towards a drastic reduction in the complexity and differentiation of the international system.

Any political philosophy alert to the perils of the accumulation and centralization of power cannot but regard with suspicion this perspective which would aim to establish at an international level the functional predominance of the political subsystem. It is only natural for such a philosophy to attempt to counter this aim by proposing the realistically Grotian objective of an international 'legal society' or, better, a constellation of 'international legal regimes' capable of co-ordinating the subjects of international politics according to a systemic logic of 'governance without government': i.e., in simpler terms, the adoption of diffuse and polycentric normative structures and forms of leadership. The 'minimal' political order ensured by an international system of this type would require only 'weak interventionism', compatible with what Paul Ekins has called 'bottom-up development'. And this should hold for the entire gamut of international issues, including the attempt to curb the destructive aggression of war by 'weak' means. In this sense a transition is needed from the logic of the Leviathan to that of the thousand fragile chains of Lilliput: from a cosmopolitan pacifism to a 'weak pacifism'.

In order to make progress towards this goal, it would be desirable to establish a network of international and above all regional and national institutions specifically directed towards intercultural communication and, consequently, towards enhancement of ethnic-cultural identities. The implicit assumption behind this proposal is that the effects of peacemaking may derive not so much from a cosmopolitan compression of ethnic-national distinctive features – which at present are rapidly and violently coming to the fore – as from a generalized recognition of such features and an acknowledgement that they form an expression of the evolutionary complexity and cultural richness of the species.

Naturally, prospects of this kind can be envisaged only if at the same time a concerted effort can be made to contain the cultural hegemony of the West, thereby allowing the development of a culture of 'human diversity' which will not regard cultural differences as 'speciated' manifestations of all that is 'other' – and hence to be combated – but will instead accept them as evolutionary differentiations confirming multilaterality and 'world-openness' as characteristics of the human species. Furthermore, it is imperative, if progress is to be made in this direction, not only for there to be recognition of the legitimate diversity of ethnic and legal systems created by different cultural traditions, but also for each national entity to be awarded equal dignity and autonomy at the international level. In opposition to the cosmopolitan attitude which looks with disfavour on multiplicity and diversity, tending to compress them within the bounds of a hierarchical macrostructure comprising only a very limited number of states, a culture of human diversity should aim towards the free self-assertion of political subjects, which should in effect also imply the free self-assertion of states.

It has for instance been calculated that in Africa there are at least five hundred cultural units which have a claim to recognition of their individual identity and political autonomy, while the African states recognized by the United Nations number no more than fifty. Over the whole planet, there are currently several thousand national entities more or less explicitly appealing for the right to self-representation in the international political arena, whereas the number of states is actually below two hundred. In the face of this explosion of requests, the great powers and the international institutions which are dependent on them are silently, and in the name of world order, putting into action a policy of, as it were, 'non-proliferation of states' (an implosive strategy openly approved by high-ranking authorities in the United States).[70] That there should be a push towards such a policy is only natural, since a multiplication of states would inevitably lead to a disaggregation of the currently existing framework of the concentration and legitimation of international power, and would therefore represent a threat to the balance of 'hegemonic stability'. But the only way to avert the risk of the atomizing and splintering effect engendered by ethnic-national particularisms leading to a 'world civil war' would appear to be the setting-up of decentralized, regional and subregional institutions through which non-coercive diplomacy can be exercised.

Finally, the dialectics of aggression–reconciliation expressed in peace-making rituals observed among primates would seem to suggest a general strategy of peacemaking which differs very sharply from that practised by international institutions over the last two centuries. Not only aggression and conflict but also reconciliation and peace need to be seen as equally natural and 'instinctive' components of human behaviour. The time has come to jettison the idea that aggression and conflict must be stamped out before stable peace can be established among nations. For not only is the elimination of aggression imposs-ible, but, if it were indeed to become feasible, then the species would be doomed to undergo severe emotional and cultural impoverishment if, as argued by Konrad Lorenz, it is true that in relations among human beings there can be aggression without love but there cannot be love without aggression; or if, again following Lorenz, we accept the truth of the statement that aggression is closely linked to emulation, exploratory behaviour and creativity, while conflict is the force that drives social and political innovation.[71] Once the elimination of aggression and conflict is seen as implausible, it is clear that any hope of averting the risk of war once and for all is an equally far-fetched proposition, barring some unforeseen – and undesirable – anthropolog-ical mutation.

It may thus be fairly stated that good reason exists to set aside the rationalistic and moralistic aspiration to the extermination of war by resorting to supranational means of repression. Yet this is precisely what the doctrine of institutional pacifism, emblematically embodied in the Security Council of the United Nations, effectively amounts to: as a philosophy of peace and war this doctrine is no less crude than the moralism and supposed enlightenment displayed by Wilson and Roose-velt in their role as founding fathers of international institutions. In opposition to this hierarchical-military utopia, work is needed towards

the elaboration of 'social structures' and 'weak' reconciliation techniques aiming at goals that are less pretentious but precisely for this
reason also more effective over the long run.

What, then, in the light of the realist theory of peacemaking I have
endeavoured to outline, do I believe to be the functions and the
organizational framework of such international institutions as would be
entrusted with the task of working towards peace by means of a 'weak'
strategy?

This is of course hardly the place for a line-by-line account of the
operational functions and organizational framework of 'weak' international institutions, intended as an alternative to existing institutions.
It is unlikely that this could be done with sufficient realism. More to the
point, however, I contend that, in such far-reaching and complex
frameworks as the international system, institutional engineering is a
mere academic exercise. I will therefore restrict my observations to a
few essential features, of use purely as a summary overview of the
direction to be taken if one were to accept the theoretical premises of
the anticosmopolitanism and 'weak pacifism' which I have proposed.

First and foremost, I argue that there would be a need for international institutions capable of performing several elementary peacekeeping activities, in the following functional sequence: first, drawing
up and constantly updating a global map of consolidated or developing
ethnic-cultural groups both within and without state boundaries; second,
guaranteeing permanent monitoring of political, economic and territorial claims made by the above groups, and of potential conflict situations
that could be triggered by such claims (such activities could in part be
facilitated by use of the communications networks which are currently
being developed and by means of electronic archives selectively accessible to specified operators); third, favouring direct interaction between
groups demanding ethnic recognition or staking out nationhood claims,
and groups involved in hostile reaction to such claims; and fourth,
carrying out non-coercive preventive diplomacy in matters concerning
disputes within state boundaries as well as those between states or
across national boundaries which have the capacity to develop into
armed conflict.

Numerous voluntary organizations are already engaged in undertakings similar to these in many parts of the world, although their activity
may be fragmentary and devoid of significant connection between
individual projects. Considerable success has been achieved, for
instance, by the community of Sant'Egidio in Rome, which has succeeded in carrying out delicate operations of non-protocol diplomacy
by the use of extremely simple measures, in particular in northern
Africa. Similarly, Amnesty International, operating according to its own

particular approach, performs .the function of monitoring political tensions within states.

Second, in order to contain the destructive effects of already existing armed conflicts, 'weak' peacemaking institutions will be required. These should offer contenders all necessary operational tools, knowledge and international connections as well as the protected physical areas needed for prompt and effective diplomacy. In addition they should encourage direct meetings between political representatives of the states involved, guaranteeing them absolute respect of diplomatic secrecy. They should be immediately and readily accessible not only to states but also to groups and minorities existing within states. Furthermore, these institutions should be in a position to act as mediators, and, upon request by the parties involved, provide arbitration and consensual interposition of peacekeeping forces equipped solely with light arms, along the lines of the model adopted in the post-war period by Dag Hammarskjöld.

An interesting example of non-coercive diplomacy and active mediation may be seen in the steps undertaken over the last few years by the ex-President of the United States, Jimmy Carter. It may be objected, however, that Carter operates on the basis of personal prestige and political authority deriving not only from his past involvement in politics but also from implicit authorization by the United States Administration. Yet it cannot be denied that his initiatives fill an immense gap existing in the activity of official international institutions, and that this void could be filled just as prestigiously and with greater effectiveness by measures taken on behalf of 'weak' international institutions.

Third, there is an urgent need to deal with the problem of weapons control, which is at present completely ignored by international institutions. This is an area capable of being addressed by highly specialized agencies, which, while possessing no direct policing powers, could be given an internationally authorized mandate to carry out fact-finding inspections even during the course of conflicts; they would then be authorized to publish their reports on the production, commerce and use of arms, including nuclear weapons and the environmental consequences of their experimental use. These agencies should operate as a sort of international Red Cross whose task would be to denounce violation of the international rules of *jus in bello* that prohibit use of certain types of weapons, such as chemical weapons or anti-personnel mines. Naturally I am by no means unaware of the difficulty inherent in this type of operation, which would inevitably clash with the secrecy of military activities and the powerful criminal organizations which control international arms traffic, frequently under cover of the complicity of the states involved.

A fourth point concerns the location of such institutions. They should be decentralized, with strong local roots, co-ordinated within homogeneous regional or continental areas and linked together through a weak 'subsidiary' centralization of a federal type. The fact that current international institutions are concentrated in the West is certainly one of the reasons, although not the major one, determining their failure. By contrast, a strong local base for alternative institutions could be assured by embedding them in the cultural and social fabric of the world's great urban areas. Over the next few decades, as a result of the massive phenomena of migration, the metropolitan areas of the contemporary world will be increasingly drawn into the dichotomy already confronting cities such as Algiers, Mostar, Sarajevo, Nicosia or Jerusalem, to name just a few in the Mediterranean basin: whether they will develop as testing grounds for multi-ethnic and multicultural coexistence, or, on the contrary, become dangerous breeding grounds of war.

Last but not least, there is the question of the financial support of these activities. Given their much lower cost in comparison with operations of warfare, their expense could be shared out proportionately among all international 'users' of peacekeeping or peacemaking operations, whether or not they individually stand to benefit from them. In any case, the costs should not be borne almost exclusively by the great powers, as is the case today with the United Nations. Quotas should be fixed, depending on the case in question, on the basis of bilateral or multilateral accords, and funding obtained by levying a tax directly on the citizens of each state. Naturally, parameters would have to be defined to ensure congruity between the number of citizens, their ability to pay and the burden of contributions imposed on each international unit.

Here, for the present, speculation should cease. It is my belief that a network of institutions and agencies similar to that which I have sketched could succeed in filtering at least a part of international conflict within its own network of permanent monitoring, preventive diplomacy and arbitration. Such institutions should, however, be truly impartial – they should be of the nature of an effective impartial third party – as is already to some extent the case with agencies such as the International Red Cross or Amnesty International. What is to be rejected is the overwhelming political domination, the cultural hegemony and legal surplus-value of the great powers. At the very least such international institutions should be put in a position to resist the predictable pressures which would be exerted by those powers.

Naturally, institutions of this kind would not themselves succeed in achieving a rapid cessation of armed conflict. Contenders would not be willing to alter their warmongering mentality or to lay down their arms immediately and face each other across a diplomatic table. They would in all likelihood continue to wage war against one another, as in fact has happened in Bosnia (despite the blockades and the military intervention by NATO), or as has predictably happened after the all-too-foreseeable failure of armed intervention by the United States in Somalia. What is minimally required, however, is that the international community should refrain from direct intervention and should make no attempt to use military force in order to prevent continuation of the conflict. The intervention of the international community should be restricted to isolating the contenders politically, thereby putting them under a form of guard from the outside, in the attempt to compel them to accept a negotiated solution to the conflict. In short: the international community should not wage war on the contenders, i.e. it should not, as it did in the Gulf War, overlay with further violence, however internationally legitimized, the violence it professes to be either repressing or subjecting to sanctions.

All this may well appear to be too weak a form of pacifism. I may perhaps be accused of advocating inertia on the part of the international community in the face of violence, destruction and genocide. However, quite apart from the fact that the military forces of the great powers have historically always intervened only after the event and frequently succeed only in heaping violence on violence, the realistic assumption on which my proposal rests is that only in and through conflict can peace be achieved. Only by overcoming the underlying reasons of conflict can the need for peace, and hence peace itself, take root among the warring parties. In other words, peace cannot, any more than democracy, be 'exported'. The fallacy of all peace-enforcing strategies – i.e. the exporting and violent imposition of peace – should be clear to all after the recent lessons of Somalia, Rwanda and signally the war between the peoples of former Yugoslavia. After more than three years of war, peace may now at length be about to be achieved in the Balkans. But it can safely be predicted that it will be a peace of reconciliation only if the deep-seated reasons underlying the conflict have been finally overcome – paradoxically, in part through the conflict itself – and have not simply been removed or repressed by military intervention from the outside. If this hypothesis is well founded, no such outcome is to be expected from the *pax cosmopolitica* imposed by western arms in the Persian Gulf; this area, as a result of the treatment it has received, remains a dangerous breeding ground of war, and is likely to remain so for some long time to come.

Notes

1 Falk, *Positive Prescriptions for the Near Future*, pp. 7–16; Held, 'Democrazia e nuovo ordine internazionale', pp. 48–50; United Nations Development

Programme, *Human Development Report 1994*, New York: Oxford University Press, 1994, pp. 87–9. The expression 'global civil society' as opposed to the idea of an 'international police' has been used by Ralf Dahrendorf in many recent articles and interviews.

2 Compare particularly Falk, *Positive Prescriptions*, pp. 7–16.

3 See A. B. Seligman, *The Idea of Civil Society*, New York: Free Press, 1992.

4 P. Costa, *Il progetto giuridico*, Milan: Giuffré, 1974.

5 See Marshall, *Citizenship and Social Class*.

6 For a tentative definition of the notion of 'human development', see the annual Reports of the United Nations Development Programme (UNDP), published by Oxford University Press, New York; compare particularly UNDP, *Human Development Report 1990*, pp. 9–16; UNDP, *Human Development Report 1992*, pp. 12–25; UNDP, *Human Development Report 1990*, pp. 90–101. Naturally the notion of 'human development', even if much weaker than the notion of 'human rights', similarly corresponds to a mostly western viewpoint.

7 Bull, *The Anarchical Society*, pp. 264–6.

8 Compare, contra, H. Bull, 'The State's Positive Role in World Affairs', *Proceedings of the American Academy of Arts and Sciences*, 1979, vol. 108, note 4, pp. 111–23; Bull, *The Anarchical Society*.

9 R. Kothari, *Footsteps into the Future: Diagnosis of the Present World and a Design for an Alternative*, New Delhi: Orient Longman, 1974, pp. 149–63.

10 Bull, 'The State's Positive Role in World Affairs', pp. 120–3. On the non-dispensability of nation states, see also the whole of chapter 11 in Bull, *The Anarchical Society*, pp. 257–81.

11 P. P. Portinaro, *La rondine, il topo e il castoro. Apologia del realismo politico*, Venice: Marsilio, 1993, pp. 122–7. 'The story is sometimes told of the man who was lost somewhere in Scotland, and asked a farmer if he could tell him which was the way to Edinburgh. "Oh sir," the farmer replied, "if I were you, I shouldn't start from here!" The doctrine that the states system does not provide the best starting point for the pursuit of world order has something of this quality' (compare Bull, *The Anarchical Society*, pp. 295–6).

12 For an effort to renew European politico-philosophical research on federalism, see J. J. Hesse and W. Renzsch (eds), *Föderalstaatliche Entwicklung in Europa*, Baden-Baden: Nomos Verlagsgesellschaft, 1991. See also G. E. Rusconi, 'Ripensare la nazione: Tra separatismo regionale e progetto europeo', *Filosofia politica*, 6 (1992), 1, pp. 63–85; for a general theoretical approach to ethnicity, nationality and global citizenship see D. Miller, *On Nationality*, Oxford: Clarendon Press, 1995.

13 On globalization see M. Albrow and E. King (eds), *Globalization, Knowledge and Society*, London: Sage Publications, 1990; E. Luard, *The Globalization of Politics: The Changed Focus of Political Action in the Modern World*, London: Macmillan, 1990, particularly pp. 138–91; for an analysis of 'transnational practices', see L. Sklair, *Sociology of the Global System*, New York: Harvester Wheatsheaf, 1991.

14 See E. Comor (ed.), *The Global Political Economy of Communication*, London: Macmillan, 1994.

15 R. Gilpin, *The Political Economy of International Relations*, Princeton: Princeton University Press, 1987, pp. 231–62; see also R. Jenkins, *Transnational Corporations and Uneven Development*, London: Methuen, 1987; G.

Gareffi, M. Korzeniewicz and R. P. Korzeniewicz, *Commodity Chains and Global Capitalism*, Westport: Greenwood Press, 1994.

16 See M. Featherstone (ed.), *Global Culture, Nationalism, Globalization and Modernity*, London: Sage Publications, 1991; B. S. Turner, *Theories of Modernity and Postmodernity*, London: Sage Publications, 1990.

17 See R. Robertson, *Globalization: Social Theory and Global Culture*, London: Sage Publications, 1992.

18 Bull, *The Anarchical Society*, p. 281.

19 See Latouche, *L'occidentalisation du monde: Essai sur la signification, la portée et les limits de l'uniformisation planétaire*.

20 Ibid., pp. 62–83.

21 Ibid., p. 10.

22 Ibid., pp. 84–110.

23 See S. Latouche, *La planète des naufragés: Essai sur l'après-développement*, Paris; Editions La Découverte, 1991.

24 Portinaro, *La rondine, il topo e il castoro*, pp. 47–8.

25 Compare my 'Citizenship in a Postcommunist Era', in D. Held (ed.), *Prospects for Democracy*, Cambridge: Polity Press, 1993, p. 266; see also U. K. Preuss, 'Citizenship and Identity: Aspects of a Political Theory of Citizenship', in R. Bellamy, V. Buffachi and D. Castiglione (eds), *Democracy and Constitutional Culture in the Union of Europe*, London: Lothian Foundation Press, 1994, pp. 137–54. On the symbolic theme of the 'foreigner' see R. Escobar, 'Rivalità e mimesi. Lo straniero interno', *Filosofia politica*, 6 (1992), 1, pp. 79–106.

26 UNDP *Human Development Report 1992*, pp. 1–11, 14.

27 UNDP, *Human Development Report 1992*, p. 1; UNDP, *Human Development Report 1994*, p. 63. The poorest 20% receives only 0.2% of global commercial bank lending, 1.3% of global investment, 1% of global trade and 1.4% of global income.

28 A. Giddens, *Sociology*, Cambridge: Polity Press, 1993, p. 534.

29 See P. Ekins, *A New World Order: Grass Roots Movements for Global Change*, London: Routledge, 1992.

30 See J. Bennett and S. George, *The Hunger Machine*, Cambridge: Polity Press, 1987.

31 UNDP, *Human Development Report 1990*, pp. 2–3; UNDP, *Human Development Report 1992*, pp. 3, 12–25.

32 UNDP, *Human Development Report 1990*, pp. 2–3

33 Gilpin, *The Political Economy of International Relations*, pp. 34–43, 270–3.

34 See A. G. Frank, *Capitalism and Under-development in Latin America*, New York: Monthly Review Press, 1969; F. H. Cardoso, 'Dependency and Under-development in Latin America', *New Left Review*, 74 (1972); C. Furtado, *The Economic Growth of Brazil: A Survey from Colonial to Modern Times*, Westport: Greenwood Press, 1984. For a critical discussion, compare Gilpin, *The Political Economy of International Relations*, pp. 67–72; Giddens, *Sociology*, p. 542.

35 See N. Harris, *The End of the Third World: Newly Industrialising Countries and the Decline of an Ideology*, Harmondsworth: Penguin, 1987; A. H. Somjee, *Development Theory: Critiques and Explorations*, London: Macmillan, 1991; U. Menzel, *Das Ende der Dritten Welt und das Scheitern der grossen Theorie*, Frankfurt a.M.: Suhrkamp, 1992; compare also Gilpin, *The Political Economy of International Relations*, pp. 65–72; Portinaro, *La rondine, il topo e il castoro*, pp. 86–8.

36 Gilpin, *The Political Economy of International Relations*, pp. 26–31, 171–230.
37 Ibid., p. 304.
38 G. K. Helleiner, *The New Global Economy and the Developing Countries*, Aldershot: Edward Elgar, 1990, pp. 3–19.
39 Gilpin, *The Political Economy of International Relations*, pp. 304, 394–7.
40 Ibid., pp. 394–408.
41 See Gareffi, Korzeniewicz and Korzeniewicz, *Commodity Chains and Global Capitalism*.
42 Non-tariff barriers include, for example, the setting of quotas, the requirement of import licences, voluntary export restraints and special countervailing and anti-dumping measures; compare Gilpin, *The Political Economy of International Relations*, pp. 204–9; B. Russett and H. Starr, *World Politics*, New York: W. H. Freeman, 1992, pp. 488–9; UNDP, *Human Development Report 1992*, pp. 5–7, 62–4; D. Greenaway, R. C. Hine and A. P. O'Brien (eds), *Global Protectionism*, London: Macmillan, 1991.
43 UNDP, *Human Development Report 1992*, p. 6.
44 UNDP, *Human Development Report 1994*, pp. 4, 63–4; Helleiner, *The New Global Economy and the Developing Countries*, pp. 193–209. As is recognized, there is a vicious circularity according to which the attempted liquidation of their debts by the developing countries could not keep up with the fall in the prices of their exports that it caused. This phenomenon has a paradoxical outcome: the more debtors pay, the more they owe; UNDP, *Human Development Report 1994*, pp. 4, 51–2.
45 Helleiner, *The New Global Economy and the Developing Countries*, pp. 128–54; Luard, *The Globalization of Politics*, pp. 127–32.
46 See G. Cannon, *The Politics of Food*, London: Century, 1987.
47 See Ekins, *A New World Order*; compare also Giddens, *Sociology*, pp. 535–7.
48 UNDP, *Human Development Report 1992*, p. 10; UNDP, *Human Development Report 1994*, pp. 5–11.
49 Portinaro, *La rondine, il topo e il castoro*, p. 92.
50 See I. Eibl-Eibesfeldt, *The Biology of Peace and War*, London: Thames & Hudson, 1979; I. Eibl-Eibesfeldt, *Die Biologie des menschlichen Verhaltens. Grundriss der Humanethologie*, Munich: Piper, 1984; Engl. trans. *Human Ethology*, New York: Aldine de Gruyter, 1989; F. de Waal, *Peacemaking among Primates*, London: Penguin Books, 1991; F. de Waal, *Chimpanzee Politics*, London: Jonathan Cape, 1982.
51 F. A. Huntingford, 'Animals Fight, But Do Not Make War', in J. Groebel and R. A. Hinde (eds), *Aggression and War: Their Biological and Social Bases*, Cambridge: Cambridge University Press, 1989, p. 33.
52 E. H. Erikson, 'Ontogeny of Ritualization in Man', *Philosophical Transactions of the Royal Society of London*, ser. B. 251 (1966), pp. 337–49.
53 Groebel and Hinde (eds), *Aggression and War*, pp. 135–7; I. Eibl-Eibesfeldt, 'Warfare, Man's Indoctrinability and Group Selection', *Zeitschrift für Tierpsychologie*, 60 (1982), pp. 177–98.
54 K. Lorenz, *Das sogenannte Böse. Zur Naturgeschichte der Aggression*, Vienna: Borotha-Schölar, 1963; Engl. trans., *On Aggression*, London: Methuen, 1966.
55 I. Eibl-Eibesfeldt, *The Biology of Peace and War*, pp. 1–6, 122–5, 240–1.
56 To be seen in Groebel and Hinde (eds), *Aggression and War*, pp. xii–xvi; compare also P. Messeri, 'Perché e come combattere: il contributo

dell'etologia', in P. Messeri and E. Pulcini (eds), *Immagini dell'impensabile. Ricerche interdisciplinari sulla guerra nucleare*, Genoa: Marietti, 1991, pp. 153–6. The Seville Statement on Violence was signed by twenty scientists from twelve different countries at the end of a meeting of natural and social scientists organized by Martin Ramirez and David Adams in Seville in May 1986. Its central thesis was that 'it is scientifically incorrect to say that war or any other violent behaviour is genetically programmed into human nature.'

57 Eibl-Eibesfeldt, *Die Biologie des menschlichen Verhaltens*, Engl. trans. p. 421; compare more generally pp. 360–422.

58 A. Gehlen, *Der Mensch. Seine Natur und seine Stellung in der Welt*, Wiesbaden: Akademische Verlagsgesellschaft Athenaion, 1978; Engl. trans. *Man, his Nature and Place in the World*, New York: Columbia University Press, 1988, pp. 3–13, 54–64, 79–92.

59 See J. Dollard et al., *Frustration and Aggression*, New Haven: Yale University Press, 1939; S. Feshbach, 'The Bases and Development of Individual Aggression', in Groebel and Hinde (eds), *Aggression and War*, pp. 78–90; L. Berkowitz, 'Situational Influences on Aggression', ibid., pp. 91–100. On 'reduction of fear', compare my *Democracy and Complexity*, pp. 35–45.

60 Eibl-Eibesfeldt, *Die Biologie des menschlichen Verhaltens*, Engl. trans. p. 422.

61 Eibl-Eibesfeldt, *The Biology of Peace and War*, pp. 123, 169–87; Eibl-Eibesfeldt, *Die Biologie des menschlichen Verhaltens*, Engl. trans. pp. 415–18. On the relationship between complexity and war, compare Groebel and Hinde (eds), *Aggression and War*, pp. 189–93, 223–29.

62 See Gehlen, *Der Mensch*, Engl. trans. pp. 54–64; N. Luhmann, *Soziologische Aufklärung*,I, Opladen: Westdeutscher Verlag, 1970.

63 Eibl-Eibesfeldt, *Die Biologie des menschlichen Verhaltens*, Engl. trans. pp. 403–8, 422.

64 J. H. Goldstein, 'Beliefs about Human Aggression', in Groebel and Hinde (eds), *Aggression and War*, p. 12.

65 De Waal, *Peacemaking among Primates*, pp. 230–71.

66 Eibl-Eibesfeldt, *The Biology of Peace and War*, pp. 219–25; Eibl-Eibesfeldt, *Die Biologie des menschlichen Verhaltens*, Engl. trans. pp. 418–21.

67 Strategies include caresses, kisses, embraces, mutual care of fur (grooming) and more intensive sexual behaviour; compare De Waal, *Peacemaking among Primates*, pp. 37–48, 110–17, 149–54, 214–22.

68 De Waal, *Peacemaking among Primates*, p. 260.

69 Bull, *The Anarchical Society*, pp. 284–95, 302–5.

70 Binder and Crossette, 'As Ethnic Wars Multiply, United States Strives for a Policy', p. 1.

71 Eibl-Eibesfeldt, *Die Biologie des menschlichen Verhaltens*, Engl. trans. pp. 391–5.

Conclusion

The Holy Alliance Paradigm and the Limitations of Cosmopolitan Pacifism

The survey of the historical origins of the international institutions which I have presented in this book reveals a structural continuity between the Holy Alliance, the League of Nations and the United Nations. This element of continuity manifests itself in what I have proposed to term 'the cosmopolitan model of the Holy Alliance': a hierarchical institutional model which superimposes the hegemonic tactics and aspirations of a narrow elite of superpowers on the sovereignty of all other countries. The Security Council of the United Nations, firmly under the control of the conquering powers of the last world war, represents this model in exemplary form. Equality before the law is denied by the Charter of the United Nations to the subjects of the international legal order, while, at the same time, an elementary theory of peacemaking, which presumes to secure for humanity a stable and universal peace through the use of superior force, receives its greatest expression within the Charter.

Following the end of the Cold War and the termination of bipolar political equilibrium in the 1980s, the world hegemony of the United States finally gave the United Nations the opportunity to exercise the role originally assigned to it by its founding fathers, and thereby to give an immediate demonstration not only of its unsuitability to guarantee peace but also of the positive dangers involved. The Gulf War, brought about through the wishes of the United States and the other western powers, became the 'first cosmopolitan war' in the sense that it was decided upon and legitimated at the highest world level in the name of international legal order and the interests of the human community as a whole. In using the United Nations as their instrument of war, the western powers declared their allegiance to the idea, which undoubtedly lies behind the Charter, that the maintenance of peace and world order requires the organization of a supranational authority with substantial military force under its control.

Such a unit has to operate, it was maintained, as an international 'police force', entrusted with the job not only of applying military sanctions against violations of international order but also of carrying out 'humanitarian' operations of peace enforcement and the promotion of democracy, a process which entirely supersedes the Westphalian principle of 'non-interference' in the internal affairs of sovereign states. The protection of human rights at an international level and the principle of non-intervention are therefore explicitly declared to be incompatible. Or rather, the idea itself of the Westphalian model of an international society composed of a plurality of sovereign states must now be thought, according to the cosmopolitan ideology, to have become obsolete. The new global order must supplant the old 'state system', which is in any case in a condition of rapid decline. This new cosmopolitan practice and ideology came fully into existence and legitimacy in the years succeeding the Gulf War and figured tragically not only in the Gulf but in Somalia and Rwanda as well.

Theorists of cosmopolitan pacifism, with the sole exception of Richard Falk, have considered the Gulf War to be a just, or at least 'justified', war. But, imprisoned in the eurocentric schema of the domestic analogy, cosmopolitan pacifism fails to perceive the dangers present in an institutional outlook which continues in traditional fashion to enshrine the hegemony of the western powers. Instead it remains stuck in the mould of a hierarchical and monocentric world order. And it deceives itself in believing that it can use the doctrine of human rights as a basis, or as the ideological flag, of an order which is universally just because it conforms to western values. It appears not to realize that the established set of international political and economic relations has been overtaken by a cataclysm and that the situation is now very far from being one of equilibrium.

The balance of hostility between the two great nuclear powers has now been replaced by an explosion of local conflicts which is, for the present at least, uncontainable. On top of this there is added the list of fresh planetary risks: population explosion, large-scale migration, ecological disorder, proliferation of nuclear weapons, increasingly unequal division of wealth between countries. The Third World is now a concept of the past, but the headlong growth of some formerly underdeveloped countries – especially those within the Pacific rim – is presenting an awkward challenge to the economic and technological hegemony of the western powers. What we are witnessing, therefore, despite the progressive westernization of the world, is an increasing differentiation, turbulence and fragmentation of the international arena. In such an 'environment' cosmopolitan pacifism reveals itself as no more than a simplistically Hobbesian theory, whose intended response to disorder is the rudimentary violence of a supranational Leviathan. Its interpretation of the mechanisms of functional interdependence in world markets of goods, finance and communications is to see these as processes of social integration of the planet which will bring about a 'global civil society'. In both of these two respects cosmopolitan pacifism shows itself to be lacking in the 'requisite variety' to map out a path to peace in a world of growing complexity. A world government which developed out of existing international institutions and which based itself on the cosmopolitan model would of necessity be a despotic and totalitarian Leviathan, condemned to resort to the use of crushing military measures in response to the inevitable proliferation of violence.

Radical Pacifism, Legal Cosmopolitanism and 'Weak Pacifism'

A radical alternative to institutional pacifism is absolute pacifism based on the moral qualities of individuals. Only, it is argued, in a community comprising individuals who have been converted to non-violence can peace be established. For war represents the eruption of violence which is already circulating through the veins of the social body. Such absolute pacifism has an advantage over institutional pacifism in that it addresses the problem of the anthropological and psychological roots of violence and allows for the contribution which is to be made to the cause of peace by the moral sensibility of individuals. In addition, with regard to the ethics of international relations currently fostered within the English-speaking academic community, it has the merit of argumentational consistency and moral vigour: absolute pacifism stands at the opposite pole to the apologetic moralism which theorists of international ethics have inherited from the medieval doctrine of the just war. Attempts to equip the concept of non-violence with strategies of resistance to oppression and 'pacific deterrence' retain great interest. But, from the viewpoint of realism, the limit of absolute pacifism is reached by what I have termed its 'moral excess': that is to say, the presumption that it is possible to deny in moral terms the existence of human aggression and to eradicate it from human consciousness. This is akin to the belief that even the most destructive forms of human conflict can be overcome through feats of spirituality and moral heroism. In the end it ignores the biological roots of aggression and the role which this plays in the interactions between both individuals and groups.

If absolute pacifism suffers from the fault of a 'moral excess' in its fideistic presumption of its ability to conquer violence as if it were an ailment of which we could rid ourselves once and for all, then legal cosmopolitanism errs for a reason which is in many respects opposite: an excess of rationality in its claim to overcome the irrationality of warfare with the rationality of law. In Kelsen and his followers the motto 'peace through law' typifies the 'logical opposition' between the two forms: law represents order, ritualization, formalization, measure, proportion, while war stands for disorder, destruction, violation of rules, disproportion. Law is the highest and purest form of rationality applied to social relations, war is the unleashing of social irrationality. The superiority of international over national law represents therefore the superiority of 'universal reason' over the subjectivism and relativism of the nation state. The cosmopolitan supremacy of the law is nothing other than the supremacy of peace and order over antagonism born of particularistic interests and conflictuality engendered by the logic of power. Peace is the essence of the rational legal ordering that unites human beings in a *civitas maxima*, a Cosmopolis of the primacy of law. From this arises trust in the possibility that the creation of an international criminal code and the institution of international courts will significantly contribute to peace. This trust has recently manifested itself in the creation of new criminal tribunals and the United Nations' first penitentiary – the International Criminal Tribunal for the former Yugoslavia with its related jail, and the International Criminal Tribunal for Rwanda – and in the persistent requests for extension of the compulsory jurisdiction of the International Court of Justice.

Clearly this cosmopolitan vision exaggerates the regulative capacities of the law, ignoring the obstacles in its path and the distortions which the normative intention undergoes in social contexts which are anything other than limited and rudimentary. In particular it overvalues the effectiveness in stopping war which can be attributed to mechanisms of international penal repression. Legal cosmopolitanism ends therefore by formalistically denying war, as if war could be prevented by decree and as if a simple *fiat* were sufficient to bring about the dismantling of military arsenals or to ensure that the production of military arms could be stopped. It ends also by overlooking the dimension, modest though it is, of the *jus in bello*, which has nevertheless proved itself to be the only one which has been effective in the attempt legally to limit the conduct of warlike activities.

That war cannot be either prevented or denied, but should instead be socially 'integrated', along with the aggression and conflict to which it is anthropologically and sociologically linked, is the realist axiom of what I have termed 'weak pacifism'. This version of political realism, unlike the ethics of international relations, regards the moral justification of war with great distrust, but does not for this reason condemn war from a moral viewpoint: it looks on war as a phenomenon so destructive and so uncontrollable as to be ethically intractable. In this respect 'weak pacifism' shares the intransigence of radical non-violence and legal pacifism: no argumentation, however sophisticated or casuistic, could justify the killing (of thousands) of innocent people within a framework of moral values not contaminated by complicity with power.

'Weak pacifism', however, unlike radical pacifism, declines to regard war as a moral degeneration or as a purely irrational regression and looks, for corroboration of its theses, to the findings reached by the ethology of war and general human ethology. A defining principle of 'weak pacifism' is that it excludes the possibility of 'making war on war'. An effective response to war can be made only by 'weak' means, i.e. in the substantially non-military forms of preventive diplomacy and 'pacification rituals'. But it does not advocate this course in tribute to the general virtue of mildness or because it is under the delusion, in Gandhian fashion, that a non-violent response morally disarms an enemy and brings about a change of hostile intention. On the contrary, it takes this form as a result of the belief that the flow of conflictuality cannot be suppressed or annulled, but should instead be patiently channelled, directed and, where fortunately possible, contained. And also as a result of the belief that aggression, however much it may lie at the heart of the propensity of *homo sapiens* towards war, plays an evolutionarily important role and should therefore be allowed to express itself freely, in the broadest measure possible.

Realistic pacifism of this nature, committed to the use of non-violent measures, forms part of a wider strategy of 'weak interventionism' which aims at a level of theoretical complexity adequate to meet the growing complexity of the international environment. This is the direction, in complete opposition to the standpoint of jurisdictional centralism, which is pointed to by the idea of an international 'legal society' embodied in a plurality of 'regimes' capable of co-ordinating international actors in accordance with a systemic logic of 'governance without government'. It is also the direction favoured by the proposal to carry out selective restructuring of 'international aid' based on a notion of 'bottom-up' economic and human growth, i.e. aid which involves intervention on a reduced scale, at a low technological level and in harmony with local values, traditions and resources. Economic and human growth, like peace and democracy, is not an 'exportable' commodity. The advancement of poor and weak countries, if and when it comes, will be the result of their autonomous capacity to organize themselves politically and economically and to defend their own collective identity through effective national means. It will depend, in other words, on their aggression and conflictuality, not on the 'aid' of the great powers or on the benevolence of the international community. Likewise, within individual countries, protection of the basic rights of democratic citizenship will depend much more on the 'struggle for law' conducted by the citizens themselves than on the protective or repressive intervention of regional or international jurisdictional bodies. Given the relations of growing interdependence and even, it may be said, of recurrent causality between internal democracy and international order, it is difficult to conceive of a more ordered and pacific world if democracy is not above all first realized within nation states.

The Non-reformability of the United Nations

The final thesis which I intend to advance, and which I consider to be supported by both the historical-political analysis and the theoretical reflections which I have undertaken in the course of this book, can be expressed in the following manner. Far from being reformed and empowered in the cosmopolitan direction of 'world government', existing international political and economic institutions – such as, in particular, the United Nations, the World Bank and the International Monetary Fund – will instead need to be subjected to substantial functional reduction. This proposal accords with the strategy of weak interventionism which I have earlier sought to justify on the theoretical level. A weakening of the military and economic functions of these institutions, and a reduction of their massive bureaucracies, would be the condition of their reformability along liberal and democratic lines. No one can be under any illusion that the greatest world powers are likely to wish to sit at the same table as the poorest and weakest countries in order to take part in a democratic decision-making process involving equality of votes over decisions regarding vital military and economic questions and the strategic balance of the planet. Under such circumstances it is necessary to recognize that the United Nations, the World Bank and the International Monetary Fund are examples of institutions which are simply non-reformable in the sense favoured by the democratic supporters of cosmopolitanism whose desire is to see them simultaneously both strengthened and democratized.

It is, however, an extremely dubious proposition that the United Nations in particular could be deprived of even a modest part of its (actual and potential) functions through a process of reform which would meet with the approval of the great powers. This would countermand the significant facility of being able to obtain international legitimation of their own 'vital interests' which the western countries are at present assured of by their hegemony within the Security Council. It is therefore realistic to maintain that the United Nations is, in absolute terms, non-reformable. If any changes are introduced, they will be in a conservative direction: that is to say, in the cosmopolitan direction of further sanctioning of the organization's hierarchical and illiberal features. It is no accident, to my mind, that the United States government has already embraced reforming theses of the kind which I have called 'autocratic cosmopolitan'. These include in particular the proposal to reinforce the Security Council through the admission of Japan and Germany as permanent members.

However, a different form of development could be brought about only by profound changes in the geopolitical and economic balance of the planet. These could lead, for example, to the secession of a substantial number of states and to the foundation of new and diverse regional or international institutions, which could even be physically dislocated from the West. It is conceivable that such a secession could be brought about by 'demographic powers' such as Brazil or India, which currently stand on the margins of international life, or by the Islamic Arabian countries, or, least implausibly, by the newly industrialized countries of the Pacific area, headed by China. It is entirely possible that the recently industrialized eastern countries will gain further strength and form a group made up, in addition to the four Asiatic 'tigers', of such countries as Malaysia, Thailand, Indonesia, the Philippines and, most potently, China.

For it is China which remains the great variable in the world equilibrium of the approaching decades. It is a country which could well regain the position it has both occupied and has thought of itself as occupying over many thousands of years, that of 'the empire at the centre of the world'. If this happens, the current geopolitical balances of the planet will suffer a radical upheaval, bringing about inevitable and important changes in the structure of the concentration and legitimation of international power. Under such circumstances, it is hard to believe that, for the United Nations and the entire western-based cosmopolitan tradition of the Holy Alliance, the final hour will not then have arrived.

Postscript to the English Edition

In this postscript I have taken the opportunity of providing English-speaking readers with an account of the critical reactions to the first edition of this work, which appeared in Italy in the autumn of 1995. I myself will also attempt to take advantage of these criticisms by endeavouring to anticipate some of the objections that may be made to the present English version (a version that corresponds to the Italian text, apart from a number of small alterations, and a different development and broader treatment of the concluding part of chapter 5). I will devote special attention to some of the issues broached either in correspondence or in public debate by several of the most important critics of my book, such as Norberto Bobbio, Antonio Cassese and Richard Falk.

The main objections raised against my critique of the cosmopolitan model and my alternative proposal of a 'weak pacifism' may be summarized in the three following points.

First, the Gulf War is presented in my book as a crucial turning-point in international relations: indeed, I term it the 'first cosmopolitan global war'. By contrast, I attribute far less importance to the 1950 Korean War, which some critics regard as similar in many respects to the Gulf War, or at least as an important forerunner. Similarly I ignore many bloody conflicts in southern Asia and sub-Saharan Africa, and I also neglect to analyse the war in the former Yugoslavia. I draw a number of theoretical consequences from the Gulf War that are contradicted or in some sense called into question by the theoretical implications derivable from the war in Bosnia. Here the role of international institutions and the great powers has been very different, and, in comparison with the Gulf War, considerably less significant from a military point of view.

Second, my book is said to attack a straw target. The polemical aspect is therefore, it is argued, overdone and, as a more serious consequence, the book falls wide of the mark from a critical point of view. At present, it is claimed, there is no risk of international institutions assuming the form of a planet-wide Leviathan, in a position to govern the world despotically, conceivably by wilfully resorting to nuclear terror. No state exists today which is capable of putting such a plan into action, or is inclined to make the attempt to do so. As far as the United States is concerned, there is no sign that it intends to move in this direction. Any imperial vocation on its part is restrained by the 'Vietnam complex' by which it is still afflicted (and, after the failure of the Somalia expedition, there may now be added to this the 'Mogadishu syndrome'), as well as by the obsessive worry over the loss of American lives and the widespread spirit of democracy. Cosmopolitanism, in the meaning I ascribe to it, is at most an abstract theory put forward by a few rather unrealistic thinkers. For this reason, my opponents object, the hard-fought battle against deadly dangers which I conduct through the pages of this book is no more than a classic case of 'tilting at windmills'.

Third, the book only partially keeps it promise (this is the most widely voiced criticism). While the *pars destruens* is relatively extensive and analytically argued, the *pars construens* is only sketchy. The notion of 'weak pacifism' is itself 'weak', and paradoxically combines realistic assumptions with expectations that are not far short of utopian. On the one hand, human aggression is viewed as an ineradicable impulse, so that conflict and war are accepted as inevitable evils, or indeed even as factors in the evolutionary process. On the other hand, one finds the optimistic hope that non- (or weakly) institutionalized spontaneous peacemaking activities may exert the same effect of conflict-attenuation as peacemaking rituals seem to achieve among anthropomorphic primates. In addition – and this is a specific objection voiced by Norberto Bobbio – the proposal of 'weak pacifism' is not the radical alternative to 'institutional pacifism' I have claimed it to be. Bobbio points out that he has explicitly presented his 'institutional pacifism' as a 'weak pacifism'. For his proposal does not claim to eliminate war once and for all, but relies on a centralized military force as a third-party player *super partes*, entrusted with the task of containing and regulating conflicts, but not of suppressing war. Furthermore, institutional pacifism itself starts from the standpoint of the natural character of human aggression.

I shall attempt to outline an answer to each of these criticisms in the following three sections.

The Korean War, the Gulf War and the Bosnian War

I have claimed, and I continue to maintain, that it is the Gulf War, and not the Korean War, that should be considered to be the first 'cosmopolitan' war. While it may be true that the Korean War was formally fought by the United States in the name (and under the flag) of the United Nations, and with a semblance of international legality, the United States received no mandate for this role from the international community. The appearance of 'cosmopolitan' consensus in support of the United States position was due, as is well recognized, to a diplomatic stratagem. The United States took advantage of the temporary absence of the Soviet Union delegate to the Security Council in order to make a unilateral decision to send troops to the aid of South Korea, which had been invaded by the North Korean army. A further factor is that, in 1950, the United Nations lacked genuine institutional universality, as it numbered fewer than sixty member states. Thus the Korean War which took place in the early 1950s is essentially to be seen as a bloody episode in the antagonism between the 'free world' and the 'communist world' which was to lead in subsequent decades to the Cold War.

The Gulf War, on the other hand, although also waged primarily at the behest of and by the United States and the western powers, received the explicit support or tacit consent of virtually all states, including the Soviet Union and the socialist countries. Unlike the Korean War, the Gulf War was waged in real terms by an extremely broad international coalition, which intended to impose sanctions by force on a state that had violated the sovereignty of another member state of the United Nations by invading the latter state's territory. From this point of view, even though not from that of the means employed and the ends pursued, the Gulf War can be said to have been a 'policing operation' designed to restore world order. Indeed this was the very motive adduced by the United States to justify its military expedition within the framework of 'global security' and the 'New World Order'.

In respect of the consequences of the Gulf War, my judgement does not differ substantially from that expressed by Richard Falk, which I described and commented on in chapter 2 of my book. Like him, I believe that although the Gulf War was extremely rapid and was with equal rapidity erased from western memory, it is destined to have long-term negative consequences on the theory and practice of international relations. (I will not dwell here on the devastations and sacrifice of hundreds of thousands of innocent lives brought about by the war, and which it still continues to cause on account of a pointlessly vindictive embargo. Nor will I go into detail concerning the permanent instability of the entire Middle Eastern area, emphasized by recent terrorist attacks against United States military bases in Saudi Arabia.)

From the time of the Gulf War onwards, a practice has developed that tends to stretch the limits of the constitutional structure of the United Nations, distorting the exercise of the main function of peacekeeping entrusted to the Security Council by the Charter. For, as Luigi Condorelli has argued, rather than engaging in peacemaking initiatives by the diplomatic or coercive means enshrined in the Charter, the Security Council has instead begun to hand over (or better: has begun to be induced to hand over) to the great powers the modern equivalent of royal 'letters of marque'. In other words, the Council has signed blank cheques to the benefit of the various states that have shown an interest in (or have insisted upon) conducting military operations aimed at peace enforcement and the promotion of democracy. Somalia, Rwanda and Haiti are cases in point. In this manner the rubber-stamp of international legality granted by the Security Council on these various occasions has, as it were, simply transformed pirates into privateers. But what the United Nations has not succeeded in doing is preventing armed conflicts from breaking out, or containing them effectively and promptly. The twofold Rwandan genocide comes starkly to mind here. Nor has the United Nations been successful in opposing discretionary use of force by the great powers, who are concerned with promoting their own 'vital interests' regardless of any normative aspect. Military interventions by these 'partial third parties' have frequently, *ex post facto*, piled violence upon violence, destruction upon destruction.

The Gulf War thus set in motion a process that has tended to drain the United Nations of authority even further. Today more than ever before, the United Nations has the appearance of a weak organization, submissive, scarcely credible and oppressed by the financial crisis brought about by the refusal of the United States and other countries to pay the huge sums they owe. The Security Council – for it is now pointless to speak of the General Assembly – is increasingly turning into a sort of empty box which overweening military and industrial powers can pack at will with whatever contents best suit their geopolitical strategies.

This brings me to the question of the former Yugoslavia. In my book I made only a few references to the Bosnian conflict because I felt it would be rash to hazard an interpretation while the war was still under way. Today, after the Dayton accords have been formally signed in Paris, the Bosnian war seems to be heading towards its conclusion, and the strategies pursued by its main protagonists over the last few years are becoming more clearly decipherable.

Many western observers have argued that it would have been better to opt for rapid and strong intervention in order to disarm the contenders and settle their ethnic and territorial controversies *manu militari*. The inertia of the United Nations, the impotence of the European Union and the uncertainty of the United States have been seen as bearing the moral as well as political responsibility for not halting the war immediately. Massive military intervention, similar to that deployed in the Persian Gulf, it is claimed, would have saved the lives of the majority of the 250,000 victims slain in the course of over three years of war. Above all, it would have avoided the horrors of 'ethnic cleansing', which some have compared to the barbarity of the Nazis. And the prolonged martyrdom of Sarajevo would have been avoided.

In support of this claim, it has been maintained that the war came to a sudden conclusion during the winter of 1995 when NATO aircraft finally adopted a hard-line response to the rain of shells on the Bosnian capital from Serb bombers, and the United States made it clear that it would no longer tolerate the war. The forceful, if belated, intervention by the police officer of the West, so the argument runs, brought the Balkan Serbs to their senses, compelling them to call an end to their primitive violence.

I have serious doubts about this interpretation. My scepticism is due mainly to the fact that such an interpretation totally overlooks the deep-seated roots of this conflict, which reach back into the depths of Balkan history. Let me briefly recall the salient features of this history, all too frequently ignored. The rivalry between Serbs and Croats and the tendency of the Serb majority to hegemonize the process of unification of the Balkans began to come to the fore as early as the nineteenth century. The 1921 San Vito Constitution which gave rise to the parliamentary monarchy of unified Yugoslavia openly recognized Serbia as playing the role of 'the Prussia of the Balkans'. And from that moment onwards the State of Yugoslavia, under the hegemony of the Serbian majority, was lacerated by ethnic and religious tensions which state centrism, monarchic at first and subsequently communist, succeeded only in accentuating and was helpless to contain.

When the centralist power of Belgrade crumbled, disintegration was inevitable. This occurred both in 1941, with the dissolution of the monarchy, and again after the death of Marshal Tito, with the ensuing crisis of his 'Popular Federation'. The Federation had emerged in 1946, thanks to the victory of the partisan movement led by Tito and supported by the communist bloc, after the end of more than five years of civil war in which orthodox Serbs fought against Croat Ustashes. The latter were headed by the ultranationalist Catholic Ante Pavelic, and from the outset had enjoyed support from the Nazi–Fascist Axis. The civil war caused over a million deaths among the Serb population alone, a fact which appears to have fallen into total oblivion today.

Just as in 1941, all signs pointed to the inevitable outbreak of a bloody civil war at the end of Tito's despotic regime. And it seemed equally inevitable that the conflict between the two main Yugoslav nationalities would also raise the lid on a Pandora's box of ethnic demands by minorities that had been repressed or sidelined by the centralist stranglehold of the dictatorship: Slovenes, Muslim Bosnians, Albanians, Macedonians, Wallachians, Montenegrins, Italians, Bulgarians and Hungarians. The conflict became particularly fierce and uncontrollable above all among the ethnic segments of the main Yugoslav nationalities present in Bosnia and in the city of Sarajevo, that is, in the area where the multicultural melting-pot assumed its most intricate aspects: here the cultural and religious distance between the religious groups was greatest on account of the presence of the Muslim minority, and the centralist tendency of the old regime had exerted its greatest pressure. The criminal atrocities of 'ethnic cleansing' and the excesses of Serb and Croat nationalism – and to some extent of the Muslims as well – must be firmly condemned. It must however also be recognized that, after an initial phase characterized by the aggressive explosion of Serb nationalism, the conflict was driven by the quest for recovery of ethnic identity and for the attainment of national autonomy by populations long oppressed by despotic regimes. If, after more than three years of slaughter and destruction, the war now seems to have run its course, this is not to be ascribed to external pressure, the ineffectiveness of which has already been amply demonstrated by the length and harshness of the conflict. Rather, the war is probably over because the entire area of the former Yugoslavia, and in particular Bosnia-Herzegovina, has ceased to be a multi-ethnic fabric on account of the violent polarization imposed by the stronger nationalities.

In my view, it is within this broader historical framework that the strategies adopted by the western powers, in particular Germany and the United States, should be interpreted. Germany, under the leadership of Chancellor Kohl, cherished the aim of expanding its economic-cultural hegemony towards both southern and south-eastern Europe, and constantly operated, without taking any military risk, in favour of the dismantling of the unity of Yugoslavia and the reduction of Serb power. This explains, for instance, why Germany immediately proceeded to recognize the independence of Slovenia and Croatia, despite the foreseeable risk that this would fuel fears and fan the flames of Serb nationalism.

The strategy of the United States, backed by its western allies, emerged clearly during the final stage of the conflict. The objective seems to have been that of assuring for itself, at very limited cost and therefore without haste – for the Balkans can hardly be said to have the strategic and economic importance of the Middle East – control over the European area that was once subjected to Soviet influence. The mainstay of this geopolitical strategy was, in its first stage, transformation of NATO, a direct descendant of the Cold War, into the military arm of the United Nations in matters concerning military operations in the former Yugoslavia. This was followed by a second stage, which effectively relegated the United Nations to the sidelines of the European playing-field. The strategic goal which thereby came to dominate was that of attributing to NATO the peacemaking functions that the Charter of the United Nations formally assigns to the Security Council. France and Spain aligned themselves with this strategy, promptly endorsed the unified Military Command of NATO, and provided military contingents to be sent to Bosnia. (A few thousand soldiers were also sent at the last moment by Italy in order to secure its place, however modest, at the table of the great powers who are going to carve up the cake of post-war reconstruction.)

The final seal was set on this metamorphosis by the operations of coercive diplomacy that led to the Dayton accords between the governments of Croatia, Serbia and Bosnia-Herzegovina, and subsequently to the concluding formalization of the accords in Paris. The culminating point of this process was the remarkable fact that in Dayton, which is a United States military base and not a decentralized seat of the United Nations, the representative of the United Nations in the former Yugoslavia, Kofi Annan, was conspicuous by his absence, not even having been invited. In Paris the Secretary General of the United Nations, Boutros-Ghali, was simply one of the invited figures performing a purely ceremonial function.

In conclusion, it is my view that there is considerable evidence to suggest that the United States, flanked by Germany and the other western powers, orchestrated the diplomatic, political and military intervention in the Bosnian conflict in such a way as to reinforce further the western presence in the southern and eastern Slav area. This strategy included instrumental use and ultimately the complete exclusion of the United Nations. Moreover, the circumstances of the war in the former Yugoslavia are far from signalling any willingness by the United States to relinquish its role as the exclusive arbiter of international controversies – those who have read this interpretation into it are clearly mistaken. On the contrary, President Clinton, impelled partly by considerations of domestic policy, has built up an exceptionally high profile in his role as direct and 'bilateral' guarantor of the peace accords, a part he is playing with unparalleled vigour.

The Dayton peace is certainly – as was stated, not without an element of envy, by the French President – a *pax americana*. Both the strong intervention by George Bush in the Persian Gulf and the moderate intervention by Bill Clinton in the Balkans can be seen as belonging to one and the same design: that of 'global security' and the 'New World

Order'. This is envisaged as being an order guaranteed by the political-military hegemony of the United States and supported by the technological and economic supremacy of the industrialized countries.

Tilting at Windmills?

The impression may have been given in certain passages of my book that I was convinced of the imminent threat of an international Leviathan, capable of bringing about imperial unification of the planet. In fact I have never even remotely entertained – much less argued – that we are facing a danger of this type. Nor have I ever suspected that some of the great powers, led by the United States, are plotting a sort of planetary *coup d'état* to abolish the pluralism of states and impose on the world a single centralized and hierarchical power structure. On the contrary, it is my belief that at the present time no superpower would be capable of undertaking the unification and imperial pacification of the whole world. No country enjoys the technological superiority and the supply of economic and military resources necessary to nurture such an unbounded ambition.

What, therefore, was I referring to when I alluded to the prospect of 'world government' and criticized it on both the theoretical and the political plane?

I was referring essentially to three tendencies with global effect. First and foremost, as I mentioned in several places in the early part of the book, I was referring to a phenomenon of a gradual concentration of international power that set in after the collapse of the Soviet empire and the end of the western/eastern bloc system. Once this equilibrium between the two nuclear superpowers had been removed, the international power-sharing mechanisms began to function in an even more asymmetric manner. Today the whole planet is gravitating in a single political, economic and cultural orbit around the industrialized powers, with the United States as their focal point.

With the one important exception of several rising economic powers in the Pacific area, the foreseeable international scenario over the coming decade seems unlikely to present any alternative to this tendency towards concentration. For the moment, no signs of a possible reversal of the tendency can be discerned such as could foster a gradual dispersal of power between a multiplicity of centres or geopolitical areas stably balanced against each other. It is for this reason that I consider the image of Cosmopolis to be pertinent. In a slightly different but equally eloquent metaphorical rendering of the same situation, it has been stated that 'the Earth is once again flat'. The steamroller effect that has flattened it has been accomplished by the new missionaries, the new merchants and the new soldiers who have invaded the 'global village', bringing in their train their western way of life, their western merchandise and their western weaponry.

In the second place, I was referring also to the tendency by a restricted number of military powers – basically the western powers – to engage increasingly in 'humanitarian' interventionism, by which I mean the propensity to use force to regulate the internal social conflicts and political crises of the weaker countries. NATO has been quick to convert to this strategy, and the United Nations has been constrained to follow suit, effectively being relegated to the function of mere formal legitimization. From the Gulf War onwards, the trend has been towards a progressive expansion of the formal role of the United Nations – in reality of the great powers – to the point of sweeping away the Westphalian principle of non-interference in the internal affairs of states. It is enough to think of the armed intervention to enforce peace and promote democracy in Iraq, Somalia, Rwanda, Haiti and Bosnia. Blue-beret interventions have proliferated, accompanied by a soaring rise in United Nations military expenditure. International war tribunals have been set up in the former Yugoslavia and Rwanda, while the first United Nations prison has been built in The Hague. Recently, NATO troops sent to Bosnia for the IFOR operation were entrusted with the task of arresting those indicted by the Hague Court (the vast majority of whom are of Serbian nationality).

Third, I was also referring to the increasing gap in economic and 'human' development between the industrialized countries, including the NICs of the Pacific, on the one hand, and the countries occupying vast areas of Asia, sub-Saharan Africa and central-southern America, on the other. The process is favoured by the ongoing drive to globalization, which is particularly evident in the sectors of finance, large-scale manufacture, information technology and the communications industry. And for all the rhetoric on global interdependence as the prelude to moral and spiritual unification of the planet, the westernization of the world is digging a deeper and deeper trench between an elite of rich countries and a large number of backward countries that are lagging far behind in the threefold thrust to industrial, technological and bureaucratic modernization.

As I mentioned in some of the pages of chapter 5, the increasing differentiation of the rhythms of 'human development' in the various continental areas is in many cases aided by the process of international economic globalization. Despite their avowed compliance with the liberal principles of multilateralism and non-discrimination, the major commercial powers have adopted complex strategies in which mercantilist competition among states, economic regionalism and sectorial protectionism coexist with policies that result in a forced internationalization of the weaker economies. The opening up of markets is being imposed in sectors where global competition favours the strongest, while elsewhere a preference is shown for playing the card of what has become known as the 'new protectionism'. These are tendencies which, it is worth adding, the international economic institutions – *in primis* the World Bank and the International Monetary Fund – have propped up and at times themselves exacerbated.

It is these phenomena, I would argue, that can legitimately be viewed as a cause for concern, as has already been pointed out by far-sighted authors such as Stephen Toulmin and Hedley Bull, who speculate that the modern world is moving towards a cosmopolitan structure. By the same token, it is these tendencies which provide the rationale for my attempt, whether it be deemed successful or otherwise, to criticize cosmopolitan claims on ethical, legal and institutional matters.

The Weakness of 'Weak Pacifism'

I would be the first to admit that my proposal of a 'weak pacifism' is itself weak from an analytical point of view. My critics contend that, although I profess to subscribe to political realism, I have put forward an abstract and insufficiently realistic proposal, imbued with a moralizing tone that is as deep-seated as my reluctance to acknowledge it. There is perhaps also some feeling that such a proposal is inadequately supported by a 'scientific' analysis of the mechanisms of international politics. Thus the idea of a 'weak pacifism', it is claimed, can embrace little more than vague and generic formulations, insightful but inapplicable.

In this English version of my book I have endeavoured to allay these criticisms somewhat, by reshaping and extending the concluding part of chapter 5. It will nevertheless become clear that I have confined myself to offering fairly general indications, without shaping my proposal into a precise institutional blueprint. This is a deliberate choice. For I do not believe in the usefulness of institutional engineering worked out on the drawing board, particularly when it encompasses vast, complex and turbulent realms such as that embodied by the international arena. The libraries of the West are full of treatises expounding in minute detail all the rules and regulations to be brought into action in various projected reforms of international institutions that are designed to usher in stable and universal peace. They make up extensive mappings of the future Cosmopolis produced by the fervid imaginations of solitary thinkers, jurists, political scientists, philosophers, moralists, theologians, visionaries.

My own aim, on the other hand, has been essentially to adopt a critical stance: I have brought up a number of radical issues and tried to provide realistic answers. It is my contention that a realist political philosophy must be given the task of voicing radical criticism, without expecting such a critique to result in a map of a possible alternative world, with all the doctrinal minutiae pedantically spelled out. Rather, in my view, it is the critique of *idola*, the iconoclastic destruction of graven images, that can unveil new horizons and stimulate the perception of alternatives that as yet remain in a latent state. But the identifications and concrete construction of possible alternatives cannot be achieved without a plurality of theoretical contributions, extensive practical experimentation and a substantial number of failures. Clearly, this is a political process that cannot happen overnight, given the many conditions and risks emerging from the radical contingency of the world.

I have attempted to explode the image of Cosmopolis by highlighting its theoretical inconsistencies and the practical risks involved. This was my first-order priority. Only as a second-order priority have I sketched a different point of view: the anticosmopolitan perspective of 'weak pacifism'. And, as a purely conjectural matter, I have finally introduced the institutional hypothesis of limited interventionism. In proposing this 'paradigm shift' I have drawn inspiration from Hedley Bull's polemics against the *western globalists*. The latter would have a global political authority actively engaged in guaranteeing not only peace but also distributive justice, ecological balance, the safeguarding of human rights, demographic containment and economic development. Now it is obvious that objectives of this type can be pursued only with the aid of the political-military tools at the disposal of the great powers. By contrast, to guarantee a 'minimal international order' – essentially to co-ordinate the political and economic strategies of individual states within a network of 'juridical regimes' and to set up decentralized circuits of preventive diplomacy – it would be sufficient, I maintain, to have much lighter institutions, which would therefore be less susceptible to the hegemony of the great powers. I believe that something similar has been recently suggested by Giandomenico Picco, one of the most authoritative United Nations officials prior to his controversial resignation in 1992. In direct opposition to Boutros-Ghali, Picco suggested that the United Nations should resume its function as a centre of diplomatic activity, exercising its authority on the moral plane as well, instead of operating more and more in the guise of a super-state that relies almost exclusively on the power of money and arms.

Naturally this does not mean, however, that peace can come about spontaneously. Nor does it mean that 'peacemaking rituals' do not need to be embodied in permanent structures and should instead find expression in the temporary succour afforded by international voluntary organizations. To put it another way, I am not suggesting that all contact with governmental organizations should be rejected, or that peacemaking should be performed as a sort of institutional non-violence. Rather – and this is how I would respond to Bobbio's objection – it means that my perspective of 'weak pacifism' does not entail the precondition that the pluralism of sovereign states must be replaced by what Bobbio describes as 'the higher authority of a world state, one single universal state'. On the contrary, what is needed is a decentralization of international power and, if anything, a multiplication of statal political units. The pacifism I preach is therefore termed 'weak' not because it starts from the assumption of the 'natural' character of human aggression and the biological inevitability of war, for I have repeatedly criticized this metaphysical and deterministic assumption, but rather, I would argue, because it holds, on the basis of the international experience of the last few centuries, that extreme forms of hostility could best be neutralized today by more effective types of preventive, flexible and decentralized intervention.

Even with these additional clarifications, I do not remotely expect the contentions put forward in this book to be shared by all my readers. I have proposed a 'paradigm shift' in the interpretation of international relations, though I am fully aware that no interpretation is grounded in neutral evaluation. I am ready to acknowledge that others may adopt a more dispassionate or utterly unconcerned attitude to the phenomena and tendencies I regard as alarming. They may even consider these developments as representing progress towards a more peaceful and well-ordered world, because this 'brave new world' would be subject, as it is inevitable that it should be, to the discipline of the mighty. Indeed, some may even believe that the strongest are, by rights, the most civilized and the most rational. Those who subscribe to such a conviction can certainly continue to maintain that in my book I have engaged in a Quixotic tilt against cosmopolitan windmills.

Florence, June 1996

Select Bibliography

International organizations

Arangio-Ruiz, G., *The Normative Role of the General Assembly of the United Nations and the Declaration of Principles of Friendly Relations*, Leyden: A. W. Sijthoff, 1972.

Claude, I. L., Jr, *Swords into Plowshares: The Problems and Progress of International Organization*, New York: Random House, 1971.

Conforti, B., *Le Nazioni Unite*, Padua: Cedam, 1994.

Falk, R. A., 'The Interplay of Westphalia and Charter Conceptions of International Legal Order', in C. A. Blach and R. A. Falk (eds), *The Future of International Legal Order*, I, Princeton: Princeton University Press, 1969.

——, Kim, S. S. and Mendlovitz, S. H. (eds), *The United Nations and a Just World Order*, Boulder – San Francisco – Oxford: Westview Press, 1991.

Gross, L., 'The Peace of Westphalia 1648–1948', *American Journal of International Law*, 42 (1948), 1.

Grove, E. (ed.), *Global Security: North American, European and Japanese Interdependence in the 1990s*, London: Brassey's, 1991.

Henig, R. B. (ed.), *The League of Nations*, Edinburgh: Oliver & Boyd, 1973.

Hilderbrand, R. C., *Dumbarton Oaks: The Origins of the United Nations and the Search for Postwar Security*, Chapel Hill: University of North Carolina Press, 1990.

Northedge, F. S., *The League of Nations: Its Life and Times 1920–1945*, New York: Holmes & Meier, 1986.

Roberts, A. and Kingsbury, B. (eds), *United Nations, Divided World*, Oxford: Oxford University Press, 1988.

Ross, A., *United Nations: Peace and Progress*, Totowa (NJ): The Bedminster Press, 1966.

Russell, R. B., *A History of the United Nations Charter: The Role of the United States 1940–1945*, Washington (DC): The Brookings Institution, 1958.

Senarclens, P. de, *La crise des Nations Unies*, Paris: Presses Universitaires de France, 1988.

Steele, D., *The Reform of the United Nations*, London: Croom Helm, 1987.

Weiss, T. G. (ed.), *Collective Security in a Changing World*, Boulder–London: Lynne Rienner Publishers, 1993.

The Persian Gulf War

Barzilai, G., Klieman, A. and Shidlo, G. (eds), *The Gulf Crisis and its Global Aftermath*, London: Routledge, 1993.
Bobbio, N., *Una guerra giusta? Sul conflitto del Golfo*, Venice: Marsilio, 1991.
Bresheeth, H. and Yuval-Davis, N. (eds), *The Gulf War and the New World Order*, London: Zed Books, 1991.
Clark, R., *The Fire this Time*, New York: Thunder's Mouth Press, 1992.
Habermas, J., 'Der Golf-Krieg als Katalysator einer neuen deutschen Normalität?', in J. Habermas, *Vergangenheit als Zukunft*, ed. M. Haller, Zürich: Pendo-Verlag, 1990.
Hawley, T. M., *Against the Fires of Hell: The Environmental Disaster of the Gulf War*, New York–San Diego–London: Harcourt Brace Jovanovich, 1992.
Helms II, R. F. and Dorff, R. H. (eds), *The Persian Gulf Crisis: Power in the Post-Cold War World*, Westport–London: Praeger, 1993.
Matthews, K., *The Gulf Conflict and International Relations*, London: Routledge, 1993.
Mowlana, H., Gerbner, G. and Schiller, H. I. (eds), *Triumph of the Image: The Media's War in the Persian Gulf*, Boulder–San Francisco–Oxford: Westview Press, 1992.
Palmer, M. A., *Guardians of the Gulf*, New York: The Free Press, 1992.
Rowe, P. (ed.), *The Gulf War 1990–91 in International and English Law*, London: Routledge, 1993.
Smith, H., *The Media and the Gulf War*, Washington (DC): Seven Locks Press, 1992.
United Nations, *United Nations Security Council Resolutions Relating to the Crisis in the Gulf*, UN Department of Public Information, DPC/1104, November 1990; Add. 1, December 1990.
Walzer, M., Weigel, G., Elshtain, J. B., Nusseibeh, S. and Hauerwas, S., *But Was It Just?*, New York: Doubleday, 1992.
Wolton, D., *War Game. L'information et la guerre*, Paris: Flammarion, 1991.

Ethics of international affairs

Beitz, C., *Political Theory and International Relations*, Princeton: Princeton University Press, 1979.
——et al. (eds), *International Ethics*, Princeton: Princeton University Press, 1985.
Bonanate, L., *Etica e politica internazionale*, Turin: Einaudi, 1992; Engl. trans., *Ethics and International Politics*, Cambridge: Polity, 1994.
——, *I doveri degli Stati*, Roma – Bari: Laterza, 1994.
Cohen, M., Nagel, T. and Scanlon, T. (eds), *War and Moral Responsibility*, Princeton: Princeton University Press, 1974.
Elfstrom, G., *Ethics for a Shrinking World*, London: Macmillan, 1990.
Ellis, A. (ed.), *Ethics and International Relations*, Manchester: Manchester University Press, 1986
Frost, M., *Towards a Normative Theory of International Relations*, London: Macmillan, 1986.

Hare, J. E. and Joynt, C. B., *Ethics and International Affairs*, New York: St Martin's Press, 1982.

Held, V., Moregenbesser, S. and Nagel, T. (eds), *Philosophy, Morality and International Affairs*, New York: Oxford University Press, 1974.

Hoffman, S., *Duties Beyond Borders: On the Limits and Possibilities of Ethical International Politics*, Syracuse: Syracuse University Press, 1981.

——, 'Superpower Ethics: The Rules of the Game', *Ethics and International Affairs*, 1 (1987), 1.

Küng, H., *Projekt Weltethos*, Munich: Piper, 1990; Engl. trans., New York: Crossroad, 1991.

Maxwell, M., *Morality among Nations: An Evolutionary View*, Albany: State University of New York Press, 1990.

Myers, R. J. (ed.), *International Ethics in the Nuclear Age*, Lanham (Md): University Press of America, 1987.

Nardin, T. and Mapel, D. R. (eds), *Traditions of International Ethics*, Cambridge: Cambridge University Press, 1992.

Niebuhr, R., *Moral Man and Immoral Society*, New York: Charles Scribner's Sons, 1932.

Nye, J. S., *Ethics and Foreign Policy*, Wye (Md): Aspen Institute, 1985.

Pettman, R. (ed.), *Moral Claims in World Affairs*, London: Croom Helm, 1978.

Schell, J., *The Fate of the Earth*, New York: Knopf, 1982.

Sterba, J. P. (ed), *The Ethics of War and Nuclear Deterrence*, Belmont (Ca.) Wadsworth Publishing Company, 1985.

Walzer, M., 'The Moral Standing of States: A Response to Four Critics', *Philosophy and Public Affairs*, 9 (1980), 3.

Warner, D., *An Ethic of Responsibility in International Relations*, Boulder – London: Lynne Rienner Publishers, 1991.

Wasserstrom, R. (ed.), *War and Morality*, Belmont (Ca.): Wadsworth Publishing Company, 1970.

Just war theories

Elshtain, J. E. (ed.), *Just War Theory*, Oxford: Basil Blackwell, 1992.

Holmes, R. L., *On War and Morality*, Princeton: Princeton University Press, 1989.

Johnson, J. T., *Can Modern War Be Just?*, New Haven: Yale University Press, 1984.

—— and Weigel, G., *Just War and the Gulf War*, Washington: Ethics and Public Policy Center, 1991.

Jones, D. V., *Code of Peace: Ethics and Security in the World of the Warlord States*, Chicago – London: The University of Chicago Press, 1989.

Kegley, C. W. Jr and Schwab, K. L. (eds), *After the Cold War: Questioning the Morality of Nuclear Deterrence*, Boulder–San Francisco–Oxford: Westview Press, 1991.

Nye, J. S., Jr, *Nuclear Ethics*, New York: The Free Press, 1986.

O'Brien, W. V., *The Conduct of Just and Limited War*, New York: Praeger, 1981.

Potter, R. B., *War and Moral Discourse*, Richmond (Va.): John Knox Press, 1973.

Ramsey, P., *War and the Christian Conscience: How Shall Modern War Be Conducted Justly?*, Durham (NC): Duke University Press, 1961.
Walzer, M., *Just and Unjust Wars*, New York: Basic Books, 1992.

Theories of international law and human rights

Bobbio, N., *L'età dei diritti*, Turin: Einaudi, 1990.
Brierly, J. L., *The Law of Nations*, Oxford: Oxford University Press, 1984.
Bull, H., Kingsbury, B. and Roberts, A. (eds), *Hugo Grotius and International Relations*, Oxford: Oxford University Press, 1990.
Cassese, A., *Il diritto internazionale nel mondo contemporaneo*, Bologna: Il Mulino, 1984; Engl. trans., *International Law in a Divided World*, Oxford: Oxford University Press, 1986.
——, *Violenza e diritto nell'era nucleare*, Rome–Bari: Laterza, 1986; Engl. trans., *Violence and Law in the Modern Age*, Princeton: Princeton University Press; Cambridge: Polity Press, 1988.
——, *I diritti umani nel mondo contemporaneo*, Rome–Bari: Laterza, 1988; Engl. trans., *Human Rights in a Changing World*, Cambridge: Polity Press, 1990.
——, *Umano-Disumano. Commissariati e prigioni nell'Europa di oggi*, Rome–Bari: Laterza, 1994.
Donnelly, J., *Universal Human Rights in Theory and Practice*, Ithaca (NY): Cornell University Press, 1989.
Falk, R. A., *The Status of Law in International Society*, Princeton: Princeton University Press, 1970).
——, *Human Rights and State Sovereignty*, New York: Holmes & Meier, 1981.
Falk, R. A., Kratochwil, F. and Mendlovitz, S. H. (eds), *International Law: A Contemporary Perspective*, Boulder: Westview Press, 1985.
Forsythe, D. P., *Human Rights in World Politics*, Lincoln: University of Nebraska Press, 1989.
Galtung, J., *Human Rights in Another Key*, Cambridge: Polity Press, 1994.
Gewirth, A., *Human Rights: Essays in Justification and Applications*, Chicago: Chicago University Press, 1982.
Kelsen, H., *Das Problem der Souveränität und die Theorie des Völkerrechts: Beitrag zu einer reinen Rechtslehre*, Tübingen: Mohr, 1920.
——, *Peace through Law*, Chapel Hill: The University of North Carolina Press, 1944.
——, *The Law of the United Nations*, New York: Frederick A. Praeger, 1950.
——, *Principles of International Law*, ed. R. W. Tucker, New York: Holt, Rinehart & Winston, Inc., 1967.
Schmitt, C., *Der Nomos der Erde im Völkerrecht des Jus Publicum Europaeûm*, Berlin: Duncker & Humblot, 1974.
Shue, H., *Basic Rights*, Princeton: Princeton University Press, 1980.
Shute, S. and Hurley, S. (eds), *On Human Rights*, New York: Basic Books, 1993.
Sumner, L. W., *The Moral Foundation of Rights*, Oxford: Oxford University Press, 1987.
Verdross, A. and Simma, B., *Universelles Völkerrecht*, Berlin: Duncker & Humblot, 1976.

Vincent, R. J., *Human Rights and International Relations*, Cambridge: Cambridge University Press, 1986.

Political theories of international affairs

Archibugi, D. and Held, D. (eds), *Cosmopolitan Democracy: An Agenda for a New World Order*, Cambridge: Polity Press, 1995.
Aron, R., *Paix et guerre entre les nations*, Paris: Calmann-Lévy, 1962; Engl. trans., Malabar: Krieger, 1981.
——, *Penser la guerre, Clausewitz*, Paris: Gallimard, 1976.
Ashley, R. K., 'Political Realism and Human Interests', *International Studies Quarterly*, 25 (1981), 2.
——, 'The Poverty of Neorealism', *International Organization*, 38 (spring 1984), 2.
Bobbio, N., *Il problema della guerra e le vie della pace*, Bologna: Il Mulino, 1984.
——, *Il terzo assente*, Turin: Edizioni Sonda, 1989.
Brown, S., *The Causes and Prevention of War*, New York: St Martin's Press, 1987.
Bull, H., 'The Grotian Conception of International Society', in H. Butterfield and M. Wight (eds), *Diplomatic Investigations*, London: Allen & Unwin, 1966.
——, *The Anarchical Society*, London: Macmillan, 1977.
——, *The Concept of Justice in International Relations*, Waterloo (Ont.): University of Waterloo, 1984.
Carr, E. H., *The Twenty Years' Crisis, 1919–1939*, London: Macmillan, 1956.
Cohen, A. and Lee, S. (eds), *Nuclear Weapons and the Future of Humanity*, Totowa (NJ): Rowman & Allanheld, 1986.
Dedring, J., *Recent Advances in Peace and Conflict Research*, Beverly Hills–London: Sage Publications, 1976.
Falk, R. A., *A Study of Future Worlds*, New York: Free Press, 1975.
——, *A Global Approach to National Policy*, Cambridge (Mass.): Harvard University Press, 1975.
——, *The End of World Order: Essays on Normative International Relations*, New York: Holmes & Meier, 1983.
——, *Positive Prescriptions for the Near Future*, Princeton: Center for International Studies, Paper no. 20, 1991.
——, *Explorations at the Edge of Time: The Prospects for World Order*, Philadelphia: Temple University Press, 1992.
——, *On Humane Governance: Towards a New Global Politics*, Cambridge: Polity Press, 1995.
—— and Kim, S. S. (eds), *The War System: An Interdisciplinary Approach*, Boulder: Westview Press, 1980.
——, Kim, S. S. and Mendlovitz, S. H. (eds), *Toward a Just World Order*, Boulder: Westview Press, 1982.
Franck, T. M., *The Power of Legitimacy among Nations*, New York–Oxford: Oxford University Press, 1990.
Gallie, W. B., *Philosophers of Peace and War: Kant, Clausewitz, Marx, Engels and Tolstoy*, Cambridge: Cambridge University Press, 1978.

Galtung, J., *The True Worlds: A Transnational Perspective*, New York: Free Press, 1980.
——, *There Are Alternatives! Four Roads to Peace and Security*, Nottingham: Spokesman, 1984.
Giddens, A., *The Nation State and Violence*, Berkeley–Los Angeles: University of California Press, 1985.
Gilpin, R., *War and Change in World Politics*, Cambridge: Cambridge University Press, 1981.
Greenfeld, L., *Nationalism: Five Roads to Modernity*, Cambridge (Mass.): Harvard University Press, 1992.
Held, D., 'Democracy: From City-States to a Cosmopolitan Order?' in D. Held (ed.), *Prospects for Democracy*, Cambridge: Polity Press, 1993.
Hurrell, A. J., 'Kant and the Kantian Paradigm in International Relations', *Review of International Studies*, 16 (1990), 3.
Keohane, R. O., *After Hegemony: Cooperation and Discord in the World Political Economy*, Princeton: Princeton University Press, 1984.
——, *Neorealism and Its Critics*, New York: Columbia University Press, 1986.
Kothari, R., *Footsteps into the Future: Diagnosis of the Present World and a Design for an Alternative*, New Delhi: Orient Longman, 1974.
Krasner, S. D. (ed.), *International Regimes*, Ithaca: Cornell University Press, 1983.
——, *Structural Conflict: The Third World against Global Liberalism*, Berkeley: University of California Press, 1985.
Mayall, J., *Nationalism and International Society*, Cambridge: Cambridge University Press, 1990.
McGrew, A. G. and Lewis, P. G. (eds), *Global Politics: Globalization and the Nation State*, Cambridge: Polity Press, 1992.
McPhail, T. L., *Electronic Colonialism*, Beverly Hills–London: Sage Publications, 1981.
ter Meulen, J., *From Erasmus to Tolstoy: The Peace Literature of Four Centuries*, ed. P. van den Dungen, Westport: Greenwood, 1990.
Morgenthau, H. J., *Politics among Nations*, New York: Knopf, 1960.
——, *In Defense of the National Interest*, New York: Knopf, 1961.
Portinaro, P. P., *Il terzo. Una figura del politico*, Milan: Angeli, 1986.
——, *La rondine, il topo e il castoro. Apologia del realismo politico*, Venice: Marsilio, 1993.
Rapoport, A., *Peace: An Idea Whose Time Has Come*, Ann Arbor: University of Michigan Press, 1992.
Rosenau, J. N. and Czempiel E.-O. (eds), *Governance without Government: Order and Change in World Politics*, Cambridge: Cambridge University Press, 1992.
Rosenberg, I., 'What's the Matter with Realism?', *Review of International Studies*, 16 (1990), 4.
Schelling, T., *The Strategy of Conflict*, New York: Oxford University Press, 1963.
Serfaty, S. (ed.), *The Media and Foreign Policy*, London: Macmillan, 1990.
Suganami, H., *The Domestic Analogy and World Order Proposals*, Cambridge: Cambridge University Press, 1989.
Toulmin, S., *Cosmopolis: The Hidden Agenda of Modernity*, New York: The Free Press, 1990.
Väyrynen, R., Senghaas, D. and Schmidt, C. (eds), *The Quest for Peace*, London: Sage Publications, 1987.

Walker, B. J., 'Realism, Change and International Political Theory', *International Studies Quarterly*, 31 (1987), 1.

——, *One World, Many Worlds: Struggles for a Just World Peace*, Boulder: Lynne Rienner Publishers, 1988.

Waltz, K. N., *Theory of International Politics*, New York: Newbery Award Records, 1979.

Economic international institutions and theories of global development

Adams, N. A., *Worlds Apart: The North-South Divide and the International System*, London: Zed Books, 1993.

Bennett, J. and George, S., *The Hunger Machine*, Cambridge: Polity Press, 1987.

Cardoso, F. H., 'Dependency and Under-development in Latin America', *New Left Review*, 74 (1972).

Comor, E. (ed.), *The Global Political Economy of Communication*, London: Macmillan, 1994.

Dicken, P., *Global Shift: The Internationalisation of Economic Activity*, London: Paul Chapman, 1992.

Dreze, J. and Sen, A., *Political Economy of Hunger*, Oxford: Clarendon Press, 1991.

Ekins, P., *A New World Order: Grass Roots Movements for Global Change*, London: Routledge, 1992.

Frank, A. G., *Capitalism and Under-development in Latin America*, New York: Monthly Review Press, 1969.

Furtado, C., *The Economic Growth of Brazil: A Survey from Colonial to Modern Times*, Westport: Greenwood Press, 1984.

Gareffi, G., Korzeniewicz, M. and Korzeniewicz, R. P., *Commodity Chains and Global Capitalism*, Westport: Greenwood Press, 1994.

Gilpin, R., *The Political Economy of International Relations*, Princeton: Princeton University Press, 1987.

Greenaway, D., Hine, R. C. and O'Brien, A. P. (eds), *Global Protectionism*, London: Macmillan, 1991.

Harris, N., *The End of the Third World: Newly Industrialising Countries and the Decline of an Ideology*, Harmondsworth: Penguin, 1987.

Helleiner, G. K., *The New Global Economy and the Developing Countries*, Aldershot: Edward Elgar, 1990.

Kelly, B. and London, M., *The Four Little Dragons: A Journey to the Source of the Business Boom along the Pacific Rim*, London: Touchstone, 1990.

Larrain, J., *Theories of Development: Capitalism, Colonialism and Dependency*, Cambridge: Polity Press, 1989.

Mason, E. S. and Asher, R. E., *The World Bank since Bretton Woods*, Washington: The Brookings Institution, 1973.

Munck, R., *Politics and Dependency in the Third World: The Case of Latin America*, London: Zed Books, 1986.

Payer, C., *The World Bank: A Critical Analysis*, New York: Monthly Review Press, 1982.

United Nations Development Programme, *Human Development Report 1990*, New York–Oxford: Oxford University Press, 1990.

—, *Human Development Report 1992*, New York–Oxford: Oxford University Press, 1992.
— *Human Development Report 1994*, New York–Oxford: Oxford University Press, 1994.
Van de Laar, A., *The World Bank and the Poor*, Boston: Kluwer–Nijhoff Publishing, 1980.
Wallerstein, I., *The Modern World System*, New York: Academic Press, 1974.

War, conflict and aggression

Buzan, B., *Peoples, States and Fear*, Brighton: Wheatsheaf Books, 1983.
Eibl-Eibesfeldt, I., *The Biology of Peace and War*, London: Thames & Hudson, 1979.
—, *Die Biologie des menschlichen Verhaltens. Grundriss der Humanethologie*, Munich: Piper Verlag, 1984; Engl. trans., *Human Ethology*, New York: De Gruyter, 1989.
Groebel, J. and Hinde, R. A. (eds), *Aggression and War: Their Biological and Social Bases*, Cambridge: Cambridge University Press, 1989.
Huntingford, F. A. and Turner, A., *Animal Conflict*, London: Chapman & Hall, 1987.
Kim, S. S., 'The Lorenzian Theory of Aggression and Peace Research: A Critique', in R. A. Falk and S. S. Kim (eds), *The War System: An Interdisciplinary Approach*, Boulder: Westview Press, 1980.
Lorenz, K., *Das sogenannte Böse. Zur Naturgeschichte der Aggression*, Vienna: Borotha-Schöler, 1963; Engl. trans., *On Aggression*, New York: Harcourt, Brace & World, 1966.
Luard, E., *War in International Society: A Study in International Sociology*, New Haven and London: Yale University Press, 1986.
—, *The Globalization of Politics: The Changed Focus of Political Action in the Modern World*, London: Macmillan, 1990.
Nieburg, H. L., *Political Violence*, New York: St Martin's Press, 1969.
Rose, S., Kamin, L. J. and Lewontin R. C., *Not in our Genes: Biology, Ideology and Human Nature*, London: Penguin Books, 1985.
Tinbergen, N., 'On War and Peace in Animals and Man', *Science*, 160 (1968), 1411–18.
Waal, F. de, *Peacemaking among Primates*, Cambridge (Mass.): Harvard University Press, 1989.
—, *Chimpanzee Politics*, London: Jonathan Cape, 1982.

Index

In addition to the names of authors who are cited within the text or discussed in a note, the index includes authors of books or essays cited more than once; the page number of the note containing the first citation and the complete reference is always shown in italics

Lightning Source UK Ltd.
Milton Keynes UK
02 July 2010

156426UK00001B/87/A